Human Trafficking

Human Trafficking

Trade for sex, labor, and organs

Bandana Purkayastha

Farhan Navid Yousaf

Polity

First published in 2019 by Polity Press

Reprinted 2020

Polity Press
65 Bridge Street
Cambridge CB2 1UR, UK

Polity Press
101 Station Landing
Suite 300
Medford, MA 02155, USA

ISBN-13: 978-1-5095-2130-2
ISBN-13: 978-1-5095-2131-9 (pb)

A catalogue record for this book is available from the British Library.

Library of Congress Cataloging-in-Publication Data

Names: Purkayastha, Bandana, 1956- author. | Yousaf, Farhan Navid, author.
Title: Human trafficking: trade for sex, labor, and organs / Bandana Purkayastha, Farhan Yousaf.
Description: Medford, MA : polity, 2018. | Includes bibliographical references and index.
Identifiers: LCCN 2018013002 (print) | LCCN 2018022967 (ebook) | ISBN 9781509521340 (Epub) | ISBN 9781509521302 (hardback) | ISBN 9781509521319 (pbk.)
Subjects: LCSH: Human trafficking. | Human trafficking victims. | Organ trafficking. | Organ trafficking victims.
Classification: LCC HQ281 (ebook) | LCC HQ281 .P87 2018 (print) | DDC 364.1551–dc23
LC record available at https://lccn.loc.gov/2018013002

Typeset in 10.5 on 12 pt Sabon
by Toppan Best-set Premedia Limited
Printed and bound in Great Britain by TJ International Ltd, Padstow

For further information on Polity, visit our website:
politybooks.com

Contents

Acknowledgments

There are many reports and scholarly collections on trafficking today. Many are easily available via simple web searches. So why did we decide to write another book? We were primarily motivated by the experiences of victims of trafficking for sex, labor, and organs. We learned how people can be trafficked repeatedly at different stages of their lives. This led us to think of a trafficking continuum, instead of following policies and remedies that tend to think of discrete forms of trafficking. As we delved into the subject, and examined efforts around the world, it was clear that many of the efforts were focused on helping victims after trafficking. The root causes – structural inequalities, wars and conflicts, the rapidly expanding political terrain in which migrants encounter new barriers to accessing rights – were rarely addressed. At the same time, without adequate resources for the future, shelters and camps can become *the* sites for trafficking and/or human smuggling. Thus, we are at a juncture when we are likely to witness ever-growing numbers of people who are vulnerable to trafficking, while our efforts to punish (the perpetrators) and rescue and reha-bilitate (the victims) are unlikely to prevent the creation of new victims. Drawing on the scholarly and policy accounts of cases around the world, we wanted to emphasize trafficking from the point of view of human security, where people are enmeshed in a global-to-local world of policies, laws, efforts, practices, and interactions, as they attempt to build lives of human dignity.

We would like to thank Jonathan Skerrett of Polity Press, our acquisitions editor, without whose encouragement this book would not have been completed. A sincere thanks to Cia Waring for reading through the document and asking us to clarify many ideas. Fiona Sewell was an amazing copy-editor. And we thank our family members for their constant support as we worked nights and weekends to coordinate our efforts across a 10-hour time divide.

Abbreviations

AIWA	Asian Immigrant Workers Advocates
ATIP	Anti-Trafficking in Persons
CAST	Coalition to Abolish Slavery and Trafficking
CATW	Coalition Against Trafficking in Women
EU	European Union
GAATW	Global Alliance Against Traffic in Women
GSI	Global Slavery Index
HRW	Human Rights Watch
ICE	US Immigration and Customs Enforcement
ILO	International Labour Organization
INGOs	international non-governmental organizations
IOM	International Organization for Migration
MOM	Ministry of Manpower
MSE	multiple systems estimation
NGOs	non-governmental organizations
NOWCRJ	New Orleans Workers' Center for Racial Justice

OHCHR	Office of the United Nations High Commissioner for Human Rights
PACHTO	Prevention and Control of Human Trafficking Ordinance
SAARC	South Asian Association for Regional Cooperation
SLBFE	Sri Lanka Bureau of Foreign Employment
SPLC	Southern Poverty Law Center
TIP	*Trafficking in Persons* [annual US Department of State report]
TVPA	Trafficking Victims Protection Act
UAE	United Arab Emirates
UK	United Kingdom
UN	United Nations
UNHCR	United Nations High Commissioner for Refugees
UNODC	United Nations Office on Drugs and Crime
US	United States
USD	United States dollar
VAWA	Violence Against Women Act
WHO	World Health Organization

1
Introduction

Over the last few decades, scholars, journalists, people in non-governmental organizations (NGOs), and policy makers have intensified their efforts to address the trafficking of human beings. A number of international and national policies and protocols have been developed and billions of dollars have been spent to combat trafficking and protect trafficking victims. According to the United Nations Office on Drugs and Crime (UNODC), since the *Protocol to Prevent, Suppress and Punish Trafficking in Persons, Especially Women and Children* (OHCHR 2000) entered into force on December 25, 2003, more than 90 percent of countries have developed legislation criminalizing different forms of human trafficking (UNODC 2016). In 2013, the General Assembly of the United Nations passed resolution A/RES/68/192 and designated July 30 as the World Day against Trafficking in Persons[1] in order to create awareness about trafficking in human beings and strengthen global cooperation to fight it. Estimates by the United Nations (UN) and international NGOs (INGOs), such as the Global Alliance Against Traffic in Women (GAATW), suggest that billions of dollars have been spent to combat trafficking since the 1990s.

Yet trafficking continues to flourish. According to the estimates of the International Labour Organization (ILO), Walk

Free Foundation, and International Organization for Migration (IOM) in 2017, 40 million people across the world were victims of modern slavery in 2016. While there are many disagreements about the data on actual number of trafficked persons (e.g. Loff and Sanghera 2004, Mugge 2017), many reports, case studies, and narratives of trafficked persons document that traffickers continue to prey upon people who are desperate to survive or move in search of better life conditions. As trafficking has grown to a billion-dollar industry according to some estimates (e.g. ILO 2014), human beings continue to be degraded to the level of commodities, smuggled across borders for profit, and trafficked for sex, labor, or their body parts.

The scholarship, activism, and policy foci on trafficking have also increased exponentially over the last few decades (e.g. Bernstein 2010, Dragiewicz 2015, Kempadoo 2012, Yea 2014). On the scholarly front, streams of research and policy analyses have generated debates and dissensions about adequate definitions and methodologies to study trafficking. Most of the research focuses on trafficking for sexual and labor exploitation. We use a slightly different approach in this book, and focus on trafficking for sexual exploitation, labor exploitation, and organs to describe the universe of trafficking. The research on this subject has begun to show that the exploitative contexts in which they are positioned make victims of one form of trafficking vulnerable to other forms over their life course. Thus, a woman trafficked for sexual exploitation might end up being trafficked for other types of labor. Or a man who has been trafficked for labor can become the target of organ traffickers. Thus, we conceptualize **trafficking as a continuum,**[2] where one form of trafficking overlaps with and can be connected to other forms of trafficking. However, the efforts to address trafficking often deal with types of trafficking separately, as discrete crimes to be punished. By examining all three forms we show that far from reflecting a series of clandestine and illegal activities, many forms of trafficking arise out of a complex series of interactions between illegal and legal (and above-ground) practices. This complexity explains why – despite so much effort – trafficking continues to flourish.

Trafficking: an old phenomenon in a new bottle?

While trafficking is increasingly in the news in our times, what is it exactly and to what extent is trafficking a new phenomenon? While we discuss the policy-based definitions of trafficking later in this chapter, broadly, **human trafficking** refers to the exploitation of human beings by others who use force, coercion, fraud, deception, and/or abduction to recruit, transport, harbor and receive, and exploit human beings for profit (UNODC 2016). The victims of trafficking do not consent to this exploitation. In other words, trafficking includes the dimensions of force, fraud, coercion (in different degrees), and diverse practices that generate profit for entities in the trafficking chain; a lack of consent on the part of the people who are trafficked is a key distinction that differentiates trafficking from other forms of exploitation. While we begin with this broad definition, each one of these terms – "force," "profit," and "lack of consent" – includes many nuances that we will discuss later in this book.

Some scholars and activists have described trafficking as **modern-day slavery** (e.g. Bales and Soodalter 2009, Walk Free Foundation 2016). With a widespread recognition of the immorality of slavery, this phrase is very effective in getting people in some parts of the world to understand the extreme forms of exploitation of human beings that continue today (e.g. Bales 1999, David 2015). This phrase also helps to frame this social problem in ways that garner support for the efforts to abolish and eradicate trafficking in human beings, so it is used widely (e.g. UNODC 2009). Yet some scholars are moving away from this phrase as they describe the contemporary structures, conditions, and facets of trafficking (e.g. Chuang 2015, Mugge 2017, Plant 2015). They argue that the term is too broad and does not help to capture many facets and underlying factors of contemporary trafficking; at the same time it appears to co-opt the conditions of slavery historically without centrally talking about racism. (We present more details on this debate in chapter 7, "Afterwords: Ongoing Debates and Unresolved Questions.")

Scholars are now looking into a number of questions including the role of states in facilitating some forms of trafficking even as the same states have laws against slavery, involuntary servitude, peonage, and debt bondage, and many have signed onto anti-trafficking protocols and devote significant resources to the eradication of some forms of trafficking. The critical questions for us today are: exactly which actors – states, corporations, crime cartels, and/or other entities – are involved in the process? How do people become victims of trafficking and what are their options for escaping from these conditions? How effective are the globally powerful policies and protocols, with their emphases on prevention, protection, and punishment, in the eradication of trafficking? Which aspects of trafficking fall through the cracks?

In order to fully understand the world of trafficking today, it is important to briefly look at the **history of trafficking**. According to many scholars (for instance, Gekht 2008, Knepper 2013, Samaddar 2015, Whitman and Gray 2015), trafficking for sexual and/or labor exploitation is not a new phenomenon. Just as most of the news stories about trafficking today focus on trafficking for sexual exploitation, the late nineteenth- and early twentieth-century discourse also focused mostly on exploitation for sex. And the Global North-based discussions of sexual exploitation of women and girls were mostly about white women and girls.

Gekht (2008) and Pattanaik (2002) point out that by 1904 and 1910 there were international agreements to stop white slave traffic. Specifically, abolition of prostitution became one of the demands of the nineteenth-century feminist movement (Outshoorn 2005). The focus of these abolitionists remained on the prostitution of *white* females, especially those who were moved overseas to serve white officers in the colonies where sexual relationships with local women were frowned upon (Pattanaik 2002). As the European powers took over the political control of vast swaths of Africa and Asia, they also organized their need for cheap labor through systems of **indentured labor** where men and women were forced to work to fulfil exploitative contracts. Slavery was officially abolished by 1927 (Fouladvand 2018), but indentured laborers were transported from one colony to another, or migration occurred from impoverished communities within Western Europe to parts of the "New World," where the migrants were held in conditions of involuntary servitude (for an overview see Samaddar 2015). Indentured labor has been historically associated with **colonialism**. Colonial powers typically took over a country to exploit its resources, for which purpose colonial powers required cheap, plentiful, and docile labor. Indentured labor met these criteria, so countries received these laborers, but made sure a range of laws and policies, from apartheid to exclusion from citizenship – with corresponding restrictions on property ownership, housing, education, well-paying jobs, etc. – ensured their unequal status. In a critical commentary on the efforts of the time, Goldman (1910) wrote:

> Our reformers have suddenly made a great discovery: the white slave traffic. The papers are full of these "unheard of conditions" in our midst, and lawmakers are planning a set of laws to check this horror... What really is the cause of this trade in women? Not merely white women, but yellow and black women as well. Exploitation of course: the merciless Moloch of capitalism that fattens on underpaid labor, thus driving thousands of women and girls into prostitution. (p. 2)

By the time the League of Nations emerged in the early twentieth century, anti-trafficking campaigners:

> managed to add a clause to the constitution that obligated the League to assume responsibility for international treaties agreed in 1904 and 1910. In 1921, the council created a permanent organization known as the Advisory Committee on the Suppression of the Traffic in Women and Children. The advisory committee decided that a worldwide social scientific study of the traffic in women would establish the facts of the trade beyond dispute and provide a substantive international agenda. (Knepper 2013, p. 36)

Initially, early twentieth-century researchers gathered data from twenty-eight countries across the Americas, Europe, and the Mediterranean. Later the studies were extended to Asia. The focus remained on trafficking in women and children for prostitution. These early discussions on trafficking – where the term was used to describe the exploitation – rarely included discussions about the exploitation for labor, or the ways in which the structures of racism and class were relevant for understanding exactly which women were the focus of rescue efforts. Similarly, the role of capitalism and colonialism remained unmarked in these discussions of trafficking.

When we examine the history of the later twentieth century and the re-emergence of trafficking on the global stage, some of these earlier trends are still evident. According to Foulad-vand (2018), the 1949 *Convention for the Suppression of the Traffic in Persons and of the Exploitation of the Prostitution of Others* emphasized criminal justice penalties for procurement for prostitution. The Nuremburg Trials reignited global attention to enslavement as the world learned about the treatment of Jews by the Nazis. Subsequently, the 1956 UN *Supplementary Convention on the Abolition of Slavery, the Slave Trade, and Institutions and Practices Similar to Slavery* expanded the definition of slave-related practices, to include:

> bonded labour, serfdom, the selling of women by their families for marriage, certain forms of abuse of women, and the buying and selling of children for exploitation [but] it was fair to say that the approach to slavery at this period was as a residual problem which flourished only in local pockets of pre-modernity, in the sex trade or under totalitarian rule. (Fouladvand 2018, p. 4)

As Gekht (2008) and others have pointed out, the recent re-emergence of the attention to trafficking has been partly due to the end of the Cold War and greater international co-operation on global crimes. Along with the criminal activities related to drugs, human smuggling and trafficking emerged as prominent international crimes. By the late 1980s and early 1990s, the United States (US) and several other nation-states, as well as large NGOs, became interested in trafficking for sexual exploitation; they became vocal advocates for better policies, protocols, and actions to control sexual exploitation, especially prostitution. These groups demanded criminal prosecution of smugglers and traffickers.[3]

By the turn of the twenty-first century, two powerful tools, which we discuss later in this chapter, were introduced. The 2000 *UN Protocol to Prevent, Suppress and Punish Trafficking in Persons, Especially Women and Children* (OHCHR 2000) includes language about mandatory criminal prosecution and discretionary language about victim assistance. The US *Trafficking in Persons* report was instituted the same year; this has become a powerful international tool seeking information about countries' efforts to combat trafficking, based on a number of quantitatively measurable items including the number of prosecutions, laws passed, special police units, and shelters.[4] Yet the 2016 *Global Report on Trafficking* points out that while many countries have passed policies against trafficking, the number of convictions remains low (UNODC 2016).

Looking beyond the policy and legal worlds, scholars have identified different facets of the current phase of globalization as critical contributors to the contexts of trafficking. The current globalized economy continues to look for cheap, contingent labor. On the demand side, there is a continuing (and, perhaps, expanding) demand for sex directly or through a rapidly growing pornography industry. With improvements in medical technology and a culture of expectation of long and healthy lives in different parts of the world, there is an ever-growing demand (often legal) for organs for transplantation. Many people are eager, even desperate for new and/or better opportunities as armed conflicts, natural disasters, and continuing inequalities, locally, regionally, and internationally, lead to their displacement and the disruption of their ways of life. Improvements in transportation and communication make distant places appear more reachable to people who are looking for better opportunities. At the same time, we are witnessing rapidly growing restrictions on legal migration. This disjuncture, between a potentially mobile population and a world of political restrictions on migrants' mobility (Purkayastha 2018), as well as the growth of legal and illegal industries and networks that trade in human beings for exploitation, leads to the conditions that facilitate the growth of human trafficking.

Regional variations

Recent international reports on trafficking show that trafficking economies exist all over the world. There are variations in the forms of trafficking that are most prevalent in different parts of the world. Women remain the largest number of trafficked persons, though the numbers of men and children have been growing. Some of this growth may be due to better monitoring and reporting. According to the *Global Report* (UNODC 2016), among those who are trafficked for sexual exploitation, women and children make up 96 percent of the victims; of those who are trafficked for labor, 63 percent are men. Men were most often targeted for organ trafficking (82 percent). This document reports that the wealthy countries are the destination for victims from the widest range of countries. For instance, victims from 137 countries were detected in Western and Southern Europe. The report points out that trafficking appears locally, regionally, and internationally. While we have been used to describing those who were made to cross international boundaries, through force, fraud, or deception, as "trafficked persons," with newer debates – some of which we discuss later in this chapter – there is a growing recognition that the phenomenon occurs at all scales, from local to global.

The UN has continued to issue periodic reports on trafficked persons. The 2016 report of UNODC shows significant inter-regional variation.

- In Northern and Western Europe, the detected victim profile shows 56 percent women, with 67 percent exploited for sex; however, labor trafficking appears to be a growing trend. Of the convicted offenders, 58 percent are foreigners to this region, often from the same countries as the victims.
- In Central and Southern Europe, most frequently detected victims are women (54 percent). As in Western and Southern Europe, the exploitation is sexual. The emerging issue is trafficking for begging and forced marriages.
- In Eastern Europe and Central Asia, the victims are more likely to be men (53 percent), with forced labor being the detected form of exploitation. Trafficking from poorer to richer countries of the region is the emerging trend.
- In North and Central America and the Caribbean, women make up 60 percent of the victims. Sexual exploitation has been detected in 55 percent of the cases. The domestic and intraregional flows show many children are among the detected victims.
- In South America, women make up 45 percent of the detected victims. Of the victims, 57 percent have been exploited for

sex. This region serves as the origin of intraregional trafficking circuits.

- In East Asia and the Pacific, women make up 51 percent of the victims. Sexual exploitation has been detected in 61 percent of the cases. This region is the destination for short-, medium-, and long-distance trafficking.
- For South Asia, the UN report does not provide the gender of the victim. However, adults make up 60 percent of detected victims, pointing to the presence of significant child trafficking, including to the Middle East. Of the detected victims, 85 percent are exploited as forced labor.
- Similarly, for sub-Saharan Africa, 39 percent of the detected victims are reported to be boys. Of the victims, 53 percent are in situations of forced labor.
- In North Africa and the Middle East, women make up 38 percent of the detected victim profile. Of the victims, 44 percent are exploited as forced labor. The report emphasizes that trafficking driven by conflict and persecution occurs along some migration routes in this region.

These overview figures provide a sense of the variations across the globe. However, the report points out that the problems of data collection affect some of these regional profiles. The report is careful to estimate profiles based on detected victims. Since many are not detected, these profiles are estimates for the years in which the data were collected. From the time of the League of Nations' attempt to collect data on trafficking, the core problem has remained: how do we collect data on victims who largely remain invisible in society? How do we even know if a person is a trafficked victim or not?

An overview on the policies and struggles to contain trafficking showcases some of the complexities of the problem.

Toward policies and protocols on trafficking: the US experience

In his account of the war on human trafficking in the US, DeStefano (2008) provides an excellent overview of the road to some of the current thinking about trafficking. While countries like the US had older laws against slavery and peonage, the late twentieth-century understanding of trafficking required sorting out smuggling, illegal migration, and migration due to fraud, coercion, and force. According to DeStefano, by the 1990s, the US had begun to develop international law enforcement standards for a number of crimes including human smuggling and trafficking.[5] This entanglement of trafficking with other criminal activities has meant most of the responses have been envisioned in terms of crimes and punishment. By 1998, the US had been in conversation with Russia, France, Germany, Italy, Japan, Great Britain, and Canada. In addition, that same year, the UN's Commission on Crime Prevention and Criminal Justice recommended the General Assembly work toward an **international convention** – which works like a treaty between countries – against transnational crime. By 2000, both the US and the UN had begun to draw up protocols and policies that specifically emphasized trafficking in women and children. Not surprisingly, these policies and protocols reflect the political advocacy of many of the groups that feel passionate about facets of human trafficking. While the US Trafficking Victims Protection Act (TVPA) initially had three objectives – prosecution, protection, and prevention – over time, the focus has been on prosecution that is reliant on the criminal justice system. Over the years, two other trends have shaped how the TVPA operates. Under pressure from activists – often from religious organizations – who wished to eradicate prostitution, the focus has been on trafficking for sexual exploitation. Further, over time, all forms of prostitution became embedded in US policy directions. In its subsequent iteration, the US policy – the Trafficking Protection Victim Reauthorization Act of 2003 – specifically prohibits money from going to organizations that do not publicly affirm their opposition to the legalization or practice of prostitution.

At the same time, especially since the 1990s, many civil infractions that were associated with immigration have been brought within the purview of the criminal justice system (often referred to by social scientists as the **crimmigration system**). Since trafficked persons typically do not possess all the papers to enable them to access justice systems within any country, their legal situation remains problematic. Thus, the worlds of migration and criminalization of their status as migrants without documents have created particularly difficult conditions on the ground for victims who wish to seek protection.

Internationally, the pressure from human rights activists led to the recognition of domestic trafficking victims. As DeStefano (2008) points out, if, as some advocates ask, all prostitution is formally included under the category of "coerced sex," then the numbers of trafficked persons would go up significantly within the US. However, the exact contours of these definitions and their translation into policy remain, in the US as in other countries, as dynamic circumstances, depending on the relative power of the groups who attempt to change the definitions.

The messy world of definitions, explanations, and data: a brief introduction

Understanding trafficking today requires us to delve into the messy world of definitions and data on trafficking. Despite the enormous effort and amount of money poured into combating trafficking, consistently valid large-scale data remain elusive. The worlds of academia, policy, and enforcement are engaged in developing adequate definitions of trafficking and refining processes to gather data. In this section we discuss some of the divergences in defining and explaining trafficking.

Trafficking: policy definitions

What exactly is trafficking? We begin with two policy-based definitions that are widely used across the world to combat trafficking. Even this brief glimpse shows that these definitions are complex, reflecting the agendas of different stakeholders (National Institute of Justice 2014). The world of policies that are designed to address trafficking range from the international level, such as the UN conventions and protocols, to a range of national laws, policies, and local efforts. The UNODC's recent report (2016) shows that over 90 percent of countries have developed legislation to combat trafficking. We provide definitions by the UN and the US[6] that have been particularly influential across the world. The UN protocols require signatories to report periodically on the actions they have taken to combat trafficking. At the same time, the institutionalization of the annual US *Trafficking in Persons* (TIP) reports as a way of shaping US foreign relations – tying some of its foreign aid to recipient countries' efforts on trafficking – has significant impact on how countries have attempted to respond to trafficking.

The UN's protocol on trafficking provides the broad framework for understanding and responding to trafficking. The UN *Protocol to Prevent, Suppress and Punish Trafficking in Persons* was passed in 2000. According to Article 3 of this protocol, human trafficking is defined as:

> The recruitment, transportation, transfer, harboring or receipt of persons, by means of a threat or use of force or other forms of coercion, of abduction, of fraud, of deception, of the abuse of power or of a position of vulnerability, or of giving or receiving payments or benefits to achieve the consent of a person having control over another person for the purpose of exploitation. (OHCHR 2000, p. 2)

According to the UNODC,[7] the definition of trafficking consists of three core elements:

1 the **action** of trafficking, which means the recruitment, transportation, transfer, harboring, or receipt of persons;
2 the **means** of trafficking, which includes threat of or use of force, deception, coercion, or abuse of power or position of vulnerability;
3 the **purpose** of trafficking, which is always exploitation. In the words of the Trafficking Protocol (OHCHR 2000, article 3), "Exploitation shall include, at a minimum, the exploitation of the prostitution of others or other forms of sexual exploitation, forced labour or services, slavery or practices similar to slavery, servitude or the removal of organs."

In addition, the UNODC *Global Report on Trafficking in Persons* (2016) provides information about human trafficking flows "within countries, between neighbouring countries or even across different continents" (p. 5). According to the report, in addition to trafficking for sexual exploitation, forced labor, and organ removal, the cases identified show that people have been trafficked for other forms of exploitation, including begging, committing crime, illegal child adoption or child selling, forced marriages, child soldiering, pornography, benefit fraud, and mixed exploitation.

By way of comparison, the annual US TIP report has some similarities with the UN definitions, but it is more limited in scope. This report defines "severe forms of trafficking in persons" as:

- sex trafficking in which a commercial sex act is induced by force, fraud, or coercion, or in which the person induced to perform such an act has not attained 18 years of age; or
- the recruitment, harboring, transportation, provision, or obtaining of a person for labor or services, through the use of force, fraud, or coercion for the purpose of subjection to involuntary servitude, peonage, debt bondage, or slavery. (US Department of State 2017, p. 3)

The specific categories identified by the TIP report are sex trafficking, child sex trafficking, forced labor or bonded labor, domestic servitude, forced child labor and unlawful recruitment, and use of child soldiers (2017, p. 12).

These definitions and their differences are important because they not only shape much of the effort to combat trafficking, they influence the data on trafficking. To which protocol countries respond, and in which ways, shapes the direction of efforts to combat trafficking. A clear point of difference between these two definitions is the absence of organ trafficking from the US description of trafficking. The UN definition includes many other forms of human degradation in its description of trafficking victims. Yet there are similarities in these approaches as well. Both, implicitly or explicitly, refer to victims who are trafficked within and across countries. Both definitions rely on gender binaries; even though the term "person" is used in the definitions, the data (including narratives) are gathered on males and females (and not people of other genders). Both are grounded in a criminal justice approach to combating trafficking, i.e. for punishing individual or group perpetrators or rescuing individual victims. These definitions recognize the power of criminal networks, but not the complex intersecting global and local *structures* that create the vulnerabilities of persons who are more likely to be trafficked. Nor do these definitions emphasize a thrust to combat the consumers of trafficked sex, labor, or organs. And little is said about the rights or quality of lives of those who are victimized through trafficking, including their ability to build lives of dignity (a key principle in understanding human rights of persons).

How do we understand trafficking?

The framework we use in this book reflects our understanding that the same individuals can be exploited for sex, labor, and organs sequentially, though sometimes these forms of exploitation occur together. We are interested in analyzing the structures – the institutions, laws, policies, patterned practices – that lead to the victimization of human beings, as well as the structures that facilitate or impede their ability to rebuild their lives if and after they are free of the trafficked condition. In charting out our approach, we draw upon several ongoing scholarly and activist debates. We present the lineage of these debates in the next section, but it is important to emphasize the key issues that shape our understanding of trafficking.

One of the key academic debates focuses on women who are in the sex trade. Since the growth of feminist scholarship and activism led to renewed attention to violence against women, sex work, and associated topics, there are debates among scholars and feminist NGOs about women in sex work as victims of trafficking or whether they chose this profession (Merry 2011). The answers to such questions are key to understanding how countries and organizations identify and count the numbers of trafficked women (and girls) and what measures they devise to combat trafficking. A related issue is adequately accounting for the sources of women *and* men's vulnerabilities to trafficking.

Another key debate is whether trafficking is a form of migration. On the one hand, the UNODC asserts "cross border trafficking flows often resemble regular migration flows" (2016, p. 12). On the other hand, migration and trafficking are often discussed separately by academics (for an exception see Purkayastha 2018). Positioning trafficking within the terrain of migration draws our attention to the rights – or lack of rights

– of migrants, including trafficked persons. We discuss trafficking as part of forced migration and recognize that trafficking takes places within countries and across international borders, with different implications about rights and access to a country's resources. We remain mindful of the overlap between trafficking and **human smuggling**. Fiona David defines smuggling in this way:

> Migrant smuggling is a related but distinct legal concept to trafficking in persons. As defined in Article 3 of the Migrant Smuggling Protocol, migrant smuggling involves two main elements: (i) intentionally facilitating the illegal entry of a person into another country; (ii) for some form of financial or material benefit. While migrant smuggling and trafficking in persons are distinct legal concepts, in reality these crime types can overlap. For example, a trafficked person may have been smuggled as part of the migration process and, similarly, a smuggled person may also become a victim of trafficking. (2012, p. 2)

While some international definitions assert that trafficking can occur even if people are not moved (see p. 3 of the 2017 US Department of State TIP report), in reality internal and international migration is mostly common to the experiences of trafficking. Drawing upon the migration literature also allows us to pay attention to the inadequacy of anti-trafficking interventions primarily through criminal justice systems. While smugglers and traffickers can be addressed through criminal justice systems, they are only one set of actors in the trafficking terrain. The actors that form the markets for the trafficked products, or those who contribute to the vulnerability, are not necessarily engaged in criminal activities according to the laws and policies of most countries. Equally important, a focus on the criminal justice system sometimes detracts from paying attention to the prevention and protection aspects of anti-trafficking efforts.

Building on the earlier definitions, we too emphasize the critical role of force and/or coercion exercised by powerful entities that profit from trading in human beings for sex, labor, or body parts within and across countries. In most people's minds, and, as we indicated earlier, in many policy circles, trafficking is most often equated with "sex trafficking." The scholarship and activism tend to address each form of trafficking separately, though there has been some change in recent years to look at trafficking for sexual and labor exploitation together. Looking at these *three* forms of trafficking together in this book allows us to unpack the meanings, assumptions, criticisms, and limitations of our thinking about trafficking. Our prior research on victims of trafficking shows that different forms of trafficking are not discrete occurrences; often the same people can be trafficked for sex or labor or organs or for other purposes at the same time or during different stages of their lives (Yousaf and Purkayastha 2015a). Consequently, while we discuss different forms of trafficking separately in the chapters of this book, we conceptualize *the forms of trafficking as a continuum* and showcase some of the structural similarities and linkages across these different forms.

Much like the data in the UNODC reports, which were the basis of our regional trafficking summary earlier, we recognize both women *and* men can be victims, though women and girls make up the vast majority of those trafficked for sex. We show that trafficking emerges and is sustained within a series of nested **glocal** structural conditions – that is, intersecting local, regional, and global conditions – that create significant inequalities and threats to people's survival and wellbeing. Consequently, we highlight the embedded inequalities and power disparities that characterize these glocal contexts in which trafficking occurs. And we pay attention to the policies, protocols, agendas, and practices of a range of actors that shape how trafficking is defined and addressed around the world.

We follow the UN protocols in thinking about trafficking as a violation of **human rights**, as these are enshrined in the UN Charters and Conventions on Human Rights. We do not rely only on the idea of rights as they are enshrined in laws and policies. Since we are interested in understanding the experiences of trafficked persons within a world of marginalization and exploitation, we discuss laws, policies, and prosecution, and fragmented goodwill initiatives and large-scale humanitarian efforts. We also emphasize that people's ability to *substantively access* political, civil, social, economic, and other human rights offers a good entry point for understanding trafficking. The idea of **human security** is based on our understanding of **substantive access to human rights**, but we think it is also important to remain aware of the historical and contemporary political-economic context in which trafficking occurs. This human security approach, as we discuss later in this chapter, emphasizes the need to look to the long-term wellbeing of the people affected by trafficking. Consequently, this approach allows us to interrogate some of the theoretical, methodological, and policy debates on trafficking.

In the next section we outline some of the key academic and activist debates that help us to better understand some of the core elements of these definitions, and outline some of the methodological problems in defining trafficking and devising responses to trafficking.

Explaining trafficking through the lineage of academic debates

The scholarly debates on different types of trafficking vary in their approaches. These divergences reflect scholars' foci on different groups (e.g. women primarily vs. human beings) and the vantage point from which they consider trafficking, for instance within a larger discussion on violence against women or through analyses of forced migration. Here we present two sets of debates. We begin with the feminist debates that relate explicitly or broadly to trafficking. Next, we turn to migration scholars who examine trafficking as a form of forced migration. These discussions overlap at times but we present these separately to explain the gaps we are seeking to address. Cross-cutting with these debates are the discussions on human rights and human security which provide an entry point to considering the experiences of the victims along with the structures that impede their access to rights.

Trafficking debates: feminist dissensions

The growth of feminist scholarship, especially the scholarship that examines individuals and groups at the nexus of intersecting structures of gender/class/race/ethnicity/age/nationality and related inequalities (widely referred to as **intersectionality**), has ignited debates relating to seemingly innocuous terms such as "trafficking" or "victims." This literature delves into violence in women's lives, how power is understood, and the structures that create people's vulnerabilities to trafficking. Since this scholarship is closely reflected in many activist organizations as well, we cite some NGOs' interpretations of these debates.

As we indicated earlier, in the nineteenth and twentieth centuries Western powers worried about white slavery, that is, the idea of white women being forced into prostitution and then moved to the colonies to provide sexual services to officers. A clear racial boundary separated those who were deemed worthy of rescue and those who were not visible in that conversation. Others who were regularly traded or moved around the world were defined as slaves or indentured labor (Seedat-Khan 2012). They were, most likely, sexually exploited under these harsh circumstances, but their sexual exploitation was not expressed as political and social anxiety. The sexual exploitation of women of different races and/or nationalities is of more recent origin; it has developed rapidly as the writings of scholars from the Global South began to challenge the views of Global North scholars who took white women's experiences as the model for understanding all women's experiences.

The debates about trafficking arose within discussions about women's subordination, violence against women, and analyses of sex work. The earliest formulations, which developed as part of second wave feminism in the Global North, focused on patriarchal power that men exercised over women. The earlier ideas of sex roles imagined women to be socialized to be homemakers within the private sphere of families. Their subordination, including victimization to violence, was explained in terms of patriarchal power within households. Over the next few decades, this framework was challenged by feminists from around the world for its homogenized conceptualization of men and women. The theoretical specifications moved from sex roles – explanations of male and female disparities in terms of their different early socialization – to a recognition of multiple and complex structures of gender, and of how structures of class, race, sexuality, nation, age, and ability intersect with gender to shape power and privilege among and between women and men (see Collins 1990, Collins and Bilge 2016, Connell 1985, Ferree 1990, Patil and Purkayastha 2017, Purkayastha 2012).

At the same time the understanding of violence against women expanded from violence perpetrated by deviant individuals within households to recognition of the ways in which private and public worlds overlapped as institutions and states facilitated and perpetrated violence themselves. For instance, scholars discussed the exploitation of women in the brothels near military bases, or actively providing comfort women for militaries (see e.g. Hicks 1995, Jordan 1995, Okamoto 2013). These types of violence clearly include the collusion of states. Today, the dominant way of understanding violence against women is to situate it within these complex intersecting structures (Ertürk and Purkayastha 2012).

Applied to the question of trafficking, however, the earlier white feminists' explanations, i.e. the gender binary framework, shaped the explanations of violence that female trafficking victims faced. As Fitzgerald (2010) and others have pointed out, the contemporary politics of trafficking continue to reflect the assumption that sex trafficking is an outcome of patriarchy: female victims are trafficked by male perpetrators. The UN and US definitions of trafficking outlined in the previous section reflect many aspects of these early feminist female-victim/male-perpetrator conceptual schemata.

The discussions of sex trafficking intersected with activist efforts to abolish prostitution. Developed within a stream of conversation about prostitution and pornography amid a growing culture of sexual choice in the Global North, some feminists (e.g. MacKinnon 1987) questioned the abolitionist tones relating to prostitution (e.g. cited in Barry 1995, Brace and O'Connell Davidson 2000, Brownmiller 1975, Dworkin 1981, Jeffreys 1997, MacKinnon 1987). Their argument tangentially touched upon the issue of trafficking by making it important to question whether force, fraud, or coercion had been used for the purposes of sexual exploitation instead of assuming that the presence of women in the prostitution industry automatically implied they were trafficking victims (also see Brace and O'Connell Davidson 2000, Choo 2016). Another strand of this conversation is linked to Kempadoo's critique of the conceptualization of women in sex work according to Global North abolitionist terms, and "that within the Caribbean arts – literature, theatre, and music – and in everyday storytelling and anecdotes, prostitutes are invariably portrayed

as an integral part of village and town life" (2001, p. 42).
Does a woman's engagement with multiple sexual partners,
for instance, in the Caribbean, mean that the woman is coerced?
More critically, how should we understand coercion and force
vs. choice? The shift in language, from sex trafficking to trafficking for sex, is a result of these shifts in understanding this
social problem.

By the twenty-first century critical gender scholars pointed
out that it was important to consider **intersections of structures** including gender/race/class/caste/ethnicity/sexuality/age/
nationality in shaping the experiences of trafficked persons. This
approach not only made visible the diverse groups of women
and men (and girls and boys) who were trafficked, it further
clarified the different sources of violence that make groups
vulnerable to trafficking (e.g. Yousaf and Purkayastha 2015a).
Kempadoo (2016, 2001, 1999) points out that the issues of
choice vs. coercion, debated by Global North feminists, do
not adequately account for the ways in which global and local
structures intersect to draw women and men into industries
providing sexual services. At the individual level, women or
men might choose to provide sexual services, and indeed it
is important to pay attention to their aspirations and agency.
Many of the participants in her research said they made this
choice. But these choices should be interpreted with reference to the *absence* of choice of other occupations, which is
a reflection of the inequalities generated by the contemporary
glocal political-economic system.

While many of the feminist debates focus on trafficking for
sex, these debates, especially the points raised by researchers
from the Global South, point to a complex terrain in which
people are trafficked. This literature offered at least four refinements in understanding trafficking that go well beyond the
specific discussion on trafficking for sex. First, using an intersectional approach means the explanations of trafficking are
configured as outcomes of more complex factors than patriarchy
alone. Second, the victims are both women and men (and girls
and boys), but they are trafficked to different trafficking
markets. It is also important to keep in mind that some women
and men are drawn into the worlds of prostitution through
their own choice, and/or through coercion and force.

Third, the distinction between exploitation for labor and for
sex cannot be rigidly drawn; such a definition of trafficking

comes closer to the trafficking-as-a-continuum approach we adopt here. Some of these refinements are already shaping policies; for instance, the ILO, Walk Free Foundation, and IOM (2017) now recognize sex work is exploitative labor. Fourth, these scholars have drawn our attention to the markets for sexual/labor exploitation, and, in doing so, made visible and implicated the consumers of these "commodities" within the terrain of trafficking. For instance, the research on sex tourism points out that ideologies about "oriental women" and their sexuality in the Global North make Asian women valuable commodities in the global markets for sex (for a discussion on the development of these ideologies, see Espiritu 2007).

Assessed through the feminist analytical lens, the criminal justice approaches enshrined in the UN or US efforts do not adequately address the diverse structural factors that create vulnerabilities to trafficking. Nor do they target the consumers of sex, labor, and organs in order to shut down those markets for these inhuman trades. In fact, Bernstein (2010), Kempadoo, Sanghera, and Pattanaik (2012), Yea (2014), Yousaf and Purkayastha (2015a), and others critique the vast global operation of anti-trafficking efforts and campaigns, which operate on a theoretical logic and framework that have little relation to *diverse* conditions on the ground (see also Doezema 2001, Downe 2007, Mahdavi 2013, Purkayastha and Majumdar 2009, Sleightholme and Sinha 1996). They emphasize the key factors leading to trafficking: these include wars, conflicts, and the negative outcomes of structural adjustment policies that create conditions of vulnerability and desperation among people seeking some measure of security in their lives. As we discuss in this book, without addressing these larger factors, it is difficult to address the sources of victims' vulnerabilities. Punishing traffickers alone is unlikely to stop trafficking. The victims simply get exploited through the same or other forms of trafficking.

Trafficking debates: migration, smuggling, and questions of rights

Situating the core idea of *trafficking as a continuum* within the migration literature yields some other insights. Trafficking involves movement, so the conditions that lead to this form of migration are an important piece of the trafficking puzzle. The literature on international migration has for more than a century indicated the struggles people go through, especially people who migrate with few resources, to establish themselves within the new country's structures and cultures. The literature on temporary migrants points to some of the challenges people face when they are not able to access political and social rights within the destination country. In addition, the literature on **forced migration**, that is, the type of migration where people are forced to move because of natural or human-made disasters, offers some direct insights into trafficking as an outcome of social inequalities, power, and violence. All these are important for understanding trafficking.

What are some of the larger factors that lead to migration, especially when people did not plan to move voluntarily? Conflicts *within* and *between* states generate migration; people who are seeking safety flee to new areas within nation-state boundaries and across them (see, for instance, Datta 2016, Njiru and Purkayastha 2015). As people flee conflict and violence they often do not have much choice in where and how long they can settle. In today's political economy, the growth of the military–industrial complex that profits from making weaponry, and from its deployment in wars and conflicts, means large swaths of people are affected by conflicts that disrupt established ways of life in many places (see SIPRI 2013, also US Department of State 2017, p. 8, for the Vatican's stance on this topic). Similarly large-scale structural adjustments, where countries are forced to make, or embark on, large-scale changes, including rescinding government-provided social and economic resources, create significant hardships (e.g. Shrivastava and Kothari 2012). Transnational corporations that extract resources such as oil, minerals, or water across the world also create conditions that can lead to the displacement of people. Many states spend more on conflicts and state security than on provisions to ensure people's economic, social, and cultural human rights. These conditions of instability and inequality make marginalized groups vulnerable to traffickers and smugglers who offer them "opportunities" to reach safer havens.

The forced migration literature documents the factors that lead to forced migration as well as the conditions people encounter after being forced to migrate. Scholars document ways in which unequal access to economic, social, and political resources mire some people in conditions of extreme marginality, which, in turn, provide the conditions conducive to trafficking (e.g. Yousaf 2018). This is similar to the point Kempadoo and her colleagues emphasized in their feminist approaches to trafficking for sexual exploitation: they also emphasized the lack of access to material resources and rights that end up creating vulnerabilities among people. Forced migrants do not always have the requisite documentation if and when they cross international boundaries. Some, like the people designated as refugees, do have documentation, but it is not clear that this documentation alone aids their transition to a new life. Life in refugee camps – or internally displaced persons' camps – is harsh (Datta 2016, Njiru 2018, Ray 2017). This is why people often turn to smugglers to escape the harsh conditions of their lives.

The worlds of temporary migration – legal short-term migration – also create vulnerabilities. The shifts and changes under the current phase of globalization have created large numbers of new jobs that are temporary, ill-paid, with few guarantees of the resources that would enable people to build stable lives. Fullerton and Robertson (2011) have written about the way the rights of labor, which had been enshrined through union movements to ensure "family wages" for stable jobs, are now being rapidly eroded. Instead there is a push to create **contingent labor**, an army of people who are forced to work temporarily at a variety of jobs for little pay (and few to no social benefits such as health care). Like the movement of indentured labor under colonialism, the current phase of globalization profits from international supplies of contingent labor with few political, economic, or social rights. These conditions enable and intersect with the rapid growth of labor trafficking.

The shifts and changes in immigration laws in different countries, and the periodic resurgence of nativist movements and their success in pressuring local and national governments to institute anti-immigrant measures, are also important aspects of the context within which trafficking occurs. These changes and movements complicate the political terrain in which trafficked persons are recognized as political subjects worthy of access to rights and resources in the destination country. While there is relatively greater recognition of victims of trafficking for sex – though this does not ensure their easy access to rights[8] – the recognition of victimhood becomes complicated for people who are trafficked for labor. In his report on smuggling at the US–Mexico border, Wuebbels (n.d.) points to the unintended consequence of clamping down on immigration to countries like the US. Bruggeman (2002) makes a similar point about trafficking to the European Union (EU). As formal channels shut down, migrants seek alternative routes to reach countries. The recent accounts of migrants and refugees streaming into Turkey, Greece, and other parts of the EU (e.g. Brunwasser 2015, Lyman and Smale 2015, Smale and Eddy 2015) have reignited the conversations about people moving out of the Middle East and North Africa, the conditions under which they get to Europe, the sexual exploitation of women along the way, and the role of traffickers and smugglers in this context. Similar conversations have emerged about South East Asian refugees and Australia (e.g. Stats 2015) and women and unaccompanied children from Central America attempting to reach the US (Musalo and Lee 2017).

While the policy-based definition of smuggling implies a person has voluntarily chosen to get to a country illegally, and, is, consequently, an undocumented migrant who can be punished for violating laws, this aspect of choice is a matter of dispute among academics (David 2012). Many academics point out that the coercion can occur at different points of a person's migration or different stages of their lives. Discussing women's migration to the United Arab Emirates (UAE), Mahdavi (2013) makes this point about female migrants who seek work in the informal economy as stricter laws restrict migration to work in a country's formal economy. In the absence of access to clearly defined rights, and channels of protest and protection, female migrants often end up providing domestic *and* sexual labor. While they may have chosen to migrate to provide domestic labor initially, their sexual exploitation – aided by political marginalization – is coerced. Similarly, Adur (2011) shows how exploitative conditions of labor, which are initially based on legal migration, can quickly change to conditions of indenture based on coercion and force. Her account of laborers on H-2 temporary or seasonal work visas to the US shows the difficulties in clearly defining trafficking without taking into consideration how conditions of migration change within a formal political terrain that deprives some migrants of access to human rights, including the ability to make choices about their work lives. Choo (2016) describes similar changes and exploitation affecting Filipina migrants who come to South Korea on temporary work visas.

Yousaf and Purkayastha (2015b) document that the shifts and changes in labor conditions – which have become more exploitative – create the contexts that facilitate trafficking in organs. Desperate people will "donate" organs to earn money to pay off debts. As their health deteriorates, they cannot work as much as before; traffickers then target their family members. The main debates in the organ-focused literature are about the ethics of receiving transplants. As we discuss in a later chapter, the political-economic structures identified by many scholars of forced migration apply to organ trafficking as well.

Samaddar (2015) has linked trafficking to a larger set of structures related to the logic of a capitalist global economy. He argued that: "studies of hunger in the 19th century, of itinerant movements, transportations of coolies, spread of famines, shipping of children, adult girls, trafficking in sex, labour, and human organs, and welfare legislations to cope with this great infamy tell us how actually we have arrived at our own time of subject formation under the conditions of empire" (p. 50).

Overall, the forced migration literature, especially from the Global South, offers three important points for considering trafficking. First, analyzing force and coercion is not simply a matter of tracing it (as do the current policies) to traffickers who commit crimes. We need to remain aware of the political-economic structures that create the conditions of vulnerability and make violence, extreme control, coercion, and force a routinized part of modern life. Second, the literature on migration directs us to question the terms on which people can cross international borders. If the global political economy generates great inequalities while countries where jobs are located shut down their borders, people who are on the move are likely to become vulnerable to smugglers and traffickers. Third, this literature emphasizes the need to look into the substantive rights of persons who are trafficked. While the human rights conventions may outline a variety of rights for migrants and trafficked persons, the reality is often different. If we analyze trafficked persons' experiences we ought to ask: which sets of intersecting local and global structures enable or impede trafficked migrants' ability to access their human rights?

Toward a framework on trafficking: combining an intersectional approach with questions of human security

The previous sections highlighted that the same people can be targeted for different forms of trafficking. As they try to move to places with better opportunities they may migrate, be smuggled, or be trafficked at different points of their journey. Traffickers target constellations of people, sorted by age, sex, and other characteristics that are likely to improve the profitability of whatever they offer as a commodity for sale.

In order to discuss the larger structural circumstances, as well as the ways in which trafficking plays out in people's lives, we use an integrated intersectionality and human security approach to discuss trafficking. Intersectionality recognizes that people are not simply male or female; they are affected by ideologies, patterned institutional arrangements including laws and practices, that create hierarchies based on their race, caste, class, religion, gender, nationality, age, and other local and global structures that create and maintain hierarchies among people. It is simply not enough to talk about how women are trafficked for sexual exploitation: we have to ask which women are trafficked (their age, class, ethnicity, race, nationality, etc.), and question the structures of their marginalization.

The human security approach draws upon the earlier work on human rights, especially the work on substantive human rights (see Armaline, Glasberg, and Purkayastha 2015, Glenn 2002, Purkayastha 2018). Typically, the human rights approach draws upon established charters and conventions to argue for the rights of people prior to, during, and after migration. Scholars and policy makers have pointed out that often the notion of human rights is set aside under the guise of national security (Robinson 2005). Kreidenweis and Hudson (2015) have pointed out that "human security can reinforce the same structuring logic of national security, reinvesting the state with the responsibility of providing security" (p. 84). We use a *human security approach*, one that remains cognizant of human rights, but focuses on substantive access to political, civil, economic, and social human rights, as critically important for understanding trafficking. This approach helps us to put the trafficking victims' experiences at the center of our efforts to understand trafficking. For instance, there is a significant literature documenting the long-term health consequences endured by trafficking victims. If we consider the long-term health consequences of trafficked persons, we need to consider their substantive access to political and social rights. There are academic studies (e.g. Banovic and Bjelajac 2012, Zimmerman, Hossain, and Watts 2011) and reports (e.g. the 2018 World Health Organization (WHO) report on female migrants and health) that provide assessments of the negative health consequences of trafficking for female migrants and trafficking victims' lives. How would trafficked persons access health care to address their health long term? Do they have the political right to access nationalized care, wherever this exists? If inexpensive government-subsidized health care is not available, how do they survive? Or how do they remain healthy enough to find and work in other jobs that will allow them to rebuild their lives? Our emphasis on human security takes these consequences into account as we assess current approaches to addressing trafficking.

Our approach recognizes that nested international-national-local structures create intersectional vulnerabilities for people, especially within unstable socio-economic-political conditions. Depending on the international and national laws and policies in place, victims of trafficking, forced migration, and smuggling may be imprisoned or put into detention camps. The rise of crimmigration in countries such as the US, where immigration and criminal justice systems are increasingly being brought together, creates further vulnerabilities for people who are forced to migrate without access to documents. Being in shelters or refugee camps does not consistently provide respite from these vulnerabilities because the conditions outside do not change (Njiru and Purkayastha 2015, Yousaf and Purkayastha 2015a). Uneven funding and shifting priorities regarding trafficking make the efforts to help people fragmented and episodic at best. While we examine the structures leading to trafficking, our framework also recognizes the role of culture, whether it is in the US or Pakistan, in fostering and justifying the conditions that make people vulnerable to trafficking.

Using this approach, the book traverses private and public spheres to document the sites of exploitation, and selected cases to illustrate the complex worlds of trafficking. We show how legally established companies and white-collar professionals can become complicit (albeit indirectly) in trafficking, alongside the worlds of smugglers and traffickers. From an intersectionality perspective, trafficking is about unequal power, privileges, and marginalization. To further emphasize the personhood of the marginalized, we keep the human security of the victims – whether they are able to survive and build lives of dignity – at the center of our discussions of policies and activist and government interventions.

In the end, this book is one attempt among many to look carefully at human lives that are being traded for profit in today's trafficking regime.

Outline of the chapters

In chapter 2, we focus on trafficking for sexual exploitation. The growing power of feminist research has drawn worldwide attention to the plight of women and girls who are trafficked for sex. Now, a number of media personalities, such as Nicholas Kristof of the *New York Times*, and prominent activists have contributed to the public awareness of trafficking for sex through a process of rescue and rehabilitation. This abolitionist framework for understanding trafficking for sex has been criticized by scholars who have drawn on case studies to question the definitions, explanations, and practices to address trafficking. We use illustrations – narratives of victims, case observations by scholars, interspersed with our own research – to document the debates about trafficking for sexual exploitation, the underlying political economic factors that promote trafficking but that are seldom addressed as part of the eradication procedures. We also discuss the human security of people who were trafficked.

Chapter 3 focuses on trafficking for labor exploitation. We discuss the overlap between forced labor and labor trafficking to outline some of the features of exploitation for labor. We situate our discussion against the background of neoliberal globalization and the need for cheap labor in the public and private spheres across the world. We argue that the shifts toward creating a vast pool of cheap labor have been paralleled by the growth of temporary work visas for a variety of low-wage workers. The immigration laws strictly control low-wage workers' access to rights and resources, facilitating the context of their exploitation. Yet many workers, burdened with debt in their home countries, and/or perceiving few opportunities to build secure lives, are looking for jobs in distant places. They end up paying money to migrate, sometimes illegally, and are then trapped in highly exploitative jobs, because of the ways their labor conditions are configured. A key discussion in this chapter is about the meaning and boundaries of trafficking when states are involved in constructing the conditions of labor exploitation.

In chapter 4, we examine organ trafficking. Unlike trafficking for sex and labor exploitation, organ trafficking often takes place after people migrate in search of work, or traffickers simply target areas where poor people live, so the person does not migrate. This chapter begins by explaining why we should consider the trade in organs as trafficking. If we follow the UN definition of trafficking, which focuses on people being forced to move against their will, then the trade in organs does not strictly fall within its purview. Nonetheless, as we have argued elsewhere (Yousaf and Purkayastha 2015b), just as sex or labor are commodified and sold through the process of trafficking, organs are harvested from marginalized groups from different parts of the world, are commodified, and yield profits to people who facilitate the supply chain. We discuss the ways in which cultural shifts – expectations of longer lives with medical interventions among the relatively privileged – forge a supply chain that includes the middlemen who identify the "donors," the people who sell organs, the medical establishment that performs the transplantation surgeries, and the legal and extra-legal establishments that move the organs to the market of recipients. While many clandestine (and consequently illegal) practices mark this phenomenon, it is perfectly possible to legally acquire and sell organs from living men and women.

The organization of organ trafficking again raises difficult questions about "choice" or force involved in the organ provider's decision-making process, since the phenomenon can only be labeled as trafficking if the victims were coerced or duped into selling their organs.

We begin chapter 5 by discussing some of the problems with the methodologies and data on which trafficking responses are crafted. Then we move on to a critical discussion of some of the policies, paying particular attention to the US TIP report since it has had a significant influence in many countries of the world. We examine the TIP reports on selected countries, including what is covered in the reports. The overall theme of this chapter is the gap between the realities of human trafficking and the policies and practices that are intended to address them. At the same time we show that the policies and data quality change, and we highlight some of the recent improvements in reporting trafficking.

Chapter 6 draws on some of the book's insights to highlight several related issues that are important in addressing trafficking. We point out the need to keep the long-term wellbeing of victims and survivors in mind in order to address the conditions that make people become vulnerable to trafficking. While anti-trafficking activists may not be involved in all the efforts to address issues such as the rights of migrants, being aware of the connections, and how these contribute to human security, is likely to create deeper positive changes. Similarly, based on a theme that is repeated in the book, we reiterate the need for better definitions and methods of gathering data, but we also introduce the need for transparency in the funding and spending efforts of governments and NGOs. The question here is the proportion of money that actually goes to victims. The chapter offers some utopian ideas for addressing trafficking but emphasizes the need to take heed of local conditions in the anti-trafficking efforts instead of using the same model irrespective of whether it fits the local needs.

Chapter 7, "Afterwords: Ongoing Debates and Unresolved Questions," provides more information on some of the ongoing debates and unanswered questions about critical issues such as modern-day slavery, feminist debates on the best approaches to addressing trafficking for sexual exploitation, the tensions between restrictive migration laws to address state security and the human security of trafficked persons as migrants, access to national organ registries, and the extent to which trafficking efforts meet the UN standards of human rights.

2
Trafficking for Sexual Exploitation

Even a casual search for documentaries on "sex trafficking," on a popular site such as YouTube, now yields many accounts of trafficking for sexual exploitation. These documentaries, typically made to raise awareness about sexual exploitation, often feature the voices of young women and girls who were trafficking victims. Some of these stories tell about the conditions that enhance vulnerability to trafficking: poverty and lack of education[1] are mentioned repeatedly. Some news reports, especially those that focus on trafficking of young, white girls in the US, let us hear, in the victims' words, about the innocuous ways in which these girls were lured into prostitution. Paired with quantitative and qualitative data, these documentaries record that trafficking for sexual exploitation continues today. Further, these accounts, implicitly or explicitly, emphasize the need to rescue the victims.

In this chapter, we examine different facets of trafficking for sexual exploitation.[2] We begin with some vignettes that show how the private worlds of homes and public worlds intersect to create the conditions for trafficking. The victims' accounts we present first, like the documentaries and news reports, show that women and girls who were trafficked were coerced, tricked, and/or forced into prostitution. We also present cases where the women thought they had some choice, but were, nonetheless, trapped into exploitative conditions. We situate victims' diverse experiences within the structural conditions

– the ideologies, interactions, and institutional arrangements – that facilitate trafficking. We consider some of the dominant efforts to address this form of trafficking: rescue the victims and punish the traffickers. Emphasizing our approach of looking at the human security of trafficked persons, we assess whether the solutions – provision of shelter and economic rehabilitation – are working in the ways we imagine them to be.

On being trafficked

UNODC (2016) reports that 23,000 victims of trafficking for sexual exploitation were detected and reported between 2012 and 2014. In Western and Southern Europe, the Americas and East Asia, "[t]he vast majority of them were females: women and girls" (p. 27). Academics and activists have been gathering information about their experiences so that there are records that bear witness. Putting the victims at the heart of the effort to address trafficking and sharing their stories in their words and voices offers the most powerful indictment of trafficking. The hope is that these narratives will encourage people to get involved in eradicating trafficking.

Narrative from the US:

I spent the first 12 years of my life in Northern Virginia. When I was only 10 years old, family members abused me. Before the abuse I was a pretty normal little girl: I loved to read, collect stamps, draw and I was a member of the Barbie fan club. Unfortunately, after I was abused, I became a different little girl. No one helped me or validated the abuse I had suffered, so part of me went into hiding and I became depressed. I didn't want to be around anyone, no longer went to school, and eventually ran away when I was 12.

When I ran away, I was a walking target for traffickers and predators who look for damaged children: I had been abused, I was depressed and was in desperate need of help. It didn't take long for traffickers to find me. Surprisingly it was a couple – a man and a woman – who found me on the streets of Washington, D.C. They took me off of the streets where I was hungry and alone and brought me into their home where they fed me and seemed to care for me. That is, until they initiated me into the world of trafficking. They used me for a few months until they no longer needed me and then sold me to another trafficker. Right in our nation's capital, I was sold into trafficking to a man named Moses. Soon after buying me, Moses took me to New York City where he trafficked me for 8 years.

During my time on the streets of New York I was abused, shot, stabbed, raped, kidnapped, trafficked, beaten, addicted to drugs, jailed, and more, all before I was 18 years old. (Richmond Justice Initiative 2016, Barbara Amaya's narrative)

Narrative from Pakistan:

I belong to a poor family...I never attended school as in my family girls are not allowed to get any education outside home...I was sold for Rs. 300,000 [USD3,000] by my family...Once sold, the girls can never return to their parents or family...After purchasing girls, they are forced into prostitution...Those who buy the girls are their owners and earn profits from them, and may sublet the girls to other parties in different cities. (Yousaf 2016, interview with a trafficked person; name withheld to maintain confidentiality)

Narrative by a Nigerian woman in Germany:

[Her father introduced Grace to a woman whose sister lived in Germany.] I was given the passport of an African woman from a different country and then transported with another woman to Germany. Once I arrived, I was told that my debt was 50,000 euro (around 67,000 USD) which I realized would take a very long time to repay. My family's contact then told me that to pay the debt, I would be working as a prostitute in brothels (which are legalized in Germany). It was then that I realized that my family's contact was a madam. I refused and called my parents to explain what was happening, but they told me to obey her and do whatever she told me to do. I didn't have any papers and didn't know my rights. She said that if I asked anyone for help, I would be deported, so I didn't think I had any choice but to become a prostitute. In Nigeria, we respect Germany. I didn't even think that they did this as a job in Germany; in Italy and Spain, we know there is prostitution. My mother begged me to do what they said. I cried every time a man slept with me, because I was brought up Christian...I worked day and night for months, doing everything they asked me, in order to get the money for my madam; and every day I cried…[I] was told by my employers that I had to have sex without condoms when asked…The women here are so desperate for money they don't care about AIDS…This is blood money, and it was killing me too. (Equality Now 2017, Grace's narrative; see Carling 2005 for a similar description)

We begin with these narratives[3] because they reflect some of the key indicators that are emphasized in the definitions of trafficking: victimization, exploitation, and use of force. Each of these young women experienced coercion and force, exploitation and victimization. The pattern of being bought and sold, and "rented," highlights how they were treated as expendable commodities. Importantly, whether they were trafficked within the country or across international boundaries, the conditions of exploitation, the force and abuse, are similar.

A common theme that runs through these narratives is the cultures of devaluing girls. While the young women from Pakistan and Nigeria directly talk about families selling them into prostitution, the young woman from the US describes abuse by family members and the absence of support that made her vulnerable to trafficking. The other theme in each narrative, explicit or implicit, is the existence of a market where these young women are sexually exploited for profit. The worlds of prostitution include those who sell women and girls, those who procure and move them, and those who profit from their prostitution. Powerless as they were during their exploitation, all three women survived, i.e. they had moved out of the range of their traffickers, and were in shelters or rebuilding their lives, at the time they provided these narratives.

Yet the descriptor "survived" has to be assessed against the women's long-term wellbeing if we want to develop an accurate representation of the experience of being trafficked. Trafficked persons experience longitudinal consequences, especially on their health. For instance, in the rest of her narrative Amaya talks about her addiction to methadone and the long-term effects of her trauma. As Zimmerman and her colleagues (2011) described, trafficked women have endured physical abuse, sexual abuse, and mental abuse. Researchers who study the long-term impact of trafficking on victims now use the term "trauma" frequently (see for instance Banovic and Bjelajac 2012, Tsutsumi and his colleagues 2008). Some describe the health consequences as being similar to post-traumatic stress syndrome, which is, most often, associated with military personnel who have participated in wars. In addition, there are several studies about the transmission of HIV through sex work (Ahmed 2011, 2015, Silverman et al. 2014, Steen et al. 2015). Given their severe exploitative situations, as Grace's narrative emphasizes, trafficked persons are most vulnerable to HIV transmission. The costs of "Innocence Lost," as Fowler, Che, and Fowler (2010) write, include the reality that victims "find it difficult to forgive themselves and overcome the shame involved. Unfortunately, some victims find it too difficult to return to a 'normal' life" (p. 1348). These long-term health conditions also affect former victims' ability to work and to build normal lives.

These three narratives fit the profile of innocent victims who were tricked or coerced into prostitution. They fit the profile of people whom rescue efforts seek to reach and rehabilitate, while pursuing, if possible, prosecution of the traffickers; two of the young women survived because of the rescue efforts by NGOs. One was still in a government-funded shelter to which she was directed by the police after she escaped.

However, the other examples we present later in the chapter show that trafficking cannot only be considered as a crime committed by deviant individuals (traffickers, family members) against hapless victims. Sometimes the lines are blurred between those who voluntarily joined the larger sex industry (e.g. as hostesses in bars), and are then coerced into prostitution, or those who "voluntarily" took up prostitution because they could earn more from this industry than from other exploitative labor markets, into which they had been trafficked. The broad similarities of experience that these narratives indicate, or the variations, as we describe through the chapter, lead us to ask several questions about who is trafficked, what are the factors that promote trafficking, and how can we envision their human security.

Data on trafficking for sexual exploitation

While the narratives above describe the experiences of young women who are trafficked within and across countries,[4] how *widespread* is this phenomenon? Many sources of data validate that trafficking is widespread. Certainly billions of dollars have been spent to combat trafficking.[5] In spite of these first impressions, *reliable* data on trafficking are somewhat scarce and many interventions rely on estimates, or they point out that their data are only based on those who are detected as trafficking victims. We discuss the specific problems with these estimates in chapter 5, but according to many international and national sources, e.g. UNODC and TIP reports, trafficking for sexual exploitation makes up the largest category among types of trafficking.[6] UNODC (2016) emphasizes that women and girls make up 79 percent of those trafficked, and the majority are trafficked for sexual exploitation. This report provides a conservative current estimate of 21,400 trafficking victims based on the number of cases prosecuted and the numbers available from helping agencies in 2006. This indicates about 17,000 women and girls are trafficked for sexual exploitation. Whether these numbers are under-counts (see e.g. UNODC 2014) or over-counts (see e.g. Gozdziak 2015) remains a matter of definition and debate. We certainly know that the data change, both with better reporting and prosecution and with better definitions and methodologies to count trafficking cases. For instance, DeStefano (2008) points out that for several years, the data on trafficking indicated 50,000 women or girls were trafficked for sex to the US, but that number has varied as the forms of trafficking are defined more precisely and the number of prosecutions is reported more efficiently (see p. 13).

Explanations of trafficking for sexual exploitation

The definition of trafficking, as we discussed in the previous chapter, recognizes movement of the victim and the use of force, coercion, and fraud as core aspects of trafficking. In addition, a key thread that runs through the narratives above as well as the data on trafficking is the *gendered* nature of trafficking;[7] there is a greater market for sexual exploitation of women than for that of men. The narratives at the beginning of this chapter emphasize the role of patriarchal power: either the women and girls were subject to force and abuse which led them to run away and be victimized through trafficking, or they were forced into trafficking by male relatives. Yet patriarchal power is not a sufficient explanation of trafficking; a variety of other structures of inequalities, which exist from local to global levels, intersect with the structures of gender to shape the worlds of trafficking.

Scholars have pointed out how the intersecting structures of gender/race sort and sift according to ideologies of desirability. Espiritu (2007), among others, earlier wrote about the ideologies surrounding women's sexuality in the context of desirability. She pointed out that these ideologies have long historical roots. The ideologies about the desirability of Asian women as objects of sexual exploitation were often developed during Western occupation of parts of East and South East Asia. As white men, who were part of the occupying forces, sought out local prostitutes or sexually exploited local women,[8] ideologies about Asian women's subservience and willingness to do anything to please men became a justification for their sexual exploitation. These ideologies also became a common trope in Hollywood cinema, and the imageries were widely circulated through media. In today's world, the Internet enables sellers to advertise to significantly larger markets.

Asian women remain profitable *sexual commodities* in the trafficking industry (Bertone 2000, Penttinen 2008). Indeed the entire **sex tourism** industry in East and South East Asia, where foreign tourists come to this region to buy sexual services from women and men, developed on this ideological premise, fueled by the economic-political structures that made a large-scale sex trade possible (Choo 2016). At the same time, racial hierarchies that set up whiteness as the epitome of beauty and desirability ensure white women remain prized commodities in this trade. Both the internal trafficking of young women like Barbara, as well as the flows of East European women into the Scandinavian countries or Russian or Latvian women into the US (US Department of State 2016, also DeStefano 2008), are shaped by these ideologies.

The **commodification** of people, that is, treating them as objects of sale, is organized according to gender/race hierarchies and works in tandem with local cultural meanings that attribute greater value to males than to females. Age remains another significant factor. Everyday cultures and interactions that normalize these types of gendered sexual exploitation of young women and girls remain important for understanding the larger context of trafficking. At the same time, scholars (e.g. Bernstein 2010 and the edited collections by Dragiewicz 2015, Kempadoo et al. 2012, Yea 2014) have insisted that we look beyond "local culture"-type explanations. Trafficking is an organized industry which includes the continuing strength of profitable markets for sex, and a range of people who profit from identifying the vulnerable, moving them, and operating the organizations through which they are offered for sale. Kempadoo (2001) has pointed out that the growth of the sex tourism industry in Barbados, Jamaica, the Dominican Republic, and Cuba has turned the Caribbean islands into backyard "playgrounds" for male and female tourists from Europe who wish to buy sex. Bernstein (2007) also argues that the sex industry has far exceeded its prior bounds to become a multifaceted and multibillion-dollar industry produced by, and itself producing developments in, other sectors of the global economy, including hotel chains and tourism. Trafficking exists, sometimes in liminal spaces, within this terrain.

The growth of the sex industry complicates definitions of trafficking. Kempadoo (2012) points out that there has been a conceptual elision between prostitution and trafficking for sex. This literature is riven by contesting feminist perspectives on women's agency or lack of agency to engage in sex work (Bernstein 2010, Bertone 2000, Cwikel and Hoban 2005, Dickenson 2006, Doezema 2002, Jeffreys 2009, Outshoorn 2015, Samarasinghe 2008, Veen 2001, Yousaf and Purkayastha 2015a, Zheng 2010). The policy definitions of force and fraud are built off the understandings of women's inability to exercise their agency. One perspective is that sex work is an occupation like other occupations: since the stigmatization of prostitution is a form of patriarchal control over women, legalization of prostitution is likely to restore women's agency and control over their own bodies. A variant of this argument is that some women may perceive sex work as self-employment leading to their economic independence. Therefore, these scholars argue that instead of relying on meta-narratives that completely ignore women's agency or ability to make choices, the analysis of prostitution or sex work needs to be contextualized to find out whether or not it involves violence or exploitation. If violence and exploitation are evident, it is likely that the women did not join the industry voluntarily.

The second perspective opposes the legalization of prostitution and argues that prostitution can never be a voluntary occupation because it always involves elements of force, coercion, and exploitation, and leads to the commodification of women's bodies and parts of their bodies mainly for men's sexual pleasure. Two INGOs – the Global Alliance Against Traffic in Women (GAATW) and the Coalition Against Trafficking in Women (CATW) – represent these two opposing views. CATW supports abolishing prostitution; it advocates that making prostitution illegal is an effective way to combat trafficking. GAATW argues that legalizing prostitution can reduce trafficking because it is the illegality of this profession that stimulates exploitation (Zheng 2010). Yet these debates do not help us to understand other specificities, sites, and contexts across the world within which trafficking for sexual exploitation takes place. (See chapter 7, afterword 2, on why feminist scholars differ on this subject.)

In contrast to the narratives at the beginning of this chapter in which it was clear the women were trafficked, scholars have also reported cases where women turn *to* the sex industry in order to escape other forms of labor servitude (e.g. Mahdavi 2013, Maternick and Ditmore 2015). While we discuss the case of domestic workers and labor servitude in the next chapter, it is important to point out that the lines between trafficking for labor *or* sex, and between choice and victimization, are not as clear-cut as the debates would suggest.

Mahdavi described the case of an Ethiopian migrant to the UAE:

> During the six months she worked for this family, she endured beatings from her madam and sexual advances from the male head of the household and his son. She had to work for up to 18 hours a day, the family often locked her in the house when they went out, and did not provide her with a dinner on the majority of weeknights. When she complained, they beat her and the male head of household made further advances towards her, uttering sexual threats that he would rape her one night while she was asleep... Limited by not having the legal entitlement to take on employment, she began by working in a restaurant in the town's Ethiopian neighbourhood. After a few

months, however, it was clear that the restaurant was not going to pay her. Then, one evening, a group of women came into the restaurant who earned their livings as sex workers at a bar called the Rattlesnake and, on discovering her potential earning power, she decided to join them right away. This marked the beginning of Meskit's entry into the informal economy of sex work. One night, after a few months at the Rattlesnake, the police raided the bar and arrested Meskit, who spent three weeks in prison. (2013, pp. 433–4)

The absence of other opportunities to support themselves becomes a complicating factor for the women who are attempting to escape situations of severe exploitation. Maternick and Ditmore describe the situation of two Mexican women who were trafficked to the US, to illustrate this complicated reality.

after leaving the coercive situation with a trafficker, they each turned to sex work in order to support themselves and their families. Returning to sex work allowed them both to gain autonomy and financial stability that was not possible in less well-paid work available to undocumented immigrants. Their autonomy and financial stability helped them each build a new life and helped prevent them from returning to a trafficking situation. (2015, p. 56)

If we were trying to define who is a victim of trafficking for sexual exploitation according to current formal definitions, we should be able to discern the point at which voluntary participation changes to enforced participation or vice versa. Yet, from the victims' perspective, it is not clear that such definitions, which often implicitly or explicitly depend on describing the point at which a young woman engages in prostitution, describe their experience of long-term extreme exploitation. Choo (2016) describes another aspect of sexual exploitation that does not neatly fit the definitions of victims of trafficking. She described the case of Filipina workers who migrated legally to South Korea on entertainment visas, and ended up working as hostesses in clubs surrounding a military base. Their work as hostesses was difficult; their labor conditions were exploitative: "Although most hostesses had a written labor contract that stipulated a minimum wage of about $850 per month for forty four hours of work and one holiday a week" (Choo, 2016, p. 126), most worked longer hours and were fined for a series of infractions that kept them perpetually underpaid.

> Customers paid $10 to buy a hostess a glass of JUICE … he also purchased the woman's company for fifteen to twenty minutes as they chatted or played pool and darts. Some clubs also had a system of "bar fines," in which a customer paid $200–$300 to take a woman out for the whole night. Other clubs had "VIP rooms" where more explicit sex-for-money exchanges took place. (p. 126)

As Choo points out, here the worlds of work and coerced sexual exploitation are not clearly separable, nor are the points at which the question of choice vs. force and coercion becomes salient. Both remained salient to different degrees. Choo also describes that when a local NGO tried to help some of these women, they used "victim of trafficking" explanations to advocate for services, which then set up other complications in terms of the rights these women had as migrants.

Overall, Kempadoo's definition of trafficking: "as *the movement, trade, and exploitation of labor under conditions of coercion and force*, analyzed from the lives, agency, and rights of women and men who are involved in a variety of activities in a transnationalized world" (2012, p. ix) offers a broad framework that can help us understand the three vignettes we presented at the beginning of this chapter, as well as the cases where women escaped from extreme economic deprivation and labor servitude into commercial sex industries. A new set of scholarship – e.g. Bernstein (2007), Dragowiecz (2015), Kempadoo, Sanghera, and Pattanaik (2012), Yea (2014, 2015a), Yousaf and Purkayastha (2015a) – is expanding our understanding of the terrain in which trafficking occurs. Without minimizing the force, coercion, and exploitation involved, these studies emphasize glocal specificities – how transnational, national, and local structures intersect – to shape exploitative conditions in which people become vulnerable to trafficking. When the trafficking industry's search for "commodities" for profit fits people's life conditions, they are most likely to be trafficked. To quote Kempadoo again, "'Trafficking of women' was complexly seen to be shaped by hegemonic and local patriarchies, globalized capitalism, and the widening gaps in income and wealth, as well as by reconfigurations of empire under late-twentieth-century globalization that reinscribed international hierarchies around notions of racial, religious, and national difference" (2012, p. xix).

Trafficking and migration

Trafficking often occurs as individuals or groups of people move or after they have moved to unfamiliar locales (where they have few networks and/or sources of reliable information and structures to support their security). Both internal and international migration can create periods of intense gendered vulnerability for women, men, and children. The lack of supportive networks appears to be a consistent theme across the cases of trafficked victims. Amaya's narrative, at the beginning of this chapter, documents that she ran away from home and ended up in Washington, DC. Other narratives on the Richmond Justice Initiative website reveal similar themes of people being trafficked when they were separated from normal networks.[9] Commenting on trafficking across international boundaries, Tyldum points out that the traffickers gain power over the women (or girls or boys or men) "by moving them across borders, away from their networks and into cultural and legal systems they are unfamiliar with" (2013, p. 106).

The data on migration show that, globally, women now make up close to 50 percent of international migrants (UN Department of Economic and Social Affairs 2016). Among those who are forced to migrate – a total of 65.3 million between 2006 and 2016, according to the UN High Commissioner for Refugees (UNHCR)'s *Global Trends: Forced Displacement in 2015* (UNHCR 2016) – there is a rapidly growing number of women and children. In 2015, half of the forced migrants were children.[10] *How* people end up being trafficked is related to *conditions* of migration.

Forced migration and trafficking

The literature indicates that economic restructuring and conflicts and disasters are major precursors of forced migration (Samaddar 2015). The TIP report on the EU shows people moving to the more economically stable parts of Europe along with migrants fleeing zones of sustained conflict. The report on trafficking in Norway[11] shows that trafficking victims "primarily originate from Eastern Europe and Africa – particularly Albania, Bulgaria, Lithuania, Nigeria, and Romania, along with...increasing numbers of Syrians [who] are subjected to trafficking in Norway" (US Department of State 2016). Both migration streams are shaped by the perceived political openness of countries to receive migrants and refugees, and possibilities for building more secure lives. Similarly, *Global Trends: Forced Displacement in 2015* (UNHCR 2016) points out that the outbreak of conflicts in Central America and parts of Africa, along with the conflicts in the Middle East, have created waves of migrants, refugees, and internally displaced people who are trying to reach safer havens in the nearby regions, i.e. the US, Europe, and parts of Latin America and Africa (see e.g. Ali 2005 on South Asia; Alvaraz Maternick and Ditmore 2016 or Maternick and Ditmore 2015 on the US; Carling 2005 on Europe).

The ambit of violence has increased over the last few decades (e.g. Ertürk and Purkayastha 2012, Sutton, Morgen, and Novokov 2008). The increase in armed conflicts within and between nation-states (SIPRI 2013) and the mass production of weapons have brought large sections of marginalized groups into the ambit of violence even if they are not involved directly in these conflicts. In these situations, sexual violence, particularly against women and girls, often becomes "normal" currency (e.g. Bangura 2013). Men, women, and children fleeing these zones may end up in refugee or internally displaced persons' camps, but life in the camps is precarious; it is nearly impossible to access the resources or rights needed to build humanly secure lives (e.g. Turner 2015, *Forced Migration Review* 2013). Nor are these places violence free; especially young women are prey to sexual exploitation, as Njiru and Purkayastha (2015) have described. Such internally displaced persons and refugees often become victims of smugglers and traffickers who promise to help them reach "safe havens" or lure them with promises of new job opportunities.

States often refer to trafficking and smuggling as distinct criminal activities (see e.g. US Immigration and Customs Enforcement 2013), and continue to build policies based on perspectives about individuals who participate voluntarily (in smuggling) or are victimized (by trafficking). Yet a series of investigative journalists have begun to describe the coming together of trafficking and smuggling. For instance, the recent massive migration from the Middle East and North Africa – of people fleeing large-scale conflict – to Europe has created conditions for successful smuggling and trafficking. In their report on migrant smuggling to Europe, Lyman and Smale (2015) point out that EU law officials state that smuggling human beings is now bigger business than illicit trades in drugs and weapons. Stories of migrants in sealed trucks have been in the news in Austria (Lyman and Smale 2015, Smale and Eddy 2015), the US (e.g. Montgomery, Fernandez, and Joseph 2017), and other countries. Scholarly work has begun to record similar realities (e.g. Mandic 2017). These cases of smuggling involve a variety of migrants, including those who end up being trafficked for sex.

The growth of smuggling has developed in tandem with the current trend in neoliberal states to construct migrants as threats to state security. Pathways to migration are rapidly shrinking in many parts of the world. At the same time, it is not easy to get a "refugee" designation that, theoretically, offers some modicum of rights.[12] Missbach and Sinanu (2014) describe examples of refugees who are tired of waiting for the rest of their families to join them, and are willing to pay smugglers to bring their wives or children. The authors describe this scenario:

> an Afghan refugee who had been living in Indonesia for three years without his wife who was still stranded as a refugee in Pakistan said: "I can't wait for much longer here. If I can't have my wife joining me here soon, I will just go by boat and use an agent. I have nothing to lose." When being asked of the risks he would face by doing that, the man replied: "I know how dangerous the journey will be, but I do not see another option. It's not like I could earn a living and have a life here in Indonesia. It's frustrating not to be able to do anything." (2014, p. 68)

Having no say in the routes smugglers choose, or even whether they actually intend to bring the wife to Indonesia to join this man, suggests that there is a significant possibility for the smugglers to profit from this man's payment *and* from traffickers who are looking for more women and girls for sex industries.

In 2004, reporting for the *New York Times*, Peter Landesman wrote about trafficked women and girls who were held in near captive conditions in an American suburb:

> The police found a squalid, land-based equivalent of a 19th-century slave ship, with rancid, doorless bathrooms; bare, putrid mattresses; and a stash of penicillin, "morning after" pills and misoprostol, an antiulcer medication that can induce abortion. The girls were pale, exhausted and malnourished.
>
> It turned out that 1212 1/2 West Front Street was one of what law-enforcement officials say are dozens of active stash houses and apartments in the New York metropolitan area – mirroring hundreds more in other major cities like Los Angeles, Atlanta and Chicago – where under-age girls and young women from dozens of countries are trafficked and held captive. Most of them – whether they started out in Eastern Europe or Latin America – are taken to the United States through Mexico. Some of them have been baited by promises of legitimate jobs and a better life in America; many have been abducted; others have been bought from or abandoned by their impoverished families.

Landesman also found that the victims were terrified of going to law enforcement officers for help because they had few papers – which had been confiscated by the traffickers – and thought they would be imprisoned. The growth of crimmigration systems within many nation-states indicates their fears are grounded in reality. As Bosworth and Kaufman (2011) point out, with the changes in laws that earlier separated civil offences from crimes in the US, immigrants who are detained under immigration powers – including asylum seekers – are increasingly housed in the same prisons as those awaiting trial or convicted of criminal charges (see also Kubal 2014 on the EU and Shamshad 2017 on India). Thus, the politics of immigration play a central role in shaping the terrain of trafficking.

Marriage migration and trafficking

Scholars have begun to document another aspect of these shifts and changes – additional restrictions – on migrants' movements. Apart from the vulnerability to trafficking within general streams of migration, marriage migration can act as a pathway to trafficking. Drawing on his research in Pakistan, Yousaf (2016, p. 58) shares this narrative:

> After completion of matriculation, I started job in a private organization and married a boy with my own choice with a hope to make a new life... After marriage, my husband sold me to a brothel owner and I was forced into prostitution... I was confined in a brothel along with many other girls and was forced to have sex with many clients a day... After spending some time there, I got a chance to escape and came to the shelter... While in the shelter, I got divorced through court... I had lost my job... After coming out of the shelter, I tried to find another job but I was not successful... my lawyer suggested me for second marriage... I developed a friendship with a boy to marry him... he took me to a remote feudal area in another province where women were treated like chattels of the land-lords... I was sold to an aunty for Rs.40,000 [USD400] who was running a prostitution ring... This time I was forced to go outside with customers for night(s)... I was not given anything except meal two times a day... When I got a chance, I fled from that place and again came to the shelter... I have no relatives where I can go... I only need a place to live and a job to survive.

The phenomenon of women's trafficking within the context of marriage is not unique to Pakistan or South Asia; nor is it confined to local marriages (for instance, see Anitha, Roy, and Yalamarty 2016 on transnational marriage abandonment in the United Kingdom (UK), or Choo 2016 on women in South East Asia who wish to migrate to South Korea via marriages). As other channels of migration shrink, migration through marriage remains an avenue for migrating for better opportunities.

Based on her study of Thai and Russian women married to Norwegian men, Tyldum (2013) showcased the issues of vulnerability, power, and exploitation leading to trafficking in women within the context of transnational marriages. Pointing to the blurred boundaries between transnational marriages in general and those that end up as conduits for trafficking, Tyldum argued that the process of transnational migration itself creates the conditions of vulnerability in which exploitation occurs. People who exploit women in transnational marriages do not create vulnerabilities for ambitious women who want to (choose to) migrate to prosperous countries. Rather, the partners exploit the women's positions of vulnerability within the processes of globalization. Migrant women leave their families and networks and move to new systems with which they are unfamiliar. Many men exploit the vulnerabilities of the migrant women, isolate them, and force them into domestic and/or sexual servitude. Tyldum notes that in contrast to the general assumption that trafficking can be identified only with reference to coercion or lack of consent (that is, women's victimization), in many transnational marriages, women themselves seek to marry foreigners despite associated risks. Further, many migrant women do not report violence or leave their homes because of economic dependency, lack of skills to communicate in the foreign language, lack of knowledge of the foreign legal system, and fear of losing their residency as they do not want to go back to their countries of origin.

Tseng's (2014) study of Vietnamese women in Taiwan also shows how marriages can turn into trafficking. Some Vietnamese women ran away from their marriages and ended up in the sex industry. Some were kept in states of servitude that would fall within the classification of trafficking for labor and sexual exploitation. Focusing on marriage migration in Australia, Richards and Lyneham (2015) also found that some marriages end up being conduits for trafficking. They argued trafficking occurs along a spectrum of large-scale, small-scale, and ad hoc operations. Marriage migration tends to fall into the last category. However, many marriages meet the UN criteria of trafficking, that is, recruitment, movement, and exploitation "for the purpose...servitude (domestic and sexual)... [and] forced marriage" (quoted in Richards and Lyneham 2015, p. 106). At the same time, by focusing mostly on the public worlds of trafficking, the efforts to address trafficking often keep these women invisible.

Virtual sexploitation

While the general understanding of trafficking is that people are moved for sexual exploitation, the widespread availability of advanced technology raises some new questions about our understanding of trafficking. Shahrokhi (2010) has described how traffickers use technology to force young girls in Iran to perform live-sex acts according to the demands of their customers sitting elsewhere in the world, while protecting the identity of the girls and the customers by not showing their faces. Shahrokhi points out that this form of exploitation is gendered, aged, and classed because it involves elite male customers who are willing to pay enough to enjoy exclusive sex entertainment from *innocent young girls*, different from ordinary *street prostitutes* or sex workers. The girls, however, are often trafficked, that is, they are forced into servitude as a precursor to being forced to perform these sex acts.

Other scholars examine the changing dynamics of trafficking and note that the Internet has aided the networking of traffickers with minimal risks (e.g. Oblinger 2015, Yu 2015). Based on her review of the EU data on sex trafficking, Hughes (2014) has noted a correlation between the rise of trafficking and the spread of digital communication. Many traffickers use fake social media accounts to trap women and girls. They also enlarge their marketing "zones" to consumers who are looking for commercial sex. Reporting on the break-up of a sex trafficking ring during the Detroit Auto show (in the US), Drew (2017) wrote "the pimps and human traffickers work together, warning each other online and on social media when the FBI is getting close." (The 2017 TIP report also acknowledges the use of the Internet to promote exploitative sex; see US Department of State 2017.)

In sum, the research on trafficking for sexual exploitation shows that the conditions of migration are centrally implicated in the ways traffickers are able to expand the range of their operations.

Questions of human security

Before we turn to the ways in which trafficking is being addressed, it is instructive to review the forms of insecurities that affect all those who are trafficked for sexual exploitation. The common themes across all the cases we discuss are economic deprivation and lack of access to rights against exploitation. These insecurities fall within human rights violations including freedom from slavery and servitude, not being subject to cruel, inhuman, degrading treatment, non-discrimination, and access to the rights that enable a person to build a life of human dignity,[13] irrespective of the place in which the person is resident. The 2000 UN Protocol on trafficking identifies several measures that states *ought* to provide victims: "(a) Appropriate housing; (b) Counselling and information, in particular as regards their legal rights, in a language that the victims of trafficking in persons can understand; (c) Medical, psychological and material assistance; and (d) Employment, educational and training opportunities ... [and] to provide for the physical safety of victims of trafficking in persons while they are within its territory" (OHCHR 2000). The central issue from a human security perspective is to question not only whether these objectives are being met, but whether the current efforts at addressing trafficking actually help to achieve lives free from threats "derived from economic, food, health or environmental security, and threats to personal, community, and political security, or human rights violations" (Tripp, Ferree, and Ewig 2013, p. 6). Or, at least, are some of these threats minimized in significant ways?

In the next section we outline some of the actions to address trafficking, and then comment on the gaps.

Addressing trafficking

In her critique on the responses to trafficking, O'Connell Davidson has argued that as "'trafficking' is popularly imagined as slavery (something universally regarded as wrong), any measure that is described as a means of combating 'trafficking' enjoys great moral purchase" (2015, p. 163). Consequently many countries and NGOs are involved in addressing trafficking. Three overlapping approaches that directly affect those who are trafficked appear to be prevalent across countries: efforts to rescue women and girls from brothels, efforts to rehabilitate them, and efforts to find, punish and deter traffickers through the criminal justice system. In the next sections, we describe some of the rescue efforts as well as efforts to provide shelter and work as part of the rehabilitation efforts. Following this, we describe groups that focus on claiming rights.

Addressing the conditions of trafficked persons: rescue, shelter, and work

Rescue

In 2004, a *New York Times* reporter published an op-ed piece describing how he bought two young girls in order to rescue them from brothels (Kristof 2004). Kristof bought two Cambodian girls and sent them home with $100 to start new economic enterprises. He attributed the trafficking of girls from rural areas to patriarchal structures in their home countries, and advocated for programs to address the low status of girls through education and job training. One girl rejoined the sex industry within the year (Chang 2013).

There is now a significant literature that is highly critical of these efforts to rescue women and girls from brothels to restore them either to their families or to shelters and other places of rehabilitation (e.g. Ahmed and Seshu 2015, Bernstein 2010, Chang 2013, Dragowiecz 2015, Kempadoo et al. 2012, Lisborg 2014, Majic 2014, Renzetti 2015, Shih 2016, Yea 2014). These scholars note that the "rescue and rehabilitate" efforts are often unsuccessful because of the ways in which trafficking for sex and its cases are envisioned. These transnational models rely on abolitionist frames where involvement in the sex industry is considered to be morally wrong; exits from these industries are considered victories. Furthermore, women in sex industries are considered to be helpless female victims; whether they are in brothels or other spaces in sex industries, their rescue is imagined to be the key to addressing trafficking.

Buying women from brothels, or raiding brothels with the police in order to shut them down – the type of activities Kristof engaged in – represent one type of effort. Shih's multisited global ethnography offers other examples of the ways in which a growing contingent of American evangelical Christian organizations promote a long-standing moral objection to sex work and prostitution within the newer lens of human trafficking (see also Bernstein 2010). Shih (2014) describes how American civilians have adopted missions to address trafficking abroad, for instance targeting women in dance bars in Thailand with offers to rehabilitate them in other industries. Here the abolitionist framing of trafficking expands from brothels to the sex industry, but operates on the basis of an imperialist understanding of other people's patriarchy. Their accounts of the rescues emphasize the women's lack of agency, and the negative effect of their non-Christian cultures for their sexual slavery: "activists commonly blame Thai religious traditions and the potency of certain 'Thai spiritual symbols' for enslaving women in the commercial sex industry. During outreach, activists frequently make contact with women who have certain religious tattoos on their body" (Shih 2014, p. 73). The narrative of these rescues, back at home in the US, includes exorcising the inferior cultural beliefs that supposedly enslaved the women. These racialized tropes serve to justify the presence of the foreigners in the rescue efforts and often erase local efforts that may exist in those places.

Shih (2016) also describes search and rescue operations within the US. She discusses how racism structures the identification of "trafficking victims":

> Outreach participants are reminded of the characteristics that they are to look for as they patrol the streets of Koreatown, a laundry list of social phenomenon [*sic*] provided by the US Department of Health and Human Service's Campaign to Rescue and Restore Victims of Human Trafficking that state evidence of sexual commerce, poverty, and migration as proxy indicators of human trafficking. The organizer gathers the group for a brief prayer, asking the Holy Spirit to "shed light on the darkness of Koreatown," and small groups of 3–4 women break out a one square mile radius of these East Los Angeles streets seeking to identify and rescue victims of human trafficking. (p. 66)

Our earlier point about the racist ideologies about Asian women's sexuality intersect with persistent ideologies about who is a migrant, and shapes who is targeted. For instance, ideologies about who is a foreigner typically depict Asians as foreigners, even though Asians have been in the US from the nineteenth century (see Kibria 2000, Purkayastha 2005, Tuan 1998). These groups work as civil society partners of the government, in these rescue efforts.

> TRLR [Thai Red Light Rescue Project] activists train outreach volunteers to look for suspicious activity, which included everything from homeless individuals sleeping at bus stations, a group of migrant workers gathered together eating in front of a taco truck, or most perilously, an attractive Asian or Latina woman walking alone – a not unusual sighting in … a highly popular "entertainment enclave." (Shih 2016, p. 79)

While there are many other organizations, such as local chapters of Coalition to Abolish Slavery and Trafficking (CAST), ethnic women's social justice organizations, and labor organizations working for the rights of immigrant women in Los Angeles, these vigilante rescue teams have made themselves part of the larger landscape of anti-trafficking efforts[14] in the US and contributed to the overwhelming focus on sex trafficking and anti-prostitution efforts in the attempt to eradicate trafficking.

The migration statuses of the rescued women are important for understanding their long-term chances of survival and wellbeing. As long as the trafficking victims are citizens of the country, the additional issues about migration status and documentation may not be significant barriers to moving ahead. The Richmond Justice Initiative's website features Holly Austin Smith, who is now a well-known author and anti-trafficking speaker. As a citizen of the country, she was able to rebuild her life. On the other hand, there are no accounts of what happened to the women discovered in the stash house in the New Jersey suburb (reported by Landesman in 2004). The national hotline established for trafficking victims receives very few calls (Lange 2011). Chang (2013) reports, based on US government reports, that between 2000 and 2006, only 616 visas were issued to trafficking victims, even though, during that period, about 50,000 persons were supposed to have been trafficked to the US each year (O'Neill Richard 2000, as quoted by DeStefano 2008). However, the rules regarding trafficking victims' visas are opaque, so it is not clear who is able to achieve legal status, and who ends up in detention centers as undocumented migrants. Choo (2016) raised similar questions about the situation of the Filipina hostesses in South Korea who arrived as legal, temporary migrants, but are subsequently coerced into practices of sexual exploitation. The South Korean NGOs that try to help them appealed for the rights of victims of sex trafficking; at the same time, their rights as migrant workers – the underpayment, extremely long hours of work, enforced channeling into sexual exploitation in their workplaces – remain unaddressed.

Shelter

A key aspect of human security is shelter. Based on her work with domestic trafficking victims' service providers in the US, Renzetti (2015) asserted:

> All of the service providers who advocated for specialized residential facilities justified this need in terms of the unique trauma that sex trafficking victims experience. As they explained, many sex trafficking victims have a history of neglect and abuse – sexual, physical, and/or psychological – dating from early in their lives; some, they said, had run away to escape their abusive home environments, which made them especially vulnerable to traffickers. While on the street, the service providers explained, they were befriended or taken in by someone who made promises to protect them and led them to believe they could not survive on their own. (p. 142)

Like Renzetti, and a number of other scholars (e.g. Agustin 2007, GAATW 2007, Kempadoo, Sanghera, and Pattanaik 2005), we found that shelters are not widely available, and most are inadequate for long-term rehabilitation of trafficked victims, understaffed, and underfunded. During our research in South Asia[15] we found that, despite the wide publicity about their work, some "model shelters," funded by INGOs, had closed after a few years because the INGOs' funding interests had shifted to other countries. In these cases, depending on the timing of moving to these shelters, victims could be out in the streets very quickly. This is not uncommon in many countries where the rescue and rehabilitation process follows the model (and funding) devised by INGOs. Looking specifically at Pakistan, Yousaf (2016) found there are no dedicated shelter homes for victims of trafficking in the country.[16] The existing shelter homes for women were established by the government for victims of different forms of violence and abuse. As a result, trafficking victims are often registered under other forms of violence and exploitation. Furthermore, with few options to build futures, many women in the shelters are poised to become victims of new phases of trafficking as criminal gangs attempt to entrap them by "planting" fake victims of violence in these shelters.[17]

Lisborg (2014) discussed the problems of enforcing the protection aspect of shelters in the EU:

A recent example of restrictions and bad practices became evident during a visit I made to a shelter in South Eastern Europe. The women and girls residing there were not allowed outside the shelter, for instance to go to a café or to buy simple things in the local shops, unless they were accompanied by shelter staff or a guard. There were bars in front of the windows in each room, according to the manager to protect the "beneficiaries" from outside dangers and, while they could walk in the yard, the main gate remained closed. Six guards were hired by the shelter, again justified by the manager as a measure designed to protect the beneficiaries from intruders. However, when asked about how many times over the years they had experienced anyone trying to break into the shelter, the manager could only mention one case where an ex-boyfriend had attempted to contact one of the women in the shelter. Other shelters and "victim protection facilities" I visited in South Asia and South East Asia had similar restrictions and practically confined victims of trafficking in the name of protection. One shelter was strategically located on a small island and frequently shelters are characterised by high walls, iron bars in front of the windows, closed gates and guards – not only to keep possible intruders out but also to keep victims in. In one particular shelter, I witnessed how child victims of trafficking who had been confined for months inside the shelter tried to communicate and interact with children from the local community outside the shelter through cracks in the walls. The children on both sides of the walls were eager to play together but not allowed to. In such ways, many trafficked persons, both adults and children, have been kept isolated and with very limited access to the local community and normal non-institutional life. (p. 23)

Without overlooking the cases of successful rehabilitation, it is clear from these examples that the shelters are not set up to promote the development of social networks, which are critical for creating new lives and futures. Nor are most shelters able to access all the resources they would need to provide for all of the victims' different needs, including stable jobs, long-term health care, secure housing, education, and training.

For longer-term survival and wellbeing, formerly trafficked persons need jobs, housing, and health care at a minimum; at present most of the efforts are not set up to consistently provide access to all of these resources.

Work

Economic rehabilitation often works through the processes set up through the rescue efforts. Many such shelters attempt to create opportunities for learning "new trades" for economic rehabilitation. The picture is often dismal. Two different processes appear to confound any good intentions. One involves the provision of resources that are not useful locally. During our own research we visited one shelter where we found a roomful of computers that had been donated by an INGO for "the empowerment of these women." The women and children in the shelter had no use for these resources because there was no one to teach them how to use these computers in ways *that would be useful to them.* Instead, they hankered after sewing machines and other resources that, they thought, would be direct routes for earning money.

Elena Shih (2014) and Anders Lisborg (2014) describe similar mismatches. Lisborg described how one group of women in Southern Europe was sent daily to care for disabled people. The disabled people's home was run by the same organization that ran the shelter so they provided transportation to the "workplace." It was not apparent how these skills would transfer to real jobs in future. Shih (2014) discussed how women in brothels in Thailand (not all of whom may have been trafficked) were encouraged to join jewelry-making enter-prises. The jewelry these women made – according to the templates set up by distant others in the jewelry-making busi-ness – became highly prized items in some parts of the US, via a global supply chain that successfully branded and mar-keted the products as "made by former trafficking victims."[18] The women themselves earned little more than the minimum wage and saw few opportunities for advancement. In both cases, the women were channeled into feminized jobs – tem-porary, considered unskilled, and consequently with inadequate pay – which then affects their ability to build secure lives for themselves.[19]

Addressing the conditions of women in the sex industry: claiming rights

In contrast to these efforts to rescue "helpless" trafficking victims, and rehabilitate them by placing them in feminized, ill-paid occupations, Kempadoo (2012) presented excerpts by sex worker rights organizations articulating what they locally considered to be important to address their exploitation. Reject-ing the politics of anti-trafficking interventions, Zi Teng (Hong Kong, China), Darbar Mahila Samanwaya Committee (Kolkata, India), and Empower (Thailand) emphasize approaches that both oppose all forms of trafficking *and* reject efforts to combat trafficking by controlling and suppressing the sex industry through the legal system. According to their perspective, these abolitionist efforts place women in the sex industries within the ambit of violence of criminal justice systems looking to "rescue victims" and to record their successful efforts in combating "trafficking," which then make up the data of the numerous national and international reports. However, most of these efforts do not address the structural conditions that lead to trafficking. Instead, all three groups mentioned here assert their understanding of the shared forms of exploitations between sex workers and other workers, and call for labor opportuni-ties and substantive rights including protection from unpaid work, the right to pensions, and the right to state benefits. These groups' activism for political and economic rights makes a different type of claim on states to address *the structures that lead to exploitative work conditions.* The conditions of trafficked persons fall within the ambit of these claims.

Apart from the issues of economic security and freedom from violence, one repeated theme of these three organizations was the urgent need to provide information and resources for the health security of sex workers.[20] Access to health care remains an unaddressed issue in the dominant anti-trafficking efforts. The feminized jobs described above do not provide health care in any country, including the US. Di Tommaso and her colleagues (2009) examined a large dataset on women trafficking victims, collected by the IOM, and concluded that access to health care was a critical factor in victims' ability to survive their experiences. As Grace's narrative at the beginning of this chapter emphasized, women who are trafficked for sexual exploitation are most susceptible to HIV/AIDS; some suggest they are more vulnerable than those who adopt sex work out of choice because of the use of drugs to control the women, the exploitative and unhygienic conditions in which they work, and the lack of power to negotiate safe sex with multiple clients a day.[21] The UN Development Programme (2007) describes trafficked women as a major source of spreading HIV/AIDS and other sexually transmitted diseases across the world.[22] Others have pointed to lifelong psychological disorders and permanent damage to the reproductive system (Birkenthal 2011, Di Tomasso et al. 2009, Tsutsumi et al. 2008). In claiming rights to health care access, and framing their needs in terms of health autonomy, organizations like Darbar simultaneously move away from the victim tropes *and* make claims for social human rights.

We have already mentioned the nexus of criminal justice systems and immigration laws in many countries that add to the complexities of navigating the trafficking terrain. In most countries, the lack of substantive political rights intersects with the impediments to access jobs, shelters, and health care, and negatively affects the life conditions of these forced migrants. Equally important, the current phase of the economy continues to create a range of ill-paid and unstable jobs for women, which further restricts the opportunities for these women to rebuild secure lives. The rapid expansion of sex tourism industries, customized "cultural" products – jewelry, clothes produced in sweatshop-type situations – and the openings for care work in homes appears to offer economic opportunities, but their success in building long-term, secure lives is an open question. In fact, they open up opportunities for different types of labor servitude, as we discuss in the next chapter.

Concluding thoughts

Yea (2014) and others have argued that the scholarship on human trafficking has exhibited a strong bias toward three topics:

> reviewing legal frameworks of counter-trafficking for various countries; describing/debating trafficking for prostitution; and understanding and critiquing the United Nations (UN) Trafficking Protocol (2000). Thus, although there are multiple possible frames through which human trafficking *could* be considered, the focus on these three topics has reinforced a tendency to discuss human trafficking as an issue of transnational crime, international law or feminism. (2014, p. 5)

Here we have examined the larger structures that shape the terrain of trafficking and taken a closer look at the human security of those who are trafficked. Despite the definitions of trafficking that are supposed to guide policy, substantively, the understanding of trafficking for sexual exploitation continues to rely mostly on gendered/racialized ideologies about patriarchal cultures and victimhood. The dominant efforts to "address trafficking" reflect these gendered/racialized understandings. While a series of new protocols and policies have been emerging in the destination countries to protect victims, e.g. the EU's victim protection plans, which include assistance for victims (European Commission 2016), such efforts remain fragmented and inadequate. In addition, as we have outlined here, little has been done, thus far, to address the underlying conditions that could make people's lives more secure. The trafficking industry is poised to grow as larger numbers of people across the world experience unsettled life conditions due to conflicts and economic distresses. These people are vulnerable to being lured by traffickers and smugglers if the causes of their vulnerability, including restrictive immigration laws, remain unaddressed. Despite the intentions of many groups, the combination of gendered/racialized definitions of women's vulnerability, the power of the rescue-and-rehabilitate schemes, the failure to address the underlying political-economic issues, and the near total separation of trafficking for sex from other forms of trafficking remain significant impediments to initiating adequate responses.

Despite the huge sums of money devoted to it, the current efforts to address trafficking for sexual exploitation remain inadequate. Consequently, many are left with few options and many get drawn into other circuits of trafficking.

3
Trafficking for Labor Exploitation

In 2012, the ILO estimated that approximately 20.9 million people were forced laborers. Some of these were as a result of state action, others were affected by private economies for sexual or labor exploitation. The ILO (2014) estimated that the forced labor imposed by private economies alone yields worldwide illegal profits of more than USD150 billion each year. Of the total number of 20.9 million forced laborers, women and girls represent the greater share of total forced labor (ILO 2012). They constituted 11.4 million victims (55 percent), compared to 9.5 million (45 percent) men and boys. In 2017, a new report jointly produced by ILO, Walk Free Foundation, and IOM estimated a higher number: 24.9 million people were in forced labor situations, while 15.4 million were living in marriages to which they had not consented. The 2017 ILO et al. report uses the phrase *modern-day slavery* to describe both groups who "were being forced to work under threat or coercion as domestic workers, on construction sites, in clandestine factories, on farms and fishing boats, in other sectors, and in the sex industry. They were forced to work by private individuals and groups or by state authorities" (pp. 9–10). Of those in situations of forced labor exploitation:

> More women than men are affected by privately imposed forced labour, with 9.2 million (57.6 per cent) female and 6.8 million (42.4 per cent) male. Half of these men and women (51 per

cent) were in debt bondage, in which personal debt is used to forcibly obtain labour. This proportion rises above 70 per cent for adults who were forced to work in agriculture, domestic work, or manufacturing. Among cases where the type of work was known, the largest share of adults who were in forced labour were domestic workers (24 per cent). This was followed by the construction (18 per cent), manufacturing (15 per cent), and agriculture and fishing (11 per cent) sectors. (pp. 10–11)

According to these data, women remain the largest proportion of victims, though not at the rate of their victimization for sexual exploitation. What is the link between forced labor and trafficking? In the first chapter we indicated that the UN definition of trafficking recognizes three interlinked elements of recruitment – movement, transfer, and exploitation – while emphasizing that the means used to get a person into an exploitative situation includes force or coercion. According to the ILO et al. report:

Forced Labour, as it is set out in ILO Convention, 1930 (No. 29) refers to "all work or service which is exacted from any person under the menace of any penalty and for which the said person has not offered himself voluntarily." Men, women, and children are forced to work in various settings across the globe, with examples of forced labour found in garment making in South Asian factories, digging for minerals in African mines, harvesting tomatoes on North American farms, working as domestic workers in East Asian homes, working on farms in Latin America, begging in European cities, and constructing high rise buildings in Gulf States…Regardless of the setting, an identifying feature of situations of forced labour is lack of voluntariness in taking the job or accepting the working conditions, and the application of a penalty or a threat of a penalty to prevent an individual from leaving a situation or otherwise to compel work. Coercion can take many forms, ranging from physical and sexual violence or threats against family members to more subtle means such as withholding of wages, retaining identity documents, threats of dismissal, and threats of denunciation to authorities. (2017, p. 28)

According to this definition, *all* forms of labor trafficking are synonymous with forced labor. However, the UNODC clearly indicates that all forms of forced labor are not trafficked

(UNODC 2016). As we will discuss in this chapter, it is some-times difficult to sort out who was trafficked and/or forced and who "voluntarily" put themselves in forced labor situations because some of the processes of recruitment, movement, and exploitation of labor are legal.

From the perspective of a human being's security, theoretical distinctions between labor trafficking and forced labor make little difference to the actual inhumane conditions of her or his everyday life. But it remains an important issue because not all laws and conventions have provisions, or attract the same amount of political will, to prevent continuing harm to the victims. When the undocumented status of migrants is a major political issue in a country, whether or not a person is the victim of trafficking is likely to make some difference in their ability to seek redress through political channels. If a state is involved in facilitating forced labor, a victim's chances of redress are almost non-existent. A further complication is that the political perception of victims, drawn primarily from the dominant effort to address sexual exploitation of women or children who were tricked into the commercial sex industry and held against their will, does not always fit those who are trafficked for labor. While many trafficked victims are tricked and trapped into ill-paid or unpaid labor conditions, others start out voluntarily, seeking opportunities in other places, and some even look to smugglers to get them to their desired destinations. It is not clear how these different paths are politi-cally regarded in global anti-trafficking efforts.

A quick look at the global prosecution figures published in the 2017 TIP report tells a sobering story of the lesser emphasis on trafficking for labor. According to this report, there has been a continuing increase in identifying the number of victims of trafficking; but the details, based on estimates provided by many governments, show that labor trafficking has not resulted in a high number of prosecutions. For instance, in 2012 a total of 46,570 victims were identified. Of these cases, 17,368 were labor trafficking victims. The number of prosecutions and convictions is smaller: 7,705 prosecutions resulted in 4,746 convictions; of these, there were only 1,153 prosecutions and 518 convictions for labor trafficking. In 2016, there were 66,520 victims identified including 17,465 victims of labor trafficking; there were 14,897 prosecutions, including

1,038 for labor trafficking. These prosecutions led to 9,071 convictions including 717 convictions for labor trafficking (US Department of State 2017, p. 34).

In chapter 2 we discussed trafficking for sexual exploitation including trafficking through marriages. In this chapter we mostly focus on other forms of trafficking, though we occasionally comment on forced labor within marriages. We begin this chapter with some vignettes of children and adults who were clearly trafficked for labor, to present some of their experiences. Then we comment on the large-scale data on forced labor and attempt to unpack some of the complexities of these data. Following this, we discuss some of the underlying economic and political factors that promote labor trafficking. We then turn to the question of human rights and security of people who are trafficked for labor, and end the chapter with some concluding thoughts.

Experiences of trafficked victims

The data provided by the 2017 ILO et al. report show that among those in situations of forced labor, the largest group were domestic workers, followed by construction and manufacturing workers, agricultural workers, and those working in fishing. The share of victims who are trafficked for labor exploitation varies regionally. For Southern and Western Europe the share is 30 percent; for North America, 40 percent; for North Africa and the Middle East, 44 percent. The lowest shares are in Central America and the Caribbean at 16 percent; the highest are sub-Saharan Africa with a share of 53 percent, and Eastern Europe and Central Asia with a share of 64 percent (UNODC 2016, p. 8).

We first present vignettes of people who were trafficked into domestic service, followed by the experiences of those in the construction and fishing industries. Even though many other groups are trafficked for labor – including child soldiers, child laborers in mines, and prisoners who are forced to work by governments, sometimes for the private companies that run the prisons as for profit businesses – these vignettes are typical of the cases that are most often reported around the world (see e.g. Cullen and McSherry 2009, Gozdziak 2016, Jureidini 2010, Yea 2015a).

The ILO et al. (2017) estimate about 67 million people, mostly women and girls, are in domestic work; 11.5 million of them are migrant domestic workers. While all domestic work need not fall into the category of forced labor, for many the work conditions are exploitative. The first vignette presents some details of trafficking for domestic labor. The second vignette, from a different country, shows some of the same patterns of force and exploitation, the blurred boundary between labor and sexual exploitation experienced by domestic workers, and additional information about the challenges posed by the (lack of) political rights of migrants.

Domestic servitude: Ghanaian girl in the US

Born and raised in a small village in Ghana, Natalia's family was struggling to pay the school fees for their children's education and welcomed the opportunity for Natalia to receive an education in the United States.

Shortly after she arrived in the U.S., the father she was living with began to physically and sexually abuse the young girl, creating a constant environment of fear for Natalia. For the next six years she was forced to clean the house, wash clothes, cook, and care for their three children, often working 18 hours a day while receiving no form of payment. She was never allowed to enroll in school as the family had promised, go outside, or even use the phone. One day, after she was severely beaten, Natalia saw an opportunity to run away from the home and a neighbor called the police. She was then taken to a local hospital for medical care. The nurse assisting Natalia was aware of the National Human Trafficking Resource Center and referred her to Polaris New Jersey. (Polaris Project 2015)

Natalia's account of the work she had to perform shows relentless work, along with abuse and extreme control over her life. Her account of her work is consistent with the accounts of drudgery, isolation, and the social and emotional costs of domestic service, historically and in the contemporary era (e.g. Diner 1983, Gurung 2015). There is a significant literature on the exploitative structures of women's work, but, in brief, feminist researchers have argued that patriarchal structures have typically separated home/private spheres from public spheres for classifying work. Thus, work that goes on within homes, tasks that typically women perform in order to feed, clothe, and care for the young, the elderly, and the wage earners, are regarded as "family work" which is not paid because it is a "labor of love." In contrast, "real" work, that typically done by men, occurs in public spheres, and is translated into wages and entitlements to social benefits from the state (e.g. Folbre 2006, Waring 1988). Despite the growing numbers of women in the public spheres of work, and their struggles to find other people to take care of the care work, ideologies about non-skilled labor within homes remain strong. As a result, even when non-family members perform this physically and emotionally taxing labor, they are severely underpaid (Flores-González et al. 2013, Romero 1992). These ill-paid structures of domestic service can, in many instances, be classified as forced labor. The exploitation becomes even more severe, as in Natalia's case, when they are not paid at all.

These larger social structures of devaluing work at home, coupled with this family's total control over Natalia's labor, constitute her exploitation. After being enticed to the US on the false promise of an education, she is forced to perform unending domestic labor. She recounts sexual abuse as well as physical and mental abuse. Some aspects of her experiences are similar to the experiences of Barbara or Grace, whose narratives appeared in the last chapter. With few or no networks, her ability to escape and survive was limited. Apart from her fear, her ambiguous political position in the country may have been an additional impediment.[1]

The main patterns of Natalia's experiences are repeated in the next case: that of a Sri Lankan woman, Juju, who was trafficked to the Middle East and ended up in a similar situation of domestic servitude.

Domestic servitude and changing migration status: Sri Lankan woman in the Middle East

Juju left Sri Lanka after her father died, leaving her mother and siblings with a substantial debt and no possibility of generating an income. She went to the government office in Colombo to ask for an overseas job, but they told her that she was too young and would have to wait a few years... Juju's mother had heard of a man who made regular trips to their village in Sri Lanka and "knew all about going to the Middle East." He was an illegal recruiter who received large sums of money from migrants and potential employers in the Gulf for brokering transactions with "less paperwork." He arranged for Juju to go to Dubai on a tourist visa (a fact she did not know at the time) and placed her in the home of a Lebanese family... After a few months, Juju settled into the home of her new family. She thought she would be a nanny to their three children, but it turned out that she was also responsible for housekeeping and tending to her employer's elderly mother. She started working around the clock and was on call 24 hours a day. Some weeks they gave her only three hours a day to sleep and no days off.... In addition to the caretaking and cleaning, Juju often had to assist in household chores such as handy work and landscaping. Most days she worked until two o'clock in the morning... When she told her boss she needed time off to rest, he told her that she had overstayed her tourist visa and would face arrest if she left their house. This was when Juju discovered that her visa was not a work permit. Her recruiter had led her to believe that he had secured a sponsorship visa for her through the employers... She thought about contacting her embassy, but worried that her government would punish her for having violated its rules about migration... Then, one day, the family invited another family for dinner and the visitors brought along their Sri Lankan nanny, a woman named Mediha... Mediha was concerned for her, and told her that she needed to leave the house immediately to find other work. When Juju said that she did not want to work for another family, Mediha mentioned some friends she had met at church who had left their jobs as nannies to become sex workers in local clubs. She said that the women made a lot of money and that it went directly to them rather than to an employer or intermediary. "But prostitution is illegal, I told Mediha." Then it dawned on Juju that she was already an illegal resident in Dubai. "I thought I'm here illegally anyway. Why not do work where I can make money and be my own boss? So that night I made my decision." (Mahdavi 2013, pp. 435–6)

Juju's decision, to move to sex work in order to gain more autonomy, starkly illustrates the effect of control and coercion on those who perform "care work" in homes. Here too, her isolation from others, which is typical of domestic workers, prevents her from finding out about other options.[2] Natalia and Juju, being young, tricked and coerced into work to which they had not consented, should have been clearly identifiable as victims. Natalia fits that model, and was helped by the Polaris Project, which now features her survivor story. However, three realities complicate Juju's classification as a victim. First is her decision to migrate to the Middle East by circumventing the established system. Second is her decision to "voluntarily" move into sex work. Third, she decides to continue working, even after she becomes aware of her status, in the commercial sex industry. Here the politics of migration, in the receiving and sending countries, contribute to her complicated position, pointing to the role of larger structures that we highlighted in previous chapters on the basis of the research by Kempadoo and her colleagues (2012).

If the intersections of gender/race/age/nationality are evident in the exploitation of Natalia and Juju, what happens to the men? Here too, as we show in the next two vignettes, intersecting structures, including legal processes, create their vulnerability to trafficking. We begin with a vignette of child trafficking, followed by a case of a group of men who sought redress as victims of trafficking.

Forced child labor in the fishing industry in Ghana

> When Ebo was 8 years old, his mother uprooted him from his hometown in Ghana and handed control of the boy to his elder sister and her husband. They promptly put him to work in highly dangerous conditions on Lake Volta. For long hours every day, he had to paddle their canoe, cast nets and perform the dangerous task of diving deep to untangle nets. When he was not working on the lake, he had to scale, smoke and package the fish for sale at the market. He was beaten and insulted whenever he made a mistake. For 8 years Ebo worked as a slave for his sister and her husband. He did all kinds of dangerous work. He made friends with another boy who had been trafficked and forced to work on Lake Volta where they fished all day in their canoe, in extreme heat and cold or in storms that sometimes capsized their boat. They were given

little to eat. Sometimes they watched as the dead bodies of children and adults floated past their canoe in the hazardous waters.[3] (UN Voluntary Trust Fund on Contemporary Forms of Slavery 2014)

Like Natalia, Ebo was a child who was forced into this form of labor. He was forced to engage in a relentless series of tasks and was not allowed to leave. Like those of the victims of sexual trafficking, his family members were complicit in putting him in this position. Working for his sister and her husband did not alter the exploitative and dangerous conditions of his everyday life. Furthermore, the conditions of Natalia's, Juju's, and Ebo's lives, much like those of the lives of Barbara or Grace reported in chapter 2, suggest that they are likely to experience adverse consequences of this relentless work, lack of sleep, and physical and mental abuse for their long-term health.[4]

Since Ebo was forced to work within the country in which he was born, it is unlikely that he had to contend with additional political status issues. However, for many men who are forced to work in the commercial fishing industry, political status and jurisdiction are important components of their exploitation. Commercial fishing industries operate ships on the high seas often for months at a stretch. For the laborers, the work is physically intensive and requires very long hours. As a recent Human Rights Watch (HRW) report documents, workers are often contract laborers. Many contractors place these laborers in debt bondage so they are unable to leave their jobs voluntarily (HRW 2018). The ILO et al. (2017) report that migrant workers are often recruited (coerced) for the low-paying and dangerous jobs so that shipping companies can reduce their costs. Some migrant workers are not able to see their families for years. At the same time, these temporary workers are often recruited under limited visa arrangements that put them at political risk of being undocumented in many of the destination countries of these ships.

The disjuncture between visas, permits, and the need for labor in many countries is most starkly illustrated through the experience of workers who are legally brought, on temporary work visas, to work in countries which refuse to grant them political rights as laborers.

Forced labor of Indian migrants in the US

The recruitment of guest workers is a lucrative business for the companies that help US employers obtain cheap foreign labor. A lawsuit filed by SPLC [in 2008] opens a window into this world ... Following Hurricane Katrina, Signal [International] sought to take advantage of a windfall of rig- and ship-repair jobs, but it lacked the necessary workforce. Signal hired Global Resources, a Mississippi-based labor recruiter, and Dewan Consultants, a Mumbai-based labor recruiter, to recruit and provide 590 Indian welders and fitters to Signal's Texas and Mississippi shipyards to allow it to take advantage of the business opportunity created by the storm damage ... Dewan ... testified ... that his firm collected between $11000 and $18000 ... from *each person* recruited to work for Signal ... In order to raise the money, the workers took on staggering debt at high interest rates, typically mortgaging the family home and land and pawning personal possessions. According to Dewan, the fees were the equivalent of two to three years' salary for a welder in India. The workers paid so much because the recruiters had told them that Signal had agreed to sponsor them for permanent resident visas that would allow each worker to settle in the U.S. permanently with his wife and children ... Upon arriving at Signal, the workers were distressed to find that conditions were not what they had been led to believe. The guest workers were housed on Signal's work site in guarded labor camps, housed in cramped 24-by-36-foot trailers, each holding 24 men who shared two toilets. Signal deducted more than $1,050 per month from each worker's paycheck for room and board, further heightening the workers' stress over whether they could afford to service their debts. Worse yet, Signal eventually announced that it would not apply for the permanent residency visas the workers had been promised.

Because the workers had entered the U.S. on 10-month H-2B [temporary non-agricultural] visas, they could not earn enough to pay back their debts. Although conditions at Signal were bad, the workers were prohibited by law from seeking alternative employment. Nor could they leave Signal; in the words of one worker, "I couldn't go back to India, still carrying the massive amounts of debts I had incurred to come to the United States. If I was forced to go back, I planned to hang myself once I landed in India, at the airport." (SPLC 2013, p. 10)

These vignettes indicate several aspects of contemporary labor trafficking, i.e. the conditions that centrally involve force, fraud, or coercion in organizing this labor (see OHCHR 2000 for the UN Palermo Protocol). Where the workers are migrants, they may have migrated legally to their destinations. Then they may find, as these workers did, that the conditions of their work are very different from what they had expected. Like the women who were trafficked for sexual exploitation, these men found both the threats (relating to their visa status) and their isolation – lack of networks – forced them to remain in the exploitative situations. But neither Juju nor the Indian men are totally helpless victims; nor are they people who had set out deliberately to break the laws of the destination country. When they were able to access supportive networks, the women and men, girls and boys, tried to find ways to address their exploitation.

Apart from the people who are trafficked across international borders, many are trafficked internally. Brokers and traffickers move many others to destinations far away, like the people trafficked into commercial fishing. Many of the poorest people *are moved by traffickers* relatively short distances – to destinations that the people are too poor to traverse to on their own – in order to work to pay off their debts. Yousaf and Pur-kayastha (2015b) have discussed how traffickers in the poverty-stricken agricultural areas of Pakistan arrange for small loans for poor men who seek money for births, weddings, and/or illnesses within their families. Then the traffickers arrange to have them work in brick kilns or as agricultural laborers to pay off their debts. Similarly, Allais (2013) found reports of men and boys being trafficked for forced labor in the agricul-tural sector in South Africa, and of boys being trafficked for street vending, forced begging, and crime. Reporting on neo-liberal expansion in India, Vakulavaranam and Prasad (2017) point out that land acquisition by governments for development purposes often displaces poor residents who end up as part of the reserve army of forced labor. Some are then trafficked for seasonal work to other parts of the country or abroad, or even become part of the labor trafficked for maritime jobs (e.g. Nonnenmacher 2014). These patterns remain under-researched in the trafficking literature.

Reflections on large-scale data on forced labor and trafficking

As we pointed out, forced labor aptly describes the conditions endured by the individuals and groups we described above. The ILO's 2012 definition of forced or compulsory labor, with its emphasis on the relationship of exploitation and coercion or force, is clearly applicable to the vignettes we have provided:

> Forced labour is thus not defined by the nature of the work being performed (which can be either legal or illegal under national law) but rather by the nature of the relationship between the person performing the work and the person exacting the work. While sometimes the means of coercion used by the exploiter(s) can be overt and observable (e.g. armed guards who prevent workers from leaving, or workers who are confined to locked premises), more often the coercion applied is more subtle and not immediately observable (e.g. confiscation of identity papers, or threats of denunciation to the authorities). Forced labour therefore presents major challenges in terms of detection, for the purposes of both data collection and law enforcement. (ILO 2012, p. 19)

How do these descriptions map onto some of the vignettes? For instance, Juju's domestic labor falls within this definition of forced labor, as do the cases of Natalia, Ebo, or the Indian men in the US. But Juju's status after she sought out sex work to escape domestic servitude is more ambiguous. Would she be included within the category of a victim trafficked for sex or as forced labor under *both* of the exploitative circumstances? Like the data on trafficking for sexual exploitation, many of the large-scale data on the subject of labor trafficking are beset with ambiguities (see also Adepoju 2005, Gozdziak 2015, Laczko 2005, Loff and Sanghera 2004).

A key problem that is relevant to the discussion in this chapter is that many globally powerful indices have typically presented data in a way that explicitly highlighted conditions *within* countries while implicitly *downplaying* the *intersecting* transnational to local processes that *create* the conditions leading to labor trafficking. For instance, the 2016 *Global Slavery Index* acknowledges that:

The ten countries with the largest estimated absolute numbers of people in modern slavery include some of the world's most populous countries: India, China, Pakistan, Bangladesh, Uzbekistan, North Korea, Russia, Nigeria, the Democratic Republic of the Congo, and Indonesia. Several of these countries provide the low-cost labour that produces consumer goods for markets in Western Europe, Japan, North America and Australia. (Walk Free Foundation 2016, p. 8)

Similarly, the ILO et al. report that: "For forced labour specifically, the prevalence is highest in Asia and the Pacific, where four out of every 1,000 people were victims, followed by Europe and Central Asia (3.6 per 1,000), Africa (2.8 per 1,000), the Arab States (2.2 per 1,000) and the Americas (1.3 per 1,000)" (p. 10).[5] These reports emphasize the causes of vulnerability *within* the countries, underscoring the lack of civil and political participation, social health and economic rights, and personal security, and the presence of refugee populations and conflict.[6] The 2017 ILO et al. report recognizes the complex nature of the structures of exploitation and points to the need to address labor rights in the informal economy, causes of debt bondage, gender, and better migration governance (but see chapter 7, afterword 3). The report recognizes conflicts and crises as sources of people's vulnerability, and points to the need to address them through humanitarian action.

We would argue that the lack of access to civil and political participation, social health and economic rights, and personal security leads to conditions that are ripe for trafficking and/ or exploitation for labor. We also agree that being in refugee camps long-term and in areas of conflict creates instability in the lives of people and enhances their vulnerability. Yet the variability in the regional share of forced labor raises a different issue: do countries recognize the trafficked labor in their midst, even if the laborers are from other countries, if their citizens are rarely perceived to be in exploitative labor situations?

The case of the Indian migrants who were trafficked to the US is a good example of this form of exploitation. While better migration governance would clearly benefit labor migrants, the issue, as we show later, is also about implementation of the existing human rights protocols regarding migrants. We are in a phase where more countries, especially the developed countries, are creating exploitative migration conditions. So it is not clear which actors should be involved in, and held responsible for, these proposed solutions, nationally or internationally. Reliance on humanitarian actions might provide temporary aid to victims, but there is little evidence to suggest humanitarian action actually addresses the structural causes of labor vulnerability and exploitation (see Roth 2015).

Low-wage labor and trafficking

The exploitative labor relationships that are evident in the lives of the Sri Lankan women or the Indian men in the vignettes occur within the current forms of globalization. The rapid spread of neoliberal globalization has led to structural adjustments across nation-states and significant disruptions in the political economies of most countries around the world (see e.g. Cagatay and Ozler 1995, Saadatmand, Toma, and Menon 2007). Sassen (2013), among others, has described the growth of two-tier economies in global cities that act as nodes for privatization and for deregulation of industries. This political economy has led to the creation of a vast "flexible" labor force; people work in jobs that rarely guarantee any stability, are typically ill-paid, and come with few, if any, benefits (e.g. Fullerton and Robertson 2011). Many jobs that earlier commanded "family wages" – that is, economic and social benefits for the worker and *his* family – have been replaced by contingent and flexible work. At the same time, a chain of brokers now structure the relations between a workplace and the worker so that it becomes very difficult for the workers to organize, negotiate, or claim better working conditions from the employer.

This phase of globalization has also created concentrations of affluence and promoted cultures of consumption (Flores-González et al. 2013). The people in the upper tier of the economy – such as knowledge industry workers, upper-tier managers, financial brokers – are able to access unprecedented levels of resources and consumption, including the consumption of personal services provided by people in lower-tier jobs. Those in the lower tier are stuck in poorly paid, unstable jobs, with few social benefits; yet they too aspire to the modernization dividend they see among those in the upper tier (see Ganguly-Scrase 2003). Many begin to accrue growing debts to meet the costs of education and health care[7] that they feel are the keys to their upward mobility. Others have to borrow just to meet the needs of food and shelter. These changes are not only evident in the Global South; they are equally evident in the Global North (though the absolute proportions of the well-off and the poor continue to vary).

Within these tiers, gendered/racialized/classed understanding of work and labor continue to sort and sift which groups – females and males of different ages, ethnicities, nationalities – are likely to get recruited for which jobs across the world. Men are frequently brought in from other countries to clean up after disasters, or for large-scale construction jobs. Construction for sporting events offers a good example: Longman's (2017) writing on the soccer World Cup stadium in Russia and Gibson's (2016) writing about the stadium in Qatar report that workers endured conditions likened to forced labor. Despite documentation by Amnesty International, HRW, and media reports, it is not clear if the trafficking in labor was discontinued in these spaces. When the labor is required by countries to clean up after disasters, as in the case of the Indian migrants in the US, similar exploitative conditions prevail. Reporting on this case of the Indian men, Preston (2008) documented that "They said they lived in sweltering labor camps, crowded 24 workers to a room, under curfew and restricted from leaving the yards, with $1,050 a month deducted from their paychecks for their upkeep."

Discussing a case in Australia, Cullen and McSherry (2009) described the case of some Chinese men who were trafficked into Australia. They arrived legally because the owner of a company – Aprint – sponsored them. But they paid $10,000 to the agent to organize their journey, and another $10,000 to the owner of Aprint, half of it as a bond repayable at the end of their employment. "The four men were accommodated in a run-down, unheated house in Melbourne…and an amount of $120 was deducted each week from their pay for accommodation and other utilities' expenses. Each man worked an average of 50 hours a week and all were paid well under the minimum rates of pay, with the rate of underpayment totaling $93,667" (p. 4). Once their debt to the owner was paid, they were sacked, and under the existing rules, were liable for deportation. Similar cases of labor trafficking are being reported from other countries (e.g. see Allais 2013, Costa 2017, Craig 2010, Ford, Lyons, and van Schendel 2012, McGrath 2012).

The case of domestic workers is related to another facet of this economy. As the economies began to shift and change over the last few decades, many societies have also seen an unprecedented number of women enter the paid-labor force (e.g. Lovell, Hartmann, and Werschkul 2007, Moghadam 2015). Many women join feminized jobs that are considered to require few skills and are ill-paid, with few benefits and often temporary. Their occupations outside homes have created gaps in the provision of hitherto unpaid care work within private spheres. Thus, there is a growing market for poorly paid domestic workers, such as maids (Romero 1992), nannies (Guevarra 2010), cooks, and elder-care workers (see Flores-González et al. 2013) around the world.[8] Governments and recruiting bureaus are involved in sending females for these jobs to other countries (e.g. Amirthalingam et al. n.d., Guevarra 2010, Parreñas 2001) and profiting from their fees and remittances. The women and men we described at the beginning of this chapter, and those in other situations of forced labor, are part of this global assembly line (also see Chang 2000, Ong 1987).

Legality and labor

However, in order to understand the conditions of international labor exploitation, we need to examine the other factors that intersect with the organization of two-tier economies. A key factor, critical for constructing the conditions of labor trafficking, is the immigration laws and labor policies set by states. Based on her work in Singapore, Yea (2015a) has pointed out that the prosperity of neoliberal states relies on the operation of their migrant regimes. Highly educated knowledge workers and wealthy investors are attractive to states; they can access political, social, and cultural rights, since states vie to attract them. The other migrants have very few rights and are often placed in the charge of their employers, further exacerbating their powerlessness relative to their employers.

The vignette we presented from Mahdavi's (2013) work illustrates a similar situation. Juju, the woman in the vignette, is desperate for work; she understands her opportunities in the global assembly line where women like herself go to the Middle East for jobs as domestic care workers. (The difference in exchange rates between Sri Lanka and the Middle Eastern countries, as well as the promise of higher wages, appear to offer attractive prospects of becoming debt free.) But local labor laws and policies include significant restrictions on the conditions in which lower-tier workers are allowed to work:

> UAE labour laws require domestic workers to abide by the kafala, which means that their residence in the country is reliant on their sponsor or kefil, who is also their employer. They depend entirely on this person not only for residence but also for assistance in accessing services such as health care. Some of the more problematic aspects of the general provisions section of the labour law that structures the lived experiences of migration include Article 3. This states that "the provisions of this law shall not apply to…domestic servants employed in private households, and the like…farming and grazing workers." Later, Article 72 adds seafarers to the list of migrant workers not protected by any labour laws. Thus, while domestic workers must abide by kafala procedures, there are no labour laws to protect them. They, like other migrant workers, are also unable to join labour unions because Laws 155 and 160 of the UAE Federal Law No. 8 of 1980 (also known as the Labour Law) ban the creation of such organizations. (HRW 2007)

While the *kafala* system in the UAE may appear to be especially harsh, a whole range of restrictive conditions structure these temporary visa categories in countries across the world. A comparison of how the labor systems governing low-wage, temporary workers operate in Singapore and the US is instructive.

Drawing upon her study of Singapore, Yea (2015a) argues that reliance on these migrants' labor, without giving them access to substantive rights, has led Singapore to practice "untrafficking" their status as victims. She argues that if "the ILO indicators for trafficking…of adults for labour exploitation [are compared] with common complaints made by male workers in the construction, shipyard, landscaping and cleaning sectors…the vast majority of cases would definitionally fall into a trafficking classification" (2015, p. 1086). So the government uses the criteria selectively to exclude less "fully fledged cases of trafficking," which presumably fall within the gray zone of banal exploitation, and thus are legal. Singapore's Ministry of Manpower's (MOM) key representative on Singapore's TIP Taskforce informed Yea (2015a, p. 1088): "A potential victim of labour trafficking in Singapore would meet two criteria; they should have their freedom of movement and association removed [they are unable to physically leave an exploitative working situation] and should be subject to physical abuse and violence [which would achieve compliance through fear and threats to personal safety] (personal communication, 18 January 2014)." Not surprisingly, MOM's records indicate very few labor-related complaints. Yea pointed out that these measures are not unique to Singapore. The city-state drew on the methodology of a study conducted in the US to assess the proportion of trafficked labor among its undocumented workers.

The case of the Indian H2B workers reported by SPLC illustrates the structural conditions in the US. The men had borrowed money and sold their assets to access the jobs in the US. But as temporary workers, they were politically positioned to be under the total control of their employers, with few labor rights (Adur 2011). According to the provisions of the H2B visas, these jobs in the US are contingent upon the employers' willingness to keep the workers. Rajan, Varghese, and Jayakumar (2011) point out that the Department of Labor has no authority to enforce the provisions of an H2B contract under most circumstances. The work conditions, including the sub-minimal living conditions that the employers provided, and their underpayment, were correctly described by SPLC (2013) as being "close to slavery."

Temporary workers, typically, have very little access to the means to complain or protest. The Indian men were unusual in how they organized and protested. The Indian workers approached the New Orleans Workers' Center for Racial Justice (NOWCRJ) and, in an act of defiance, went to Washington, DC, where they began a hunger strike to draw attention to their cause. But in engaging with this form of protest they also became undocumented migrants, since their status depended on working for this employer; this, in turn, made them vulnerable to the enforcement regimes of US Homeland Security services. Employers, are, of course, better positioned to work with government agencies to control agitating workers. In 2010, commenting on an unusual victory that SPLC was able to win for these workers, a *New York Times* editorial pointed out:

> In an internal e-mail message, a Signal official disclosed that ICE [US Immigration and Customs Enforcement] had promised to go after workers who had walked off the job, "to send a message to the remaining workers that it is not in their best interests to try and 'push' the system." The workers, with the help of the New Orleans Workers' Center for Racial Justice, pushed anyway. They took Signal to court with a host of charges... The United States Citizenship and Immigration [*sic*] Services, an arm of the Department of Homeland Security, has concluded that the workers, part of a group of 500 men recruited to work in Gulf Coast shipyards after Hurricane Katrina, had been subject to involuntary servitude and were entitled to visas set aside for victims of human trafficking. (*New York Times* 2010)

In sum, in both nation-states, labor laws are constructed to uphold the state's interest in restricting temporary migrants' access to rights. Different arms of the government assist in upholding this political process. The unequal and exploitative power relationships that define forced labor, including trafficked labor, are a reflection of these laws.[9]

Other aspects of local laws and practices add to the structures of exploitation. Destination governments are often reluctant to regulate and punish labor brokers for infractions. The Signal International case was unusual in that both the Indian and US-based brokers were punished. In most countries, the layers of contractors shield various links on the exploitation chain. For instance, Jureidini (2010) described the case of brokers in Lebanon who appeared to work with impunity to profit from the fees they charged their subcontractors, who passed on the charges to the potential employees. The potential employees incurred significant debts to meet these charges, which, in turn, kept them within conditions of labor servitude as they struggled to pay off their debts.

With near-total control over these temporary migrants, employers are able to extract forced labor. Domestic workers are especially vulnerable because they often work alone, with few avenues of access to the outside world or resources. The work is relentless and often involves many more hours than were originally contracted for (see the case of Nepali domestic workers in the US, in Gurung and Purkayastha 2013). Further, the lines between sexual labor and care labor often get blurred within domestic workspaces. Mahdavi (2013) discusses the case of another domestic worker who wanted to borrow some money from her employer in order to pay an existing debt. He proposed she engage in sexual relations with him in order to earn this money. Such sexual exploitation is not uncommon. Amrithalimgam et al. (n.d.) report that the Sri Lanka Bureau of Foreign Employment (SLBFE) received over 12,000 complaints in 2009, 96 percent from women who reported sexual exploitation, violation of terms of contract, and non-payment of wages. However, these were records of women who went to the Middle East through formal channels. For those like Juju in the vignette, who had bypassed the local government restrictions, the multiple layers of restrictions – within the country and at the destination – intersect and shape their silence about their exploitation.

Yousaf's research in Pakistan (2016) highlighted other problems faced by trafficked victims in domestic spheres. Discussing the case of an Afghan woman who had been sold into domestic service (and sexual exploitation), he pointed out that linguistic problems often prevent victims from reaching out for help. Additionally, even though many countries assert that trafficking victims are supposed to receive help for rehabilitation, to what extent the criminal justice system – for instance, the police in this case – provides such help remains an open question.

The lack of regulation of many jobs, existing labor laws that do not apply to many labor sites, or the enforcement of these laws and policies also create conditions of labor servitude. While some domestic workers have been able to organize for workplace rights,[10] these rights are not consistently available to the vast number of women who work, around the world, in conditions of domestic servitude.

When the delinking of labor and political rights is often justified as a way of protecting the nation-state against uncontrolled migration that threatens the nation's way of life,[11] these measures lead to the exploitative conditions that fall broadly within the ILO's definition of forced labor. These migration regimes, the movement, recruitment, and terms of service for temporary workers, promoted by different states, deny rights to the "temporary" migrants, and contribute centrally to the problem of trafficking.

Labor, trafficking, and questions of rights and security

By comparison with the case of women who are forced to work in the commercial sex industry, labor trafficking is more difficult to prove, since exploitative conditions of labor exist within terrains that are partly legal and visible. The UN definitions of trafficking that emphasize three interlinked elements of recruitment, movement and transfer, and exploitation (UNODC 2016) are not wholly adequate for interrogating the chain of governments, brokers, contractors, and employers that facilitate the recruitment, movement, and exploitation of trafficked laborers. Thus, the questions of the human rights and human security of those who are trafficked for labor reveal additional complications of legalities, experiences of exploitation, and paths of redress.

On the one hand, article 4 of the Universal Declaration of Human Rights (1948)[12] proclaims, "No one shall be held in slavery or servitude; slavery and the slave trade shall be prohibited in all their forms." Article 8 of the International Covenant on Civil and Political Rights (1966)[13] and articles 6 and 7 of the International Covenant on Economic, Social and Cultural Rights (1966)[14] clearly state that no human being shall be held in slavery or forced labor, and everyone has the right to favorable working conditions and decent living. On the other hand, the cases of labor trafficking show that these rights are often not accessible because people are *already* constituted as groups that are not worthy of all available rights. According to the human rights charters, states are responsible for ensuring the human rights of all persons within their territory, irrespective of their political status (Armaline et al. 2015). In practice, the ability of temporary migrants to access labor rights remains an open question, depending on the power and willingness of civil society groups to convince one or another government entity to navigate the terrain of human rights conventions, national laws, and local policies to ensure trafficked persons can access rights.

Furthermore, according to the UN Palermo Protocol and the US-based TVPA, the designation "trafficking victim" theoretically entitles the person to a particular legal status and its attendant benefits. Yet, as we discussed earlier, countries are actively involved in ensuring low-wage immigrants have restricted access to the victim designation. States use two "interrelated techniques of governmentality" (Yea 2015a, p. 1090) for the production of a discourse on victimhood. Victimhood is asserted through repeated public affirmations of a particular type of victim and victim behavior. Women and children who are trafficked for sexual exploitation *in the commercial sex industry* fit this discourse on victimhood. Chang (2013) and others have shown how domestic workers and laborers in a large number of exploitative industries are rendered invisible through the hyper-visibility of the rescue-and-rehabilitate discourse focusing on women and girls in the sex industry. Thus, along with the problem of trying to go up against the states that confer few labor rights on temporary workers, the definitions of victimhood, with the attendant images of helplessness, often work against those who wish to challenge their marginalization. Since the charges of exploitation are also hard to prove in the absence of witnesses or other forms of evidence, few complaints of labor trafficking are recorded in most countries (ILO 2012). In these circumstances, exploited workers, like the Sri Lankan woman Juju, simply seek other options, including in the sex industry.

Another aspect of migration is related to these questions about rights and security. As the EU and the US have restricted the paths to legal migration (and restricted the number of legal temporary migrants allowed to enter each year) the opportunities for smuggling have increased (Bruggeman 2002, Wuebbels n.d.). Many scholars have noted that lower-tier migrants pay agents to move them to their job destinations. Based on the assessment of force, fraud, and/or coercion during their recruitment, movement, and transfer, we could describe their cases as trafficking. But from the point of view of law enforcement, those who are smuggled are willfully breaking the law to enter a country. The rapid growth of increased cooperation between immigration and criminal justice systems that we discussed in the earlier chapters points to further challenges of sorting out undocumented migration facilitated by smuggling and trafficking. From the perspective of the person paying the money, these processes – trafficking and smuggling – may not be clearly distinct. Both involve money; both are exploitative. Often the "traffickers" and "smugglers" are the same entities or people within the same operations. And, irrespective of the states' distinction between good victims (who were trafficked) and deportable migrants (who were smuggled), these exploitative channels of migration remain a part of the harsh reality for accessing low-wage jobs.[15] (For more on the contradictions between state vs. victims' security, see chapter 7, afterword 3.)

As we discussed in chapter 1, the forced migration literature documents ways in which unequal access to economic, social, and political resources places people in conditions of extreme marginality, which, in turn, creates the conditions for trafficking (e.g. Samaddar 2015). Many of the cases of labor exploitation we have discussed in this chapter exemplify these insights. Significant gaps emerge between the definitions of trafficking, the good intentions of the protocols, and the realities on the ground. Howard (2014b) describes young males, some less than 18, who go to Benin in search of jobs in mines.[16] They insist it is their choice, because this work gives them a better chance to improve their lives. In the absence of other opportunities, this work may act as a stepping-stone to a better option for their survival and future. Formally, this case, of under-age children in mines, is defined as trafficking. Our own data from Pakistan show young males making similar "choices" to work in brick-kilns, in order to protect their sisters and mothers from being trafficked for sex and labor and organs (Yousaf and Purkayastha 2015b).

Addressing the exploitative conditions of labor trafficking

By comparison with trafficking for sexual exploitation, with a few exceptions, it is harder to find accounts of international activism to combat trafficking for labor per se. As we have described in this chapter, the legality of the condition of temporary migration often makes it difficult to address trafficking for labor that is not directly for sexual exploitation. Some of the organizing focuses on justice for migrants and addresses the politics of detention and deportation (e.g. Golash Boza 2015). Indeed, new literature has started to argue that many states are beginning to abandon the principles of protection even for refugees in their quest to stop migration (see *Forced Migration Review* 2013, Leenders 2009, Musalo and Lee 2017, Permoser 2017). In this section we focus primarily on local activism that attempts to address exploitative labor conditions (irrespective of whether the people have been trafficked).

Using the US as an example, we identify several types of women's activism that have touched on issues that affect trafficking. Many of these social-justice-oriented efforts address larger conditions of labor exploitation, which can, on occasion, work together with some legal protections for trafficked victims to provide limited solutions for victims.

Chang (2013) described the case of Damayan Migrant Workers Association, through which a survivor of domestic labor trafficking brought a lawsuit against her diplomat employer; it was later successfully settled. To *also* confront the Philippines government about its complicity in these labor exchanges, Damayan leveraged the fact that Filipina women's earnings as domestic workers abroad contribute billions of dollars to the Philippines economy. Some South Asian American women's groups, like Workers Awaaz in New York City, used US domestic violence laws (the Violence Against Women Act, or VAWA) to bring charges against exploitative employers (Varghese 2006). Carvajal (1996) reports that groups like Sakhi and Workplace Project in Long Island have focused on getting the information about workers' rights to immigrant communities. Chang (2013) also discussed the Cambodian American organization Banteay Srei, which works to make victims aware of their rights when they are processed as criminals after law enforcement raids. This program has other components such as peer-based learning, early prevention, and cascading leadership training, and it specifically addresses the trauma experienced by the Cambodian community as they fled the genocide in their home countries. The National Domestic Workers Alliance, which began organizing in the New York area, won initial victories to institute legal protocols on the number of hours, days off, normal pay, and overtime pay for domestic workers; since then they have organized nationally and have worked with the ILO and activist groups in other countries, to push for comparable rights globally.

Similarly, the Asian Immigrant Workers Advocates (AIWA) fought for immigrant women workers' rights in the much-publicized case against Jessica McClintock (in the US). This case is particularly interesting since the organization of layers of contractors through which the work of these immigrant women contributed to the profits of the designer is similar to the organization of many forced labor situations. AIWA successfully launched a case against the use of, and profiting from, sweatshop labor, a case that has been replicated elsewhere (see Elkins and Hertel 2011 on university-based organizing against sweatshop labor). The three-year struggle lead to McClintock paying the immigrant women the wages owed to them, and a multilingual national hotline was set up for garment workers to anonymously report workplace violations. The organization also trains workers in English and in health and safety (including identifying and changing hazardous workplaces), creating grassroots organizing networks and leadership, along with working toward better labor laws (Chun, Lipsitz, and Shin 2013).

In contrast to the successes we described above, there are other cases where migrants (trafficked laborers) are punished. Chang (2013) and others have discussed how the introduction of higher annual deportation quotas in the US has led to a pattern of workplace raids in immigrant-dominated workplaces. Chang describes the 2008 raid of the Agriprocessors kosher meatpacking plant in Iowa, where 389 workers were arrested, detained in a cattle exhibition hall, mistreated by ICE agents, and, without the provision of sufficient linguistic (translation) or legal support, encouraged to plead guilty to identity theft – using false papers – and many were deported[17] (see also Argueta and Rivas 2010). The owners and plant managers were not initially targeted, even though *they* had violated many of the terms of the US Fair Labor Act, and the requirement in immigration laws for employers to check the papers of all employees. Lydersen (2008) reports that when the owner and plant manager were indicted they confessed that *they* had provided the false papers to the undocumented migrants.[18] Chang (2013) argues that even though the *owners and managers* violated the second clause of the TVPA (2000), i.e. "the recruitment, harbouring, transportation, provision, or obtaining a person for labor or services through the use of force, fraud or coercion and for the purpose of subjecting that person to involuntary servitude, peonage, debt bondage or slavery," many of the immigrants, who qualify as victims of trafficking, were deported. Similar harsh raids in other parts of the US have revealed how owners and managers *encouraged* immigrant workers to buy false working papers from people within their networks (Abraham and Ballou 2007). After some raids, some of the women were released, but under precarious migrant conditions where they have to check in regularly until the immigration service decides to deport them. In most families that were already struggling economically, their older children had to find work for the family to survive, setting up a fresh round of labor servitude. Similar raids have continued across the US (e.g. Chozick 2017) with long-term consequences (see Gowans 2017).

Concluding thoughts

While many of the cases of organizing we described in the last section, and the adjustment of status for the Indian men who worked for Signal International, represent success, the immigration raids indicate that the answer to the larger question about the human security of trafficked labor is much more complicated. Sustainable success in changing and challenging exploitative labor situations often depends on the support of the majority groups in a society. The successful campaigns by governments in separating "good" immigrants from "bad" immigrants, along with a general rise of anti-immigrant sentiments in many countries around the world, typically undermine the possibility of such alliances. While we mentioned the use of the VAWA in the US to challenge some domestic workers' labor exploitation, in the first attempts to advocate for that bill, white feminists rejected proposed alliances with immigrant women, arguing that the addition of immigrant women's claims would simply lead to failure to pass the bill. Similar experiences abound in accounts of labor organizing; not all labor unions are willing to form alliances with immigrant labor groups, including trafficked and/or forced labor, rationalizing that the resentment against immigrants is likely to lead to the failure of their efforts.[19]

Despite some successes, clearly, these groups rarely achieve long-term human security. Their aspirations for more secure lives, in the midst of little to no substantive access to economic, social, and political resources, simply mire them in precarious conditions of living in the places to which they migrate in search of work. Around the world the coming together of formal, legal, political, and economic shifts complicates how labor trafficking is understood on the ground.

Two other points are important. First, as Howard (2014b) pointed out, the "binaries – consent/coercion, normal/abusive, legitimate/exploitative – which shape our understanding of trafficking, have to be extended to include important ambiguities, contingencies, and the structural contexts within which migration and trafficking take place and are experienced by those involved in labor migration" (p. 125). Second, while the dominant rhetoric about trafficking describes a move away from sex industries as a primary solution to addressing trafficking in general, some of the slave-like labor described here reminds us that sometimes, a move to sex industries is the preferred option for people suffering from other forms of servitude. The vignette of the Sri Lankan woman in this chapter showed her desperation as she chose work in a commercial sex industry to escape the conditions of her domestic servitude.

If the human security of persons rests on their ability to build lives that are economically, socially, and politically secure, with good health and no active threats to survival, then people who are most vulnerable to labor trafficking are far from reaching these conditions of life. Notwithstanding the activism and legal victories we describe here, the harsher reality is that many remain vulnerable to repeated rounds of trafficking for sexual exploitation, trafficking for labor exploitation, or organ trafficking.

4
Organ Trafficking

In 2016, Pope Francis issued a statement describing human trafficking for the purpose of organ removal[1] as a crime against humanity; his statement was further supported by the Pontifical Academy of Sciences (Vatican Radio 2017). It is interesting to begin with this declaration by the Vatican because even though scholars and experts were reporting organ removal for trafficking from the 1980s, according to the UNODC (2015) many such accounts were not taken seriously at that time.[2] Even now, trafficking for organs has a checkered presence in the policies and efforts to combat trafficking.

Among the major protocols and legal instruments that recognize this form of trafficking is the UN *Protocol to Prevent, Suppress and Punish Trafficking in Persons, Especially Women and Children* (OHCHR 2000). Article 3(a) of the Protocol explicitly mentions "the exploitation of the prostitution of others or other forms of sexual exploitation, forced labour or services, slavery or practices similar to slavery, servitude or the removal of organs" (UNODC 2016, p. 26). Two protocols define the European efforts: the Council of Europe Convention against Trafficking in Human Beings, and the Council of Europe Convention against Trafficking in Human Organs. The US TIP assessments do not include organ trafficking. A series of other declarations, such as the Istanbul Declaration on Organ Trafficking and Transplant Tourism (Transplantation Society and International Society of Nephrology 2008), have directed our attention to the markets for organs.

In spite of the protocols and declarations, data on organ trafficking are very sparse. We have some information about some aspects of organ trafficking, but most are estimates. In 2007, the WHO estimated that 2-5 percent of the organs that were transplanted were obtained illegally. In 2011 Haken estimated that the illegal trade generated profits of between USD600 million and USD1.2 billion. According to the data gathered by UNODC, between 2012 and 2014, 120 cases of organ trafficking were detected in ten countries in different regions of the world (UNODC 2016). In the Middle East and North Africa region, 3 percent of the trafficking victims are trafficked for organs, which is the highest share reported by region (UNODC 2016, p. 8). The 2016 UNODC report also estimates that of those targeted for this form of trafficking, 82 percent are men and 18 percent women.[3] These data indicate that trafficking for organs is not always recognized or reported. As the UNODC (2015) emphasizes, there is research on this subject, but it does not consistently get to the judicial and law enforcement authorities, so there is inadequate recognition and punishment of this form of trafficking.

Compared to the other forms of trafficking, organ trafficking is a relatively new phenomenon. The first successful transplants were carried out in the 1950s; by the 1990s, according to UNODC (2015), hospitals in over 100 countries were practicing transplantations, including transplantation of kidneys, livers, pancreas, and bowels. The actual medical process is typically legal and organs are obtained from deceased and live donors. Huge waiting lists for organs in countries around the world indicate there is a demand. The UN, WHO, and other agencies have established parameters within which organs should be obtained for transplantation (see e.g. UNODC 2015). However, medical confidentiality prevents easy sharing of the details of organ transplants, which, in turn, increases the difficulty of assessing whether trafficking was involved in the process of transplantation.

Trafficking exists within the interstices of the visible world of transplantation. As we show in this chapter, who is targeted varies: sometimes people are victimized after they have migrated in search of work; at other times, traffickers seek poor individuals who are desperately searching for better economic opportunities, wherever they live. Sometimes organs are forcibly extracted from victims who were trafficked or kidnapped for other purposes.

> The issue of forced removal of organs in the context of trafficking in persons and migrant smuggling in North-Eastern Africa gained renewed international attention in July 2016, when the Italian authorities arrested 38 people suspected of being members of a transnational organised criminal group involved in these crimes. The investigation revealed that Eritrean migrants, who had been kidnapped along the route to North Africa and who were unable to pay ransoms, were killed to remove their organs. The organs were then sold for around US $15,000. (UNODC 2016, p. 67)

However, organ removal may or may not occur in the context of migration of the individual; that is, the individual (donor) may not move even though his or her organ is transported. The recipient typically moves to receive the transplantation. When they move internationally, they are subject to migration rules and policies, including those governing tourists.

We do not discuss all forms of organ trafficking in this chapter. We focus on kidney trafficking to illustrate our points. Although the illicit practice of organ trafficking involves many different human organs, kidneys are in most demand (Ambagtsheer, Zaitch, and Weimar 2013, Meyer 2006, Mullins 2007, Naqvi et al. 2007, Pearson 2004, Scheper-Hughes 2004). We draw upon scholars such as Lock (2001), Manzano et al. (2014), Scheper-Hughes (2013), and Yea (2010) who have been highly critical of the discussions that characterize the organ trade as a victimless process.[4] In addition these scholars, and we, highlight the political economy of trafficking fueled by economic-political-cultural globalization.

We begin by sharing some narratives and vignettes that have been reported in scholarly outlets to illustrate the condition of people who sell organs. Since the distinction between trafficking and trade (selling and consumption) of organs is obscured through the linguistic conventions about *donations* of organs, we pay attention to some of the nuances of these terms. We discuss the structures that facilitate such trafficking, including the role of brokers and medical personnel who act as the chain between the person whose organs are extracted and the person who ultimately benefits from the organ. Then we discuss how labor servitude often precedes organ trafficking. We also describe three main types of responses, and their limitations, to address the issue of trafficking. We end the chapter by discussing how deleterious health effects in the aftermath of organ trafficking set up other family members for labor and/or sexual servitude. Thus, this form of trafficking remains a critical part of the continuum of trafficking in human beings.

Narratives

"I had to repay a loan of Rs.165,000 [USD1,650]. Despite working so hard I realized I could not repay the loan…Here one other person had done this before…Two years ago, I sold my kidney…They [agent and doctor] had promised me Rs.200,000 [USD2000], but I received only 180,000 [USD1,800] after deduction of food expenditure during my stay in the hospital…I had to take loan again when my wife was about to deliver a baby, then my child fell ill and needed blood bottles, and then my mother fell ill. Now again my loan has amounted to Rs.85,000 [USD850]. I, my wife, and children work in the brick kiln. If I feel ok then we earn Rs. 300–350 [USD3–3.5] daily." (Yousaf and Purkayastha 2015b, p. 644)

"No," corrected Viorel, a 27-year-old unemployed kidney seller from Moldova's capital city, Chisenau. "We [kidney sellers] are *worse* than prostitutes because what we have sold we can never get back. We have given away our health, our strength, and our lives." (Scheper-Hughes 2003b, p. 200)

In the same *banguey* of unemployed stevedores I encountered an unanticipated "waiting list," which comprised angry and "disrespected" kidney sellers who had been "neglected" and "overlooked" by the medical doctors at Manila's most prestigious private hospital, St. Luke's Episcopal Medical Center. Perhaps they had been rejected, the men surmised, because of their age (too young or too old), their blood (difficult to match) or their general medical condition. Whatever the reason, they had been judged as less valuable kidney vendors than some of their lucky neighbors who now owned new VCRs, karioke machines and expensive tricycles. "What's wrong with me?"

a 42-year-old man asked, thinking I must be a North American kidney hunter. "I registered on 'the list' over six months ago, and no one from St Luke's has ever called me," Mr S. complained. "But I am healthy. I can still lift heavy weights. And my urine is clear." Moreover, he was willing, he said, to sell below the going rate of $1300 for a "fresh" kidney. (Scheper-Hughes 2003b, p. 202)

The vignettes showcase four aspects of trafficking in organs.[5] First, the men are looking for ways to move out of debt or poverty, or to supplement their low earnings. There is a market for these organs, and the price of kidneys varies depending on the place and person whose kidney is being acquired. Nonetheless, the first and second vignettes clearly indicate the men's sense of being exploited. At the same time, there is a recurrent theme of masculinity, in the first and third vignettes, of these men trying to be the family provider. Second, like some of the narratives on trafficking for sexual exploitation, some of the individuals express their choice to sell kidneys. But, as we discussed in chapter 2, we need to consider the larger political economic conditions that shape the "choices" for these individuals. This point is especially critical because of the legality or illegality of the organ trade, and consequently the classification of this process as trafficking (whether force or coercion was used) hinges on the assumption of free choice and donation. Third, as is evident in the third vignette, the organizational structure that harvests the organ and moves it to the receivers is often visible and legal. While many clandestine (and consequently illegal) practices also mark this phenomenon, it is possible to legally acquire and sell organs. Fourth, there are significant health impacts of donating organs, and for poor people, the consequences include the long-term loss of their ability to work.

What's in a name? Transplanting, donating, harvesting, and trading in organs, or is it trafficking?

A key challenge in talking about organ *trafficking* is to understand the language through which organ transfer practices are described. We mentioned earlier that the latest data on trafficking for organs show that only twelve countries reported the phenomenon (UNODC 2016). These reports probably reflect the problems with understanding and reporting. UN definitions of trafficking emphasize the use of force, coercion, or threat in securing organs, yet it is not always clear whether the discussion and reporting on organ trafficking *always* consider the issues of force, coercion, or threat, and, more importantly, exactly how these terms are understood.

A review of the literature shows that the transfer of organs is understood in many different ways, including as donations and transplantations, or as donor and recipient, or as harvesting and trafficking. These sets of definitions are rooted in different understandings about individuals' choices (and capacity to choose). Gunnarson and Lundin (2015) have argued that proponents[6] of a market solution would see the organ sellers as autonomous, freely choosing agents who own their bodies. If we consider the third vignette in the previous section, it is clear that the man wanted to sell his kidney. Even in the other cases, where poverty and unemployment are clear in the narratives, the men indicate *they* sold their kidneys.

However, is it important to take into account the context of their choice? If we were to frame organ trafficking in the way in which Dragiewicz (2015), Kempadoo et al. (2012), and Yea (2015a) framed trafficking for sexual exploitation, the question of choice would have to be considered with reference to the structures in which trafficking takes place. Cohen (2003), Schepher-Hughes (2001, 2003a, 2004, 2006, 2013), and Yousaf and Purkayastha (2015b), among others, have emphasized that poverty, including debt penury, leads people to consider the sale of an organ as a choice. Yousaf and Purkayastha quote an organ broker, who described himself as a former donor:

> Here people are poor, some have to marry their daughters off, so they work at brick kilns. They work in such a hot weather but they don't receive the wages they deserve. People remain hungry, some fall ill. As people came to know about selling kidney, they presented themselves. Here people don't have sufficient land for agriculture...and there is no business. They are all uneducated and ignorant and know nothing. They take loans...if they don't work they don't get food. If they are in tension and there is no solution then people have to do

something for their children. They sacrifice their bodies for their children. People do it due to poverty; nobody does it happily. All the men had to pay loans...their wives are abused and humiliated, they can't go anywhere...they can do anything to protect their honour. (2015b, p. 645)

Recognizing these *contexts* of restricted choices, many of the scholars who discuss the globalized structures facilitating the transfer of organs use the term *trafficking* to describe the trade in general.

Similar to the discourse on the other forms of trafficking, the language describing trafficking of organs is laden with power. In the case of organs it is particularly challenging, but important, to interrogate the language because some parts of these operations are legal. Gunnarson and Lundin (2015) argue that thinking as binaries of victims (who had no choice) and donors who exercised choice restricts us from understanding the realities of people who give up their kidneys. These authors argue for developing an understanding of a more contextualized concept of victimhood.

The discussion of victimhood related to organs is broadly similar to debates about trafficking for sexual exploitation and the relative benefits of legalization. Some scholars (e.g. Barnett and Saliba 2004, Clay and Block 2002, Dworkin 1994, Gregory 2011) argue that individuals should have control over their own bodies and the right to make the decision regarding selling their body parts. Therefore, legitimizing the trade, or selling or buying of human organs, would help to balance the gap between demand and supply of human organs, and minimize the exploitation involved in organ trade. The illicit nature of this act increases the exploitation of organ sellers, whose organs can be removed through deceptive claims that they need surgery (Bindel 2013). Hence these scholars argue it would be fair for both buyer and seller if they were able to enter into an open (legal) agreement. Conversely, other scholars (e.g. Cohen 1999, Joralemon and Cox 2003, Zutlevics 2001) challenge this argument, stating that a legalized free market in human organs would lead to commodification of human beings and their bodies, where poor persons would be viewed more as a "reservoir of spare parts" (Scheper-Hughes 2006, p. 16) rather than human beings with dignity. We would additionally argue that the use of the terms "seller" and "donor" might imply a choice, but, assessed within a context of deprivation, it would be an error to consider this selling as falling outside of the realm of trafficking.

We also emphasize that terms such as "harvesting" and "transplantation" with roots in the imagery of medical-scientific procedures downplay the reality – the structures of inequality – of the person whose organ is transplanted and the person who acquires the kidney, as do the joined terms "donor" and "recipient." Paying heed to these controversies, and our own interests in human security, leads us to use the term "organ provider" throughout most of this chapter to emphasize that a human being provides the organ within a specific context. Along with specifically designating the circumstances under which people sell their kidneys, the term "buyer" is still appropriate for the person who spends money to acquire a kidney. Both terms indicate the different social locations of buyers and providers within glocal, intersecting structural contexts. Using these terms enables us to interrogate why and how this form of trafficking occurs without using the binary terms – "victims" and "exploiters" – at the outset. While there are transplants that involve organs from deceased persons, the discussion on trafficking is about the living providers and the buyers.

The global industry in organ trafficking

Organ trafficking is a function of modernity. Scholars have discussed the roots of organ trade, relating it to the use of organs historically for a variety of purposes, including medical explorations in Europe (e.g. Richardson 2006). Crowley-Matoka and Lock (2006) have discussed the cultural moorings that promote a mechanistic view of the world and separate the "self" from the "body," paving the way for the cultural justification of the use of the organs of human beings who are alive. Additionally, Lock (2001) has described how the shifts in the bio-ethical framework, as well as commodity fetishism, have redefined organs as commodities, and organ transplants as "normal" and desirable practices.

The current explosion of a globalized trade in organs is facilitated by the growth of medical innovations and technologies that enable doctors to remove organs from one person and transplant them into another legally and/or illegally. Beginning in 1954, when the first living-related kidney transplant was successfully performed in the US (Ambagtsheer et al. 2013), the unprecedented advances in the practice of organ transplantation and the availability of immunosuppressive drugs have made it possible to successfully transplant human organs from living and non-living donors.

Cohen (2003) pointed out that the sale of kidneys often occurs in places where there is already a significant penetration of other medical – i.e. surgical – technologies into people's lives. In his study, he argues the Indian government's drive to reduce its population growth had already brought poor women to hospitals for tubal ligation.[7] The kidney transplant surgeries are a part of this longer stream of experience for some women in India. In other regions of India, where women are not so drawn into the realm of surgical procedures, it was more likely that men rather than women were selling their kidneys. The studies across the world certainly document that surgery to remove kidneys occurs where advanced medical facilities are available.

Kalindi Vora (2008) has argued that contemporary capitalism created a key shift in our understanding of resources that we need, or can acquire, to live good lives. In her discussion of the material and cultural understanding of "excess," she argues:

> The idea that a second kidney is excessive is one example of a new mode of abstraction allowed for by the expanding commodification of human biological materials. Scholars in Science and Technology Studies have referred to the way that the sciences of life construct and articulate new historical modes of capitalism as "biocapitalism".…As the product of a specific idea of excess, that is, the idea that there are parts that the body doesn't need, the kidney is "freed" to have an existence separate from the body that produced it.

At the same time, there has been a growing cultural expectation, among the relatively affluent, of living longer. Access to these "excess organs," from "donors," via "transplantation," facilitates this cultural expectation (Meyer 2006, Pearson 2004,

Scheper-Hughes 2003a, 2003b, 2013, Yousaf and Purkayastha 2016). Further, Ikels (2013) asserts that if there were ambivalences earlier about surgically removing one person's organs to benefit another,

> bioethicists helped to remove this roadblock via two justifications: (*a*) the assurance of voluntary informed consent to the procedure by the autonomous donor; and (*b*) the presumed psychological benefits to the donor of altruistically helping save (or improving the quality of) a life, initially the life of a blood relative, then that of an emotionally related person, and finally even that of a stranger. (p. 95)

This, too, is a cultural shift. According to Ambagtsheer et al.:

> Transplantation is becoming a victim of its own success, with demand for organs far outpacing supply. In the United States, in 2007, 21,489 deceased donors were reported to the Global Database on Donation and Transplantation. As of the end of February 2010, 105,966 patients were on waiting lists for transplantation. At the end of 2010 in the European Union (EU), 47,773 patients were waiting for a kidney. The average waiting time for a deceased donor kidney, for example, is now 3–5 years. An estimated 10 people in the EU die every day waiting for an organ. (2013, p. 3)

While these figures do not indicate trafficked kidneys from live donors, they provide a sense of the growing cultural expectation for organs. This growing global demand has led to a global illicit trade and trafficking in human organs, at the time when countries have begun to make it illegal to trade in organs (Ambagtsheer et al. 2013, Kelly 2013).

The extensive research of Schepher-Hughes (2004, 2006, 2013) on commercial transactions of human organs and organ trafficking in different countries, including Turkey, Moldova, Israel, the Philippines, and the US, along with other research (e.g. Budiani-Saberi et al. 2014 on India, Columb 2017 on Egypt, Moazam, Zaman, and Jafarey 2009 on Pakistan, Panjabi 2010 on India and China, and Yea 2010 on the Philippines), shows a well-organized chain of different actors, markets, and institutions, some legal and some illegal, that sustains a global web of organ trafficking (e.g. Schepher-Hughes 2003b, 2013).

Migration and movement[8] remain critical to this process. Organ providers have often moved within the country in search of economic opportunities (see e.g. Yea 2010 on the men in the slums of Manila, or Yousaf and Purkayastha 2015b on Pakistan). Often, prior episodes of labor trafficking are part of this process through which they sell organs. Some of the providers may have moved as internally displaced persons. Others may have migrated internationally as refugees fleeing conflict zones or economic and natural disasters. Certainly the literature on Egypt suggests that refugees from the East African countries are part of the groups who provide organs (see Kelly 2013 for a review of this literature).

Shimazono (2007) described the larger process of people traveling overseas for transplantations as "transplant tourism." According to Shimazono, such transplant tourism can include four types of transnational travel: movement of a buyer of an organ to a country where the provider[9] is located; movement of a provider to the country of the buyer; movement of both buyer and provider from the same country to a third country where an organ transplant can be performed; and movement of both buyer and provider from two different countries to a third country where an organ transplant can be performed (also see Budiani-Saberi and Delmonico 2008).

The following news report in the *Los Angeles Times* illustrates some of these facets of organ trafficking.

Seven years after leaving his village in northern India to find work in the bursting metropolis of Mumbai, Sundar Singh Jatav was struggling in a menial job at a video game shop. The $2.50 daily wage was hardly enough with his family back home deep in debt.

So, in late 2015, when his boss introduced him to a man who promised to solve his financial problems, Jatav listened – and was shocked.

"He suggested I sell my kidney," said Jatav, now 23.

What happened over the next several months would upend his life – and reveal a high-level kidney trafficking network inside one of the most reputed hospitals in India's financial capital.

At least 14 people, including four doctors and the hospital's chief executive, have been arrested since July when police, acting on information provided by Jatav, stopped a kidney transplant involving a 48-year-old patient who had presented forged documents purporting that the organ donor was his wife. The ring is part of what one news outlet dubbed the "Great Indian Kidney Racket."

Because the country harvests relatively few organs from people who die in accidents – the most common source of kidneys in the U.S. – the vast majority of transplants here involve living donors who give up one of their two kidneys.

To reduce the chances that money is changing hands, which is illegal in India and almost everywhere else, the law allows, with rare exceptions, only a spouse, child, parent, sibling, grandparent or grandchild to act as a donor.

For patients who don't have a relative with a suitable kidney or don't want to put a loved one through the small risk that donation entails, there is another option: a shadowy market-place in which well-off patients can buy organs from strangers. The sellers are often impoverished, recruited from small towns by middlemen and made to present falsified papers – sometimes in collusion with doctors. (Bengali and Parth 2016)

While several countries have begun to institute a series of laws to control trafficking, journalists have reported that traffickers and kidney buyers are able to evade these laws (e.g. Columb 2017). Campbell and Davison (2012) report in *The Guardian* that

[e]vidence collected by a worldwide network of doctors shows that traffickers are defying laws intended to curtail their activities and are cashing in on rising international demand for replacement kidneys driven by the increase in diabetes and other diseases. Patients, many of whom will go to China, India or Pakistan for surgery, can pay up to $200,000 (nearly £128,000) for a kidney to gangs who harvest organs from vulnerable, desperate people, sometimes for as little as $5,000.

Many go to five-star facilities for these transplantations in India or China (Cohen 2011).

Shimazono (2007) further pointed out that the international movement of potential recipients is often arranged or facilitated by intermediaries and health care providers who arrange the travel and recruit providers. The Internet has often been used to attract foreign patients. Several websites offer all-inclusive "transplant packages"– the price of a renal transplant package ranges from USD70,000 to USD160,000. Campbell and Davison (2012) reported that a reporter from *The Guardian* contacted an organ broker in China who advertised his services under the slogan, "Donate a kidney, buy the new iPad!" He offered £2,500 for a kidney and said the operation could be performed within ten days.

Thus, the markets, the buyers, the facilitators of transplants, and the providers are part of this chain that links legal and illegal realms.

Questions of human security

Class/gender/age intersecting with other locally relevant inequalities shape the global trade in who provides organs, who facilitates the sales, who carries out the transplants, and who acquires the kidneys. While the different linguistic conventions and the overlapping legal and illegal realms of trafficking can obfuscate its realities, the exploitation, fraud, and coercion are most evident if we assess the human security of the providers, or their lack of security, within these intersecting global-local realities that shape the contexts of their victimization.

In her review of the anthropological literature on organ trafficking, Ikels (2013) has emphasized a paradox among people desperate for a kidney: many are hesitant to ask their relatives for organs. Among others, Ikels points to the research of Moniruzzaman in Bangladesh (2010, 2012) and Scheper-Hughes in Israel (2008) who found kidney seekers were aware of the risks involved for a person to donate his or her kidney. They were, consequently, unwilling to put their relatives at risk, but "did not hesitate to put others at risk by buying a kidney because organs were available" (Ikels 2013, p. 93). To address the growing charges of Western bio-imperialism by critics of these procedures, Cohen (2011) points out that the trade no longer reflects simple binaries of Westerners vs. the Global South. He described the diasporic Indians from the US who return to India to acquire organs, and who then claim to set up a longer-term relationship with the provider's family, most often paying for their children's schooling. Nonetheless, it is clear that intersectional privileges of the North American resident – whether they are of Indian origin or not – work in their favor as they buy organs from the poor(er) Indian providers. And, to date, there has been no evidence that the organ provider's human security improves over the long term.

Economic insecurity is the most significant reason for kidney sales. The narratives of providers suggest that people are inclined to sell their body parts to manage family crises and to escape the vicious cycle of exploitation. Cases from different countries show a consistent mismatch between their anticipated earnings and actual earnings, and, consequently, their decision – "choice" – to sell a kidney to improve their circumstances does not help them or their families to escape the vicious cycle of exploitation in the long run.

Cohen (2003) quotes one woman:

I sold my kidney for 32,500 rupees. I had to; we had run out of credit and could not live. My friend had had the operation and told me what to do. I did not know what a kidney was; the doctors showed me a video. It passes water; it cleans the blood. You have two. You can live with one, but you may get sick or die from the operation or from something later. You have to have the family-planning operation because without a kidney childbirth is very dangerous. I had already had *that* operation. What choices did I have? Yes, I was weak afterwards, sometimes I still am. But generally I am as I was before. Yes, I would do it again if I had another to give. I would have to. That money is gone, and we are in debt. My husband needs his strength for work, and could not work if he had the operation. Yes, I also work. (p. 666)

Yousaf and Purkayastha (2015b, p. 647) report this account:

I sold my kidney because I had to pay a loan amounting to Rs.150,000 to the brick kiln owner. Although my whole family was working in brick kiln, the amount of loan was increased with the passage of time. I had to take loan repeatedly for the treatment of my mother, then my son fell ill, and I had to marry my daughter. After working the whole day we earn only Rs.400-500, whereas just to feed the whole family we need Rs.600 daily. What else we can do to survive if don't take loans?

Similarly, Yea (2015b) reports on the men in Manila slums:

Al said that he decided to sell a kidney because he had migrated from a poor rural area in provincial Luzon to Manila in order to find work and send money back to his parents who were struggling on their farm. He recounted:

"After the operation I was paid US $2000 and I sent every single cent back to my parents. Since coming to Manila my work has been only casual and not enough for my own needs, let alone to send money back home. I didn't tell my parents what I was planning to do, but after I gave them the money I told them how I had earned it. They were really angry with me and upset, but they still accepted the money. I don't have much contact with them now ... It makes me happy that I could keep my promise that I could support them." (p. 130)

Al's admission parallels those of many Filipino migrant workers who must negotiate the mismatch between anticipated and actual earnings. For overseas Filipino workers, this can produce considerable shame (*hiya*) and scrutiny within the home community, but Al's experience shows that internal migrants are not immune to these cultural codes around shame and obligation either.

Apart from the questions about the ability of these individuals to make a choice in the way in which we may assume autonomous individuals can make a choice, their victimization is starkly apparent if we examine their longer-term experiences. Ikels (2013) points out that the structure of choice or consent often does not consider the lack of information on longer-term effects on health (also see Crowley-Matoka and Lock 2006, Joralemon and Fujinaga 1997, Yousaf and Purkayastha 2015b). Yet this is the key to understanding victimization. Like the man in the second vignette at the beginning of this chapter, most providers in the Global South share experiences of pain, sorrow, and helplessness after selling their kidney:

I cannot do any hard work; if I do, I feel pain and take some rest and then start work again because we have to feed our little children ... nobody is here to support us ... who gives anything without any purpose ... We eat if we do work with our hands ... We pray nobody else should do this again when we feel pain. (Yousaf and Purkayastha 2015b, p. 646, interview with a male victim of organ trafficking in Pakistan)

Those who worked in physically labor-intensive occupations were especially affected because their earnings were dependent on their ability to work at the same pace within the same circumstances. Their wages decreased significantly with their declining ability to work, which, in turn, affected their provider role (in the case of men or women). They were left with little choice other than taking loans from the moneylenders to feed their families, especially during their times of illness, which, in turn, increased the vulnerability of other members of their families to new rounds of trafficking.

The other way to understand the relation of exploitation and victimization is to examine the mismatch between the health security of the buyer and that of the provider. Ikels (2013) summarized the studies on organ recipients, and found that they were informed about the risks and benefits of transplants. Ikels also points out that

> [i]nternationally, anthropologists have been concerned that the presentation of organ donation as nearly risk-free, at least in the case of kidneys, has been based on outcomes in high-tech hospitals in developed countries. Should there be postoperative complications or infections, donors usually have ready access to care through insurance. The risks to donors in developing countries can be very different, and the situation is complicated by the issue of transplant tourism. (2013, p. 96)

In our study (Yousaf and Purkayastha 2015b) we found that the doctors had never told the providers about consequences of a kidney removal for their lives. Their kidneys were extracted with minimal post-transplant care. They were discharged from the hospitals within a few days of the transplant, and later, if they felt any pain or developed some health-related issue, the doctors were never available for medical care (also see Moazam et al. 2009, Monirurzamam 2010, Naqvi et al. 2007, Scheper-Hughes 2000). Thus, the global circulation of the ideologies of risk-free "scientific-medical" procedures, without taking into account the structural realities in which the providers are enmeshed, contribute significantly to the long-term health and economic insecurity of the victims' lives. Even though they may have seen kidney sales as one option to improve their lives, their exploitation through the withholding of information – or the provision of misleading information – made them *victims of trafficking.*

Cousins (2016) describes another aspect of the problem:

> In June, 2014, 50-year-old Sita Tamang and her husband, Krishna, from Hokse village in Kavre district, 30 km from Kathmandu, Nepal, were approached by a broker – the middleman between an organ seller and recipient. You don't need two kidneys, he said; one is sufficient. "You can sell your kidney for a lot of money."
>
> The couple were convinced that selling a kidney would lift them out of poverty, so they travelled to India for illegal operations. "I took the decision to sell my kidney for the livelihood of my four children," Sita says. "With the money we got by selling our kidneys, we made a house but unfortunately the house was destroyed in the April 25 [2015] earthquake."
>
> As a result, the family of six have been living in a makeshift tent in sub-zero temperatures. "It is difficult to carry loads, and difficult to breathe and I have blood in my urine and stool," she explains. "We have become weak. We can't even work normal tasks after selling our kidney." (Cousins 2016, p. 833)

With the growth of conflicts and disasters that we discussed earlier, this scenario may not be an isolated case. We earlier alluded to the rapid growth of forced migrants around the world – the total refugee population in 2016 would rank them as equivalent to the twenty-first-largest country in the world (UNHCR 2016). Years of living in camps without many resources (see Njiru and Purkayastha 2015) point to another potential space that might be targeted by organ traffickers. Indeed the representation of refugees among the "commercial donors" in Egypt (see Kelly 2013) indicates this is already a possibility.

Thus, the questions relating to human security and whether providers' lives are improved – in terms of being free, or at least better off, as far as economic, food, health, and/or environmental security, and other threats – confront us with the long-term patterns of victimization of the providers, even though they may have chosen to sell organs.

Addressing organ trafficking

At present, there appear to be three types of responses to organ trafficking. First, some countries have addressed the legal trade by setting up country-wide waiting lists and registries. Second, some doctors have tried to engage others in their profession to stop unethical practices (Holmes and Sagalyn 2017). Third, and most widespread, is the attempt to use the criminal justice system to punish those who break the law.

Many Western countries – which have already set up systems of obtaining organs from deceased persons – have organ registries. Glen Cohen (2014) describes the Eurotransplant and Scandiatransplant systems, but asks whether foreigners should be able to access kidneys from a US registry. These registries then raise additional questions about the legally bounded geographic spaces in which certain types of transplants are possible, and available mostly to some groups of people. (The debate about this appears in chapter 7, afterword 4.) We know that a growing series of migration laws and policies – including for the purposes of tourism – make it easier for people in the Global North to travel to procure organs. The financial advantages of strong currencies further facilitate their choice to travel elsewhere for organs. For people in the Global South, the draconian migration laws and policies, as well as their inability to access organs from the registries, make it harder for them to access organs legally. Inevitably then, the trafficking in organs is most likely to occur in the Global South, or at least, with the organs of poor people from the Global South.

According to Martin (2012), the 2008 Declaration of Istanbul on Organ Trafficking and Transplant Tourism attempts to curb international trade in organs and travel for commercial organ transplantation, known as "transplant tourism." The Declaration provides ethical guidance for policy makers and doctors working in transplantation medicine. The members of the Declaration's Custodian Group and its emissaries gather reports of trafficking and illegal trade in organs and bring them to the attention of the relevant authorities, to prompt reform. Following this declaration, several countries have banned organ tourism and prosecuted those involved in the process.

The criminal justice system of finding and reporting people involved in these trades is sporadic at best. Despite some highly publicized cases of punishing medical establishments and personnel who were illegally involved in the trade, without systematically addressing the linguistic-cultural shifts that normalize these processes of "donations" and "recipients," and the cultural expectation that the acquisition of a kidney from a live person is risk-free for the provider, or is a victimless process, the efforts at addressing this form of trafficking are going to be inadequate, at best.

Concluding thoughts

As we have discussed in earlier chapters, underlying political, economic, and social structures create vulnerability and draw people into the terrain of trafficking for sex and labor. Trafficking for organs arises from the same causes and is very much a part of the trafficking continuum. However, trafficking for organs is marked by its relative invisibility as a trafficking issue. It does not draw much international attention, partly because the expectation of organ transplants has become so acceptable culturally in the Global North and among affluent people in the Global South. It is almost normalized as a part of modern, developed life. The discourse about donors and transplants – i.e. the association with modern, scientific processes – seems to separate the organ from the personhood of the provider. Thus, the moral outrage that seems to drive the crusades against trafficking for sexual exploitation is muted, at best, in the case of organs. Also, the male victims do not fit the gendered discourses of helpless victims of sexual exploitation. Since the presumption is that women are helpless, the helplessness of men becomes relatively invisible. Another, intersecting reason for the invisibility of organ trafficking arises from the lack of data, and countries' willingness and ability to even report on organ trafficking. So we end this chapter by highlighting the tragic consequences of not addressing the underlying structural conditions in which trafficking occurs.

One of the men Yousaf and Purkayastha (2015b, p. 647) interviewed in Pakistan said:

> I sold my kidney … I had to repay a loan of Rs.80,000 [US $800] of my sister … Due to the outstanding loan, brick kiln owner was going to sell my sister. He said he will receive money from the buyer after selling her … She asked me to help her … I sold my kidney to help her … I also took a loan to marry off my daughter.

This narrative shows that young men may sell kidneys in order to protect their family members, especially women and children, from hunger, illness, and sexual abuse by the more powerful. His sister's vulnerability to being sold for sexual exploitation makes this man "choose" to sell his kidney. But his exploitation does not change the larger condition; the family is positioned to be a target of traffickers seeking to buy and sell other human commodities: sex and labor. Thus, trafficking remains an endless cycle in their lives.

5

The Other Side of Trafficking: A Look at the Data and Policies on Trafficking

As we discussed trafficking for sexual exploitation, labor, and organs in the previous chapters we touched on some of the inadequacies of the data and policies on trafficking. In this chapter, we take a look at a selection of data and policies to show why inadequate data and gaps in policies matter for our understanding of the worlds of trafficking. While the women and men who are trafficked remain at the center of our concern, here we take a look at the practices and products of experts and policy makers to highlight the impact of these data and policies in defining and directing how to address trafficking.

We begin with a look at some of the methodological issues inherent in some of the data that are widely quoted to assert the presence and seriousness of trafficking. Following this, we turn to the policies.

Methodologies and the worlds of data

On September 25, 2015, the General Assembly of the UN in its resolution A/RES/1 adopted a set of seventeen goals to eradicate poverty and achieve universal peace as part of a new sustainable development agenda to be achieved by 2030. Goal 8.7 specifically requires all states to "Take immediate and effective measures to eradicate forced labour, end modern slavery and human trafficking and secure the prohibition and elimination of the worst forms of child labour, including recruitment and use of child soldiers, and by 2025 end child labour in all its forms."[1] Despite growing global understanding of human trafficking and the investment of billions of dollars annually, still it is extremely difficult to estimate the number of people who are trafficked for diverse forms of exploitation and calculate the huge volume of profits, at multiple levels, generated by the clandestine acts that constitute human trafficking.

Since the early twentieth century, various organizations have been making efforts to obtain reliable estimates of trafficking across the world. Knepper (2013) notes that the first international research to understand and estimate (women) trafficking was conducted under the auspices of the League of Nations in the 1920s. The extensive fieldwork for the research was organized in twenty-eight countries and 6,500 interviews were conducted in fourteen different languages. The field research unveiled several challenges in estimating trafficking, e.g. difficulty in approaching hidden populations, and unreliable or exaggerated statistics by different organizations lacking empirical support. The research concluded that the issue of trafficking in women was extensive, but could not provide any numbers of trafficked women and stressed developing international cooperation to address the problem. Knepper further notes that even after the lapse of so many decades, the situation is not much different today. Despite growing global attention to the issue of trafficking, we do not have any reliable statistics on how many people are trafficked each year across the world. Owing to the clandestine nature of the phenomenon, difficulty in identifying trafficking activities, and lack of capacity in and coordination of concerned law enforcement agencies, it still remains a daunting task to estimate the extent of trafficking (Jones 2010). Moreover, as different countries define trafficking differently based on certain assumptions about the phenomenon, it becomes almost impossible to compare countries based on their available national statistics (Allain 2014, Hepburn and Simon 2013).

In his discussion of the interplay of US law, donor policy, and NGOs in Latin America, David Guinn stated:

> It is virtually impossible to obtain reliable data on trafficking in Latin America or indeed anywhere else in the world. Clearly, the status of trafficking as an illegal enterprise plays a part in this difficulty; however, reasonable, reliable statistics can be found about many aspects of other organized crime. Nor is it adequate to blame the region, with its lack of resources and sophistication, though those play a part. For example, even the United States with all of the resources available to it has trouble acquiring reliable data as the number of trafficking victims has drastically fallen from the 1999 Central Intelligence Agency estimates of 45,000–50,000 victims to current estimates of 14,500–17,500 victims. (2008, p. 121)

Other scholars have criticized the imprecision and inadequacies in methodologies and estimates (e.g. Brennan 2014 on Dominican migrants to Argentina, and Lima de Perez 2015 on Brazilians in Spain and Portugal).

What is problematic about these data? As we indicated earlier, especially in chapter 3, part of the answer lies in the definitions themselves that shape the collection of data; the other part of the answer can be traced to the policies of powerful countries, funders, and NGOs that shape the ways in which data are gathered and anti-trafficking activities are justified. There are a few international-level influential reports now that provide some estimates or data on trafficked persons, including the UNODC *Global Report on Trafficking in Persons* (2016); the Walk Free Foundation's *Global Slavery Index*, which includes trafficked persons in its definition of slavery (2013, 2016); the ILO's (2012, 2014) reports on forced labor, which also include trafficked persons; the US Department of State's annual *Trafficking in Persons* report; and the 2017 report on *Global Estimates of Modern Slavery: Forced Labour and Forced Marriage* jointly produced by the ILO et al.

We use the GSI as a starting point for this discussion. According to the GSI estimates (Walk Free Foundation 2016), there are 45.8 million people living under conditions of modern slavery across the world. This index is supposed to be an independent counterpoint to government data and is supposed to be accessible to, and reflective of the efforts of, a wide variety of governments working on addressing "slavery." The GSI is marketed as "the most accurate and comprehensive measure of the extent and risk of modern slavery, country by country, currently available" (quoted in Howard 2014a).

In the methodological appendix of the 2013 report, the GSI lists the following:[2]

A weighted combined measure of 3 factors:
   a) Estimate prevalence of modern slavery in each country (this makes up the majority of the Index measure, accounting for 95% of the total)
   b) A measure of the level of human trafficking to and from each country (accounts for 2.5%)
   c) A measure of the level of child and early marriage in each country (accounts for 2.5%)

The estimate of the number of people in modern slavery, country by country, is based on two types of information. The first type of information was obtained from a review of the public record, also referred to as secondary source information – published reports from governments, the investigations of non-governmental and international organisations, and journalistic reports across all media…

From the information gathered from secondary sources and analysis by the research team, **an estimate was made of the prevalence of slavery in each of the 162 countries. These estimates were then presented to experts with personal knowledge of a country, a region, or an industry, often with a promise of anonymity. They compared the information that had been collected with their own knowledge and suggested which points might be exaggerations, which might be under- or over-estimates, and which might be indicative of the social reality. In the process, they often suggested further sources of information. The experts were asked to frame their response within a specific working definition of slavery so that there would be conceptual comparability between their assessments…**

recent research has made possible an additional and different type of information – information about prevalence gained through **representative random sample surveys**…Because this type of information does not exist for many countries, the Index uses representative sample data to **statistically extrapolate the prevalence of modern slavery for select countries that have not yet had random sample surveys…**

The aim was to use both statistical comparisons where available and expert knowledge to group countries along the hypothesised range of prevalence proportions. For example, the prevalence ratio from the UK study was assumed to be relevant to other European island nations such as Ireland and Iceland, whereas **the prevalence ratio for USA was assumed to be relevant to developed Western European countries such as Germany**. Clearly, this method does not have the precision of a global random and representative sample; rather it is the best estimation that can be derived from the extrapolation within an assumed range…As **a rule, human trafficking flows from poorer countries to richer countries, and the modern slavery that occurs in the richest countries tends to be the enslavement of foreign-born persons, not of their own citizens.** (Walk Free Foundation 2013, pp. 110–13)

While we mention some contours of the general debate about the use of the term "slavery" in chapter 7, afterword 1, several scholars have been critical of the ways in which this concept affects the *quality* of the data. Broome and Quirk (2015), among others, have questioned the conceptualization of "slavery"; they are especially critical of the index for assigning *fixed* meanings to "[c]hallenging and contested concepts, such as slavery,…which are presumed to be universally applicable irrespective of cultural context" (p. 814). In other words, the contours of the exploitative structures are presumed to be similar across the world even when it is inaccurate to use this descriptor. The report's persistence in using the term "slavery" and ascribing this descriptor to exploitation of human beings raises several questions. The concept and the data may not be valid or reliable. This question of validity rests on the principles of good science; researchers are expected to produce data that can be verified by their peers. The definitions, and the data gathered, are expected to describe the phenomenon they are studying. Researchers are also expected to indicate the limits to which the data can be generalized, that is, the extent to which these data actually indicate the realities, and when it should not be used to describe a social phenomenon. While the footnotes of these reports indicate some of the limitations of the data, the validity of the concept – slavery – does not appear to be a subject of discussion. In fact there is growing use of the term by many actors across the globe, a sort of ascription of a set of conditions following this group's success in framing exploitation in these terms.

Despite greater use by actors, the concept is not neutral; slavery conjures certain types of human degradation. As Yea (2014) points out, "instead of thinking about human beings in chains…it is essential that trafficking is recognised as involving various degrees of the removal of freedom, very often indirectly through debt bondage, threats, deception and being taken advantage of and exploited while being in an inferior and vulnerable position" (p. 21). The very fact that slavery might conjure up visions of persons in chains (for instance, in places like the US in the nineteenth century) suggests that many countries can rationally claim there is no slavery within their borders. This disjuncture between international discourse and local realities is likely to negatively affect the quality of the data. In addition, while it is clear that some people continue to be enslaved, like the example we featured in chapter 4 from UN reports of migrants who are captured and held by criminal gangs for organ trafficking, the vast majority of persons trafficked for labor are not in these extreme conditions. Janie Chuang (2015) has pointed out that the terms "slavery," "forced labor," and "trafficking" are tied to very precise legal edifices. The use of a broad term such as "slavery" complicates how data can be gathered about these social harms and how these harms are to be legally addressed. In fact, in chapters 2, 3, and 4 we present cases where individuals suffered significantly, but their experiences did not fit some of the existing definitions neatly. The experience of those trafficked persons was not slavery as it is commonly understood across the world, but, their exploitation was better described, as Yea (2014) described it, as being a long pathway where they are severely exploited and experience loss of freedoms and substantive rights. Evidence for this type of a concept would require longitudinal data gathered over people's life courses. The concepts have to also be more sophisticated to capture these complexities.

Similarly, the use of these categories to classify countries and people can be very problematic in various locales. For instance, contesting their rank in the lowest tier of the slavery index, the Haitian government has pointed out that it was one of the first societies in the world to *outlaw slavery*, a history of which the country is very proud. The attribution of modern-day slavery to Haiti undermines this history by ascribing a term outside its historical referents (Bodeau 2013). Neil Howard presents a similar criticism on the basis of his work on Benin (2014a, 2014b). Howard states that the assignment of a fixed, dividing line between adulthood and childhood ignores local understandings of childhood and adulthood. Since age is also used to assign individuals to helpless victim status, sometimes 17-year-old males, who are considered to be old enough to make their own choices about work in Benin, are placed within the category of children. Reviewing the literature on trafficking, Gozdziak (2015) comes to a similar conclusion about the economic aspirations and contributions of children.

Another problem is that the index relies on estimates by country experts; the basis of their designation as "expert" is not transparent. As Tyldum and Brunovskis (2005) point out:

> because numbers and estimates arrived at by expert opinions or involved NGOs cannot be subject to methodological scrutiny or evaluations of external actors, numbers are given weight not based on the methods used to arrive at them (i.e. registration methods, update frequency, or coverage), but based on the authority of the person or organization that provided the estimate. (pp. 27–8)

Equally important, the appendix states that irrespective of the views of the "experts" they were asked to adhere to "a specific working definition" of "slavery" to facilitate cross-country comparisons. This predetermined definition is a key part of the problems of this index.

Moving on to the actual methods of collecting data, Bales (2013) has talked about data derived from national surveys in a few countries including Haiti. Bodeau (2013) points out the government in Haiti is not aware of any such survey. In the earlier chapters we argue that glocal contexts matter for understanding trafficking (see for instance Yea 2014). Here the contexts are flattened if not erased in the quest for a top-down mode of gathering data.

Furthermore, the dataset claims to be comprehensive, but the first paragraph shows detailed data were only available for some countries. Thus, an extrapolation of the relevance ratio for the US onto Germany and other Western European countries seems to overlook the specificities of structures in the EU and in each of these countries. Further, McGrath and

Mieres (2014) argue, "The US State Department's annual Trafficking in Persons (TIP) report classifies countries' efforts to combat trafficking (used synonymously with 'modern slavery') according to a scale from Tier 1 (the best), through Tier 2 and the Tier 2 watch list to Tier 3 (the worst)," and this system has been criticized for allowing its diplomatic alliances and conflicts to influence its rankings. But the GSI relies partly on TIP reports, further exacerbating the problem.

Scholars have discussed the power these benchmarks wield over less powerful countries. Guinn (2008) discusses how governments are pressured to follow the understanding and dictates of the US TIP report rankings of Latin American countries for sex trafficking: "the United States has gone so far as to link HIV/trafficking program assistance to groups that explicitly condemn prostitution and sex trafficking" (p. 126), which is a particular problem for countries in Latin America where prostitution is legal. Howard (2014a) further notes that the close association of the GSI and TIP rankings creates the danger of pressuring countries like Benin to act in ways that are likely to further victimize those in difficult or forced labor situations:

> countries like Benin are tarred with the brush of slavery when arguably this is inappropriate. For another, the diplomatic pressure that powerful states bring to bear as a result of the TIP report or the slavery index can often lead governments such as Benin's to criminalise the work or migration that forms a key part of the economic strategies of the poor.

As we have pointed out, the GSI's ranking of countries suggests that countries are to be blamed for the presence of "slaves" in their midst. Several scholars (including Chang 2013, Chapkis 2003, Dragiewicz 2015, Guth et al. 2014, Kempadoo et al. 2012, McGrath and Mieres 2014) have been critical of assigning the responsibility for "slavery" and the plight of the "slaves" to the national governments of the less "developed" countries. The last highlighted section of the GSI methodology indicates that, despite significant bodies of research that provide contrary evidence, the authors of the index believe in the lack of the complicity of developed countries in contributing to the causes of trafficking within their own countries and transnationally. These assumptions shaped the data in their GSI reports and made the data unreliable.

While we have presented a somewhat detailed criticism of the GSI, estimates are typical of the other reports as well. In 2016, UNODC conducted a multiple systems estimation (MSE) in the Netherlands to test this particular methodology for estimating the total number of victims there. Then it used that method for generating its latest *Global Report on Trafficking in Persons* (2016).

> The MSE is a capture-recapture method applied to lists of victims detected and recorded by different local authorities. The analysis, conducted on the combination of these different lists, is used to estimate those victims that are never detected, and extrapolate a number for the entire victim population in that country.
>
> One key advantage of the MSE method is that it estimates the total number of victims on the basis of information on victims of trafficking detected by national authorities. This is the same basis used by the *Global Report*. The MSE is a cost-effective and relatively simple method but can be applied only in countries with the capacity to detect and keep reliable records of victims of trafficking. (UNODC 2016, p. 47)

This reliance on estimates and extrapolations also affects the accuracy of the data presented in the *Global Report*. The report indicates that 63,251 victims of trafficking were detected in 106 countries between 2012 and 2014. Further, this report highlights the differences between overlapping concepts of trafficking, forced labor, and slavery, as

> Trafficking victims may be exploited for other purposes than forced labour or slavery, enumerated in article 3(a) of the UN Trafficking in Persons Protocol. In addition, while forced labour requires coercion or threat of punishment, in the context of trafficking in persons, victims can be trafficked by other means, including abuse of power or a position of vulnerability. For minors, the consent is always irrelevant in the determination of a trafficking case. (UNODC 2016, p. 15)

Thus, estimates of forced labor and slavery presented in other reports might not reflect the clear picture of diverse forms of exploitation involved in human trafficking.

According to the ILO's *Global Estimate of Forced Labour* (2012), 20.9 million people were victims of forced labor globally. The ILO has classified forced labor "into three main categories or forms: forced labour imposed by the State, and forced labour imposed in the private economy either for sexual or for labour exploitation" (p. 13). The methodology employed to estimate the magnitude of forced labor is available in the report (see pp. 21–30). But here too the units of incidents were aggregated to estimate the number of cases. The ILO discusses how national surveys would improve the data but these presuppose that other conditions for successful surveys – population frames, including the population of trafficked persons – exist in every country. That said, its capture-recapture sample by geographical stratification by form of forced labor, and its aggregate data that were subject to capture-recapture sampling without stratification, improve the data quality compared to the GSI. The ILO's conceptualization of forced labor and trafficking – while upholding the reality of blurred boundaries between "labor" and "sex" trafficking – make it relatively more useful than the other indexes for conceptualizing trafficking and its solutions.

The US annual TIP report also provides significant data on human trafficking, and ranks countries based on their efforts to combat trafficking in accordance with the minimum standards provided in the TVPA. According to the 2017 TIP report (US Department of State 2017), 66,520 victims of trafficking were identified across the world during 2016. In the next section, we discuss in detail the issues involved in ranking, criteria of ranking, and the implications of TIP reports for fighting trafficking by other countries; here we want to highlight the particular methodology used in the making of TIP reports. The methodology section of the 2017 TIP report states that "The Department of State prepared this Report using information from U.S. embassies, government officials, non-governmental and international organizations, published reports, news articles, academic studies, research trips to every region of the world, and information submitted to tipreport@state.gov" (p. 25). This simple generic description of methodology does not provide any information about the "real sources" of data and "experts" that provided or analyzed the data. Further, contrary to the UN Trafficking Protocol (OHCHR 2000), the

TIP report does not consider organ trafficking a form of human trafficking.

The recent collaborative work of three leading organizations – the ILO, Walk Free Foundation, and IOM – also provides estimates of modern slavery, including human trafficking, in the report entitled *Global Estimates of Modern Slavery: Forced Labour and Forced Marriage* (2017). Focusing on two main issues or forms of modern slavery – forced labor and forced marriage – the estimates indicate that there are 40 million people across the world who are victims of modern slavery, including 25 million people in forced labor and 15 million people in forced marriage. While defining modern slavery and associated concepts, the report states that "Although modern slavery is not defined in law, it is used as an umbrella term that focuses attention on commonalities across these legal concepts" (2017, p. 9). The report used combined methodology drawing on a variety of data sources, including fifty-four national probabilistic surveys involving interviews with more than 71,000 respondents across forty-eight countries, administrative data from IOM databases, and validated sources and systematic review from the ILO supervisory bodies.

Although the report used an innovative methodology to include data/information from diverse sources, experts have pointed out its limitations to precisely estimate modern slavery. For example, Mugge (2017) highlights several significant issues related to the methodology. First, the survey data were collected only from forty-eight countries and it is unclear how regional and global estimates of slavery were generated from the data. Further, countries are grouped together based on geographical proximity to generate regional average scores, on the basis of which different regions of the world are ranked. The regional average scores do not reflect any variation within the regions regarding the prevalence of modern forms of slavery. For example, Bangladesh and Japan have the same average regional score. This (regional) ranking is very different from the ranking of countries in the GSI. Second, the report states that the estimate of "[forced] labour imposed by state authorities was derived from validated sources and systematic review of comments from the ILO supervisory bodies with regard to ILO Conventions on forced labour" (pp. 11–12). However, the report does not provide any information about the "validated sources" or the "experts" who validated the sources of information. Third, the concept of modern slavery as defined in the report is based on the definition of forced labor provided in the ILO Forced Labor Convention of 1930. However, as we discussed in chapter 3, economic inequalities and labor exploitation are now so much engrained in the global political economy that it is very difficult to draw a distinction between "voluntary" and "forced" labor. Fourth, to estimate modern slavery and rank regions based on the prevalence of slavery, the report uses statistics combining forced labor and forced marriage. According to Mugge, this is a "dubious fusion," as the issues have diverse roots and require different interventions. Acknowledging the challenges in defining and estimating modern forms of slavery across the world, the report states that "Due to limitations of the data, as detailed in this report, these estimates are considered to be conservative" (2017, p. 9).

In a comprehensive review of the methodologies and data on trafficking, "Data and Research on Human Trafficking," published by the IOM, Laczko and Gozdziak (2005) and their colleagues pointed out earlier there are inherent challenges in studying hidden populations. Nonetheless, instead of the methodologies having improved in the interim, Gozdziak (2015) concluded that sweeping generalizations continued to be made on the basis of small samples and anecdotal research. She renewed calls for caution in using overgeneralized data to make sweeping recommendations on trafficking. Similarly, Weitzer (2011) discussed how the numbers of trafficked persons get inflated because the original reported numbers often come with a number of caveats, but as these get included in the regional or country-wide estimates the caveats are ignored. Weitzer also described the contrasts between the number of victims reported and those who were actually identified as victims in the US: "between 2001 and mid-2008, 1379 trafficking victims in the US were identified. This figure remains but a tiny fraction of the number of persons allegedly trafficked into the US during this period of time [estimated between] 108,750 [and] 131,250" (2011, p. 1351). The estimates in the thousands, vs. the sharply lower number of identified victims, raise questions about the reliability of the estimates.

In her paper "Trafficked Enough?" Yea (2015a) similarly examines the ways in which people are classified as trafficking victims, to show the degrees of imprecision entrenched in the process as countries attempt to show progress on sex trafficking without admitting to being the recipients of labor trafficking. Tseng (2014) discusses a similar phenomenon in Taiwan, where immigration officials are quoted as looking for sex trafficking victims, often among those who are being exploited for labor, so that the official efforts to address "trafficking" appear to be vigorous – and earn them higher rankings in the international reports. (There were few corresponding efforts to address the exploitative conditions of labor.) The awareness of these ambiguities has led many scholars, including Dewey (2008), Sanghera (2016), Zhang (2007), and others, to point to the need to center studies and reports on the question of *how* trafficking victims negotiate their work and exert agency within situations of coercion, in order to produce data that will help in creating and promoting effective anti-trafficking efforts (also see Yea 2015a, Yousaf and Purkayastha 2015b).

To sum up, these ambiguities about data matter for the purposes of designing and implementing anti-trafficking efforts. First, when the data are being constantly revised or based on estimates, without robust transparency, we do not know exactly how the data categories are changing, and ultimately we do not know the extent of the problem. Nor do we know exactly what is being done to solve the actual conditions that victims encounter. Without minimizing the harsh circumstances of trafficked persons, our need to address the human security of victims – however large or small the numbers – requires the development of reliable data on trafficked victims and how they are trafficked.[3]

The next section on policies illustrates this nexus between understandings, policies, and data-gathering efforts.

Worlds of policies

Policies are key instruments through which interventions are designed and resources are channeled to address trafficking. Here, we analyze some key international policies and then assess their efficacy by looking at the intersection of these policies with local policies in Pakistan.[4] We examine the UN

Protocol on Trafficking (OHCHR 2000), the US TVPA, and methods embedded in the TIP reports, along with the policies in Pakistan and the country's attempts to comply with TVPA.

Evolution of the concept of trafficking

According to scholars (Boris and Berg 2014, Cullen-DuPont 2009, Doezema 2010, Kempadoo 2012, Segrave, Milivojevic, and Pickering 2009), the concept of trafficking emerged as a distinct phenomenon – separate from slavery or forced labor or common prostitution – with certain assumptions based on gender, race, morality, and nationality, to protect white women from forced sexual exploitation (Boris and Berg 2014, Lee 2007, Quirk 2007). Altink (1995) argues that the term "traffic in women" was deliberately used, separate from "slavery," to avoid any conflation of prostitution with exploitative labor. Various international instruments were adopted during the first half of the twentieth century to fight trafficking mainly focused on sexual exploitation of women, with varying assumptions about consent and coercion involved in the process. (See Yousaf and Purkayastha 2015a for a detailed commentary on earlier international instruments on human trafficking and their limitations in addressing the issue.) As we discuss in the preceding chapters, and especially chapter 2, many of these assumptions persist today.

The rapidly changing globalized world and the limitations of various earlier adopted international instruments in addressing emerging forms of exploitation (Raymond 2002) led, by the late 1990s, to a realization that the definition of trafficking needed to be revisited to expand its scope to include other forms of exploitation (Cullen-DuPont 2009). Moreover, during this period trafficking came to be referred to as modern-day slavery (Quirk 2007), which led to the adoption of another international protocol under the auspices of the UN to approach trafficking as a new form of slavery.

The UN Trafficking Protocol 2000

Despite the fact that several international instruments were adopted in the twentieth century to address trafficking of women, Gallagher (2010) observes that the term "trafficking" itself was not defined until December 2000, when member states of the UN General Assembly adopted the *Protocol to Prevent, Suppress and Punish Trafficking in Persons, Especially Women and Children, Supplementing the United Nations Convention Against Transnational Organized Crime* in resolution 55/25. While providing a broader definition of trafficking, the Protocol was the first legally binding instrument to address the malaise at the global level. Article 2 of the UN Trafficking Protocol describes its following three main purposes (also referred to as the three Ps):

(a) To prevent and combat trafficking in persons, paying particular attention to women and children;
(b) To protect and assist the victims of such trafficking, with full respect for their human rights; and
(c) To promote cooperation among States Parties in order to meet those objectives. (OHCHR 2000)

The purposes provide a broader framework for fighting human trafficking globally. Article 3 of the UN Trafficking Protocol provides a definition of key terms:

(a) "Trafficking in persons" shall mean the recruitment, transportation, transfer, harbouring or receipt of persons, by means of the threat or use of force or other forms of coercion, of abduction, of fraud, of deception, of the abuse of power or of a position of vulnerability or of the giving or receiving of payments or benefits to achieve the consent of a person having control over another person, for the purpose of exploitation. Exploitation shall include, at a minimum, the exploitation of the prostitution of others or other forms of sexual exploitation, forced labour or services, slavery or practices similar to slavery, servitude or the removal of organs;
(b) The consent of a victim of trafficking in persons to the intended exploitation set forth in subparagraph (a) of this article shall be irrelevant where any of the means set forth in subparagraph (a) have been used;
(c) The recruitment, transportation, transfer, harbouring or receipt of a child for the purpose of exploitation shall be considered "trafficking in persons" even if this does not

involve any of the means set forth in subparagraph (a) of
this article;

(d) "Child" shall mean any person under eighteen years of
age. (OHCHR 2000)

This protocol expanded the scope of the definition of trafficking and stated that human beings can be trafficked for
sexual exploitation, forced labor, domestic servitude, organ
removal, or other forms of exploitation. However, scholars
also highlight some limitations of the UN Trafficking Protocol.
Specific emphasis on women and children in the title of the
Protocol marks continued concerns about sexual exploitation
of women and children, and linking women and children
together reinforces the assumption that women lack agency
and need (male) protection (Cullen-DuPont 2009, Loff and
Sanghera 2004). Moreover, owing to the lack of consensus
among delegates and activists, while drafting the UN Protocol,
regarding links between trafficking and prostitution, the Protocol did not explain "exploitation of prostitution of others
and other forms of sexual exploitation" or servitude (Davidson
and Anderson 2006, Ebbe 2008, Gallagher 2010). In addition,
the UN Trafficking Protocol has been adopted as part of the
UN Convention against Transnational Organized Crime,[5] which
reinforces the assumption that trafficking is an issue of transnational organized crime (Liempt 2006).

Although the UN Trafficking Protocol defines trafficking
as a process that may involve movement of persons leading
to their exploitation, its supposed roots in organized crime
allow states, as we discuss in the earlier chapters, to treat it as
a matter of regulating or stopping undesired migration (also
see Burke 2013, Kara 2011). Noticing this response shift,
Limoncelli (2010) argued the 2000 Protocol drew upon the
anti-trafficking movement as a humanitarian issue to protect
the sexual exploitation of women, to control *women's movement in order to protect* them from exploitation. Allain (2014),
Doezema (2010), and Hyland (2001), among others, also point
out that the measures about protection and provision of services are not binding on member states. Similarly, the issue of
victimization – predicated on the lack of choice – is at odds
with grounded realities (e.g. Doezema 2010, Goldberg 2014,

Kotiswaran 2014, Yousaf and Purkayastha 2015b). In 2012, the UNODC appeared to recognize the broader concept of vulnerability:

> Abuse of a position of vulnerability occurs when an individual's personal, situational or circumstantial vulnerability is intentionally used or otherwise taken advantage of, to recruit, transport, transfer, harbour or receive that person for the purpose of exploiting him or her, such that the person believes that submitting to the will of the abuser is the only real or acceptable option available to him or her, and that belief is reasonable in light of the victim's situation. In determining whether the victim's belief that he or she has no real or acceptable option is reasonable, the personal characteristics and circumstances of the victim should be taken into account. (UNODC 2012)

Even so, Elliott (2015), among others, has noted that for trafficked persons it is near impossible to prove vulnerability or contextual coercion to a law enforcement official.

In addition to the UN Trafficking Protocol, the OHCHR developed the *Recommended Principles and Guidelines on Human Rights and Human Trafficking* in 2002 to guide member states to protect the rights of trafficked persons while implementing anti-trafficking interventions, stressing that "The human rights of trafficked persons shall be at the centre of all efforts to prevent and combat trafficking, and to protect, assist and provide redress to victims" (OHCHR 2002, p. 1). Although the *Recommended Principles and Guidelines* provide a human-rights-based framework to address trafficking, they are developed mainly focusing on trafficking that involves transnational movement. For example, the introductory statement describes trafficking as an "abusive form of migration," which gives the impression of trafficking as a process that involves (cross-international-border) movement; and the framework provides little guidance in terms of protecting the rights of those who have been trafficked internally, like many people whose cases we discuss in the previous chapters.

The UN Protocol and its global reach

Many regional and international organizations have completely adopted the definition of human trafficking provided in the

UN Trafficking Protocol, or adopted the definition as a base and added further provisions to make it more effective in their particular context. For example, realizing that the UN Trafficking Protocol does not explain what constitutes exploitation of a position of vulnerability, the European Commission adopted the UN definition of trafficking with the explanation that "A position of vulnerability occurs when the person has no real or acceptable alternative but to submit to the abuse involved" (European Commission n.d.).

However, there are some regional organizations that have adopted trafficking definitions which are much narrower in scope than the UN definition. For example, according to the South Asian Association for Regional Cooperation (SAARC) *Convention on Preventing and Combating Trafficking in Women and Children for Prostitution*, trafficking "means the moving, selling or buying of women and children for prostitution within and outside a country for monetary or other considerations with or without the consent of the person subjected to trafficking" (SAARC 2002, p. 1). As is evident from the definition, this Convention conflates trafficking with prostitution and only focuses on women and children, ignoring other persons and forms of exploitation involved in trafficking.

Even though many international and regional anti-trafficking instruments exist, individual countries tend to have their own definitions of trafficking which are different from the UN and regional definitions of trafficking. For example, many countries in South Asia have their own country-specific definitions of trafficking that reflect neither the regional Convention on trafficking nor the UN Trafficking Protocol. Thus, these co-existing sets of definition make it very complicated to understand what counts as trafficking and reported trafficking data; it is also nearly impossible to compare the countries even in one particular region of the world. (For a detailed commentary on definitions and anti-trafficking interventions in South Asia, see Yousaf and Purkayastha 2015a.) Tuesday Reitano (2017) highlights similar issues in Africa and explains how the concept of trafficking defined by the West fails to capture the complex realities on the ground in the African context. Despite launching the regional African Union Initiative against trafficking in 2010, individual states have shown little interest in actually fighting the Western-defined trafficking.

With this understanding of the checkered effects of the UN Protocol, we turn to the US TVPA and its reach.

Trafficking Victims Protection Act of 2000

In October 2000, a couple of months before its adoption of the UN Trafficking Protocol, the US enacted the TVPA to address the issue of human trafficking, which has had global implications. The TVPA defines *severe* forms of trafficking under Sec. 103 (8) as:

(A) sex trafficking in which a commercial sex act is induced by force, fraud, or coercion, or in which the person induced to perform such act has not attained 18 years of age; or

(B) the recruitment, harboring, transportation, provision, or obtaining of a person for labor or services, through the use of force, fraud, or coercion for the purpose of subjection to involuntary servitude, peonage, debt bondage, or slavery. (US Department of State 2000)

Although the TVPA used gender-neutral language to define trafficking, it is focused only on "severe forms" of trafficking i.e. sex trafficking and labor trafficking. The TVPA definition differs from the definition of the UN Trafficking Protocol as it defines sex trafficking and labor trafficking separately – not recognizing prostitution as labor – and identifies victims of sex trafficking as a special category, to receive more attention or privilege in policy implementation (Maternick and Ditmore 2015, Peters 2013, 2014). Moreover, as we highlight in the previous section, the US definition of human trafficking does not include exploitation of human beings for organ trafficking. Other scholars (e.g. Hepburn and Simon 2013, Kotiswaran 2014, Peters 2013) highlight that the TVPA includes only some activities as severe forms of trafficking, which helps to construct an ideal type of deserving victims. Along with the efforts of the civil society abolitionists we discussed earlier, to punish engagement in sex work, the law is most often used to support only ideal or deserving victims, especially those who belong to other repressive cultures. Although victims of trafficking can apply for a special T visa that allows them to remain in the United States, there are annual caps, and the visa is contingent upon their passing as *deserving victims* (US Citizenship and Immigrant Services n.d.).

The TVPA also provides minimum standards for the elimination of trafficking in persons. Since 2001, the US Department of State has been issuing an annual TIP report that ranks countries across the world on three different tiers based on the evaluation of their compliance with the minimum standards provided in the TVPA. The 2017 TIP report (US Department of State 2017, p. 28) explains different tiers as:

TIER 1 The governments of countries that fully meet the TVPA's minimum standards for the elimination of trafficking.

TIER 2 The governments of countries that do not fully meet the TVPA's minimum standards but are making significant efforts to bring themselves into compliance with those standards.

TIER 2 WATCH LIST The governments of countries that do not fully meet the TVPA's minimum standards, but are making significant efforts to bring themselves into compliance with those standards, and for which:

a) the absolute number of victims of severe forms of trafficking is very significant or is significantly increasing;

b) there is a failure to provide evidence of increasing efforts to combat severe forms of trafficking in persons from the previous year, including increased investigations, prosecution, and convictions of trafficking crimes, increased assistance to victims, and decreasing evidence of complicity in severe forms of trafficking by government officials; or

c) the determination that a country is making significant efforts to bring itself into compliance with minimum standards was based on commitments by the country to take additional steps over the next year.

TIER 3 The governments of countries that do not fully meet the TVPA's minimum standards and are not making significant efforts to do so.

A 2008 amendment to the TVPA provides that any country that has been ranked Tier 2 Watch List for two consecutive years and that would otherwise be ranked Tier 2 Watch List for the next year will instead be ranked Tier 3 in that third year... The Secretary of State is authorized to waive the automatic downgrade based on credible evidence that a waiver is justified because the government has a written plan that, if implemented, would constitute making significant efforts to meet the TVPA's minimum standards for the elimination of trafficking and is devoting sufficient resources to implement the plan.

As we have mentioned earlier, the TVPA is a significant piece of legislation, with global implications, to hold countries accountable for not showing enough commitment to addressing trafficking in their territories (Bernat and Zhilina 2010, Palmiotto 2015). We have also mentioned in the previous section that the annual ranking of countries in different tiers is likely to be based on questionable data and methodologies, and to impose evaluation criteria based on the US-defined policies instead of the UN Trafficking Protocol.[6] Since the US itself is one of the leading destination countries or global markets for trafficked persons (Bales and Soodalter 2009, Batstone 2007, Cullen-DuPont 2009, Hepburn and Simon 2013, Schauer and Wheaton 2006, Zhang 2007), ranking countries on the basis of compliance with the TVPA's minimum standards, instead of actual trafficked persons, is misleading in assessing countries in terms of prevalence of trafficking. Therefore, as we have discussed in the earlier chapters, the US, despite itself struggling to control the increasing volume of trafficking in the country, imposes its own politically defined standards for evaluating the performance of other countries (see also Chapkis 2003, Hua and Nigorizawa 2010, Kotiswaran 2014, Peters 2014, Srikantiah 2007). For several years, the US was not included in the TIP ranking, but after a lot of criticism, the country was added in the process of Tier Placement in 2010 and has, since then, been ranked in Tier 1 each year.[7]

Low ranking of countries or their failure to comply with the TVPA's minimum standards can lead the US to establish sanctions, withdraw its foreign assistance, and impede these countries' access to global financial institutions. Regarding funding restrictions for Tier 3 countries, the 2017 TIP report clearly states:

> Pursuant to the TVPA, governments of countries on Tier 3 may be subject to certain restrictions on assistance, whereby the President may determine not to provide U.S. government nonhumanitarian, nontrade-related foreign assistance. In addition, the President may determine to withhold funding for government official or employee participation in educational and cultural exchange programs for certain Tier 3 countries. Consistent with the TVPA, the President may also determine

to instruct the U.S. Executive Director of each multilateral development bank and the International Monetary Fund to vote against and use his or her best efforts to deny any loans or other uses of the institutions' funds to a designated Tier 3 country for most purpose [*sic*] (except for humanitarian, trade-related, and certain development-related assistance). (US Department of State 2017, p. 29)

However, as *The Guardian* reports, the ranking of countries in the TIP report is not only dependent on their performance to fight trafficking (Kelly 2015). As we mention in the previous section, because of US foreign policy interests, the ranking of many countries is upgraded in the TIP report despite the fact that the countries fail to comply with the minimum standards. At the same time, Wooditch (2011), among others, claims that the ranking in different tiers, as well as funding from the US, has not helped to improve the situation in many countries. The US provides funding to NGOs to fight human trafficking, especially in low-tier countries; but funding is granted to only those NGOs that work within the US-government-defined standard to address trafficking, do not lobby for the legalization of prostitution, and do not work on behalf of trafficked women who do not fall within its narrowly defined category of victims of severe forms of trafficking (Birkenthal 2011, Haynes 2014, Hua and Nigorizawa 2010, Musto 2010, Wooditch 2011).

Furthermore, the TIP report's narrow scope draws attention away from the deeper structural causes. As we have discussed earlier, structural adjustment policies, the shifting terrain of jobs and the flexibilization of labor, and the expanding scope of armed conflict – in which the US is centrally complicit – are absent from these classifications on efforts.

In the next section we examine the case of Pakistan, where there is no shortage of rules. We show how compliance with the TVPA instead of the UN Protocols, however, creates many gaps in actually addressing trafficking.

Anti-trafficking legislation in Pakistan

The Constitution of Pakistan specifically prohibits slavery, forced labor, and trafficking in human beings and requires the state to take the necessary steps to protect people, especially women and children, from all forms of exploitation. For example, article 11 of the Constitution (first published in 1973 and since amended) proclaims:

(1) Slavery is non-existent and forbidden and no law shall permit or facilitate its introduction into Pakistan in any form.
(2) All forms of forced labour and traffic in human beings are prohibited.
(3) No child below the age of fourteen years shall be engaged in any factory or mine or any other hazardous employment. (National Assembly of Pakistan 2012)

Despite these provisions in the Constitution, the concepts of slavery and trafficking were not defined until 2002 and there was no specific legislation in Pakistan to deal with the issue of human trafficking. In October 2002, the government of Pakistan promulgated the Prevention and Control of Human Trafficking Ordinance (PACHTO), defining trafficking and setting the legal basis for addressing the issue in the country. Section 2(h) of PACHTO defines human trafficking as:

obtaining, securing, selling, purchasing, recruiting, detaining, harbouring or receiving a person, notwithstanding his implicit or explicit consent, by the use of coercion, kidnapping, abduction, or by giving or receiving any payment or benefit, or sharing or receiving a share for such person's subsequent transportation out of or into Pakistan by any means whatsoever for any of the purposes mentioned in section 3.[8] (Federal Investigation Agency n.d.)

In addition, PACHTO describes purposes of trafficking and prescribes strict punishments – from seven to fourteen years' imprisonment – for all those who are involved in the process of trafficking, including recruiters, exploiters, and abettors. However, due to the narrow scope of the legislation, which defines trafficking only in terms of crossing international borders, the people who are trafficked internally are not officially categorized as victims of trafficking and are deprived of the victims' rights provided in the UN Trafficking Protocol.

Thus, the men who are trafficked to pay off debts would not fall under the purview of trafficking.

Moreover, PACHTO has not, till this year, distinguished between human trafficking and human smuggling, so it has also been used (more frequently) to deal with cases of illegal migration or human smuggling. As a result, law enforcement agencies tend to conflate trafficking with smuggling or illegal migration (US Department of State 2017). In chapter 2 we have discussed the case of the Afghan girl who was trafficked to Pakistan in her early childhood; law enforcement agencies considered her as an illegal immigrant rather than a victim of trafficking. The country is in the process of passing a bill on human smuggling in 2018; perhaps the passage of this bill will change the pattern of implementation.

Other ambiguities abound. Although the definition of trafficking provided in section 2(h) of PACHTO is gender-neutral, section 6(iii) of PACHTO and the Prevention and Control of Human Trafficking Rules (PACHT Rules, notified in 2004 by the government for the implementation of PACHTO) contradict the definition by specifying the provision of services based on gendered assumptions about victims. For example, according to rule 3(2) of the PACHT Rules,

> In case the victim is an un-accompanied child or a destitute woman, the court before whom such victim is produced may pass an order to keep him in a shelter home established by the Government or by the Non-Government Organizations for accommodation, food and medical treatment. (Federal Investigation Agency n.d.)

According to the definition here, shelter and other services can only be provided to "an un-accompanied child" or a "destitute woman"; hence, men, transgenders, or others who do not fall into the predefined category of deserving victims are not entitled to these services.

Thus, on paper, there is a lot of effort to address trafficking, in terms that are legible to international reports like TIP. For the protection of victims of trafficking, the National Action Plan for Combating Human Trafficking announced by the government of Pakistan in December 2005 also envisages replication in other areas of the country of the model shelter established by the IOM and the US embassy (Ministry of Interior, Government of Pakistan 2015). Safe and secure accommodation is supposed to have a properly secured building with appropriate living conditions, access to telephones, access to medical care and psychological counseling, the possibility of legal assistance, the opportunity to have a translator, and a separate place for conversation, ensuring the confidentiality of information about the person placed in the accommodation. In reality, cases of trafficking are dealt with by the generic government-run shelters mainly established for victims of domestic violence, which lack facilities and resources to provide services to trafficked women.

What happens to the victims of forced labor that we have described earlier? Sometimes the local law enforcement officials deal with the cases of internal trafficking as other crimes under the Penal Code or other laws (Hussein and Hussain 2012). For example, in Pakistan, bonded labor or debt bondage – considered to be the most prevalent form of trafficking in the country – is prohibited under the Bonded Labor System (Abolition) Act (1992). However, the Act prescribes less serious punishments for the perpetrators than does the anti-trafficking legislation (also see Hepburn and Simon 2013, Kara 2011, Sanghera 2016). Furthermore, it lacks any mechanism for the protection and support of victims of bonded labor or debt bondage to address their long-term vulnerabilities (Yousaf and Purkayastha 2015b). In addition, the Act has rarely been used or implemented to convict perpetrators of these crimes in the country (US Department of State 2017).

If we examine the impact of the TVPA and TIP reports in Pakistan, against this background of local laws and policies, we can trace how a disjunctured process emerges, creating gaps in addressing trafficking. According to a stakeholder from an international organization that was involved in the process of designing anti-trafficking legislation and interventions in Pakistan, one of the main reasons that the government initiated anti-trafficking legislation was its ranking in Tier 3 in the TIP report of 2001 (Yousaf 2016). Since the government was concerned that being noncompliant with the TVPA's minimum standards would lead to cuts in US aid, it promulgated the legislation to improve its ranking in the TIP report, which was consequently improved from Tier 3 to Tier 2. In addition, according to HRW (2002), Pakistan was the major ally of the US in the war against terrorism, so Pakistan's ranking was improved in the TIP report because of the political interest of the US government. The stakeholder asserted that the anti-trafficking legislation in Pakistan was drafted quickly, after reviewing the legislation of some other countries instead of analyzing the situation or nature of trafficking in the country. During that period the government was more active in taking anti-trafficking initiatives because international organizations and donor agencies were providing financial and technical support to address trafficking in a particular way. However, after the donor assistance and resources were exhausted, the government found it difficult to sustain or implement the counter-trafficking interventions through its own limited resources.[9] Yousaf (2016) also points out that the consequence of these gaps, in understanding and addressing trafficking on the ground, makes it likely that the data that are provided for international reports like TIP are based on the local understanding of trafficking (conflated with smuggling) even though these are being distilled as "trafficking" data at the international level.

Overall, these policies fall short of addressing the structural problems and range of trafficking. Nor are the individual vulnerabilities and the needs, both short-term and long-term, of trafficked persons addressed adequately. The international protocols draw attention to the problem but the gaps in conceptualization as well as the competing definitions lead to contradictory impacts of these protocols on countries.[10] The power of the US directs countries to comply with its TIP report standings. In the process the shortcomings of the US definitions are added to the terrain of international compliance. The US TIP report describes the situation in many countries. In countries like Norway, the focus of trafficking and compliance appears to fit the TVPA requirements and the UN Protocol. But in a country like Pakistan, with very different local conditions, the effect of the need to comply with TVPA standards shapes the direction of efforts in ways that do not address the pervasive conditions that affect the vulnerabilities of people who are trafficked for sexual exploitation, labor, and organs.

These brief reviews of the worlds of data and worlds of policies provide a glimpse into the significant gaps between how trafficking data are produced, how and why policies are written and coded in particular ways, and the money and effort to address trafficking. The overall picture indicates a lot of activity, but there seem to be few concerted efforts to improve labor rights, advocacy, and transnational efforts for better immigration laws, raising consciousness about different types of trafficking among people who benefit from trafficking (including organ trafficking) in order to draw them into the anti-trafficking efforts. Sustained and long-term support for trafficked victims falls through these data and policy gaps.

6
Envisioning a Trafficking-Free World

Our discussions of the continuum of trafficking for sexual, labor, and organ exploitation in this book show that many actors – including UN agencies, governments, NGOs, activists, and academics – are engaged in understanding, defining, implementing policies and practices, and gathering data and information on trafficking. New alliances are being forged; for instance, the recent joint efforts by the ILO, Walk Free Foundation, and IOM to redefine the directions of action to address trafficking. Given these trends of growing awareness and involvement in anti-trafficking efforts, can we envision a trafficking-free world? The answer to this question partly rests on our ability to critically think about the different facets of trafficking, including how we think about victims and survivors, and how we conceptualize the terrain within which trafficking occurs and survivors try to rebuild lives that are secure economically, politically, socially, and culturally.

We have drawn upon the UN criteria on trafficking, understanding the process to include the actions of actors who recruit, move, receive, and/or hold human beings for exploitation, and accomplish these actions through the use of deception, coercion, abuse of power, abuse of positions of vulnerability, and threats or actual use of force. We have examined intersecting structures of gender/race/class/sexuality/age[1]/nationality to discuss some of the reasons that make people vulnerable to different forms of trafficking. Significant social inequalities link those who are trafficked and those who are more privileged consumers of sex, labor, and organs within and across countries. We have found, repeatedly, that continuing socio-economic inequalities play a very significant role in constraining the life chances of these human beings. As a result, their long-term human security, including their access to economic, political, and social resources, among them health care, remain in jeopardy. Thus, a starting point for our reflections on trafficking, based on the continuum we presented here, is to think about the aspects of victims' lives that are not being emphasized sufficiently in the current discussions and anti-trafficking efforts.

Since many actors are involved in the world of anti-trafficking efforts, the victims are presented according to the perspectives of these actors. NGOs that seek to raise awareness and resources often use survivor narratives and descriptors such as "modern-day slavery" to frame trafficking. These emphases – through the selection of stories and language that are meaningful to the *intended audiences of the NGOs* – often bring many other groups into a common frame of understanding about the experience of victims. Governments might use the language of criminal justice to highlight some aspects of trafficking; they too might share survivor stories or profiles of young, helpless people to create political support for their efforts. Many of the survivor stories, including many of the vignettes we present in this book, describe the extreme, inhumane conditions that shape the lives of helpless victims.

Since we do not have effective ways to actually gather more systematic information on victims, we repeatedly rely on these survivor narratives, with an implicit or explicit emphasis on victims' helplessness, to convey the impact of trafficking. At the same time, this helplessness, i.e. the victims' inability to act, becomes central to the iconic accounts of trafficking-related exploitation. Without minimizing the experiences of human beings who were subjected to the most extreme inhumane conditions, we have presented vignettes of victims' helplessness, as well as their agency within a variety of exploitative conditions. It has allowed us to show that victims make choices whenever they can, but if the larger structures continue to deprive them of substantive access to resources to address the human insecurities of their lives, their choices do not lead to the outcomes they seek (see also Gozdziak 2016). Indeed, many victims end up within other circuits of trafficking.

Understanding that victims are not always totally helpless raises the difficult question of our readiness to recognize them as victims, and help them, even if they were involved in making some decisions that may have made them more vulnerable to victimization through trafficking.[2]

The repeated narratives about truly extreme injustices, followed by stories of the individuals' survival, with fewer details about the process through which they achieve long-term survival, leave several gaps in our understanding of the effects of trafficking on victims. Often the survivor stories show that NGOs or local government agents help to rescue victims or direct them toward agencies that might help. Barbara Amaya's case, which we present in chapter 2, shows this profile. In addition, Barbara described her long individual struggle to rebuild her life. We do not know about the availability of social benefits that may have helped or impeded her struggles. Relatively few narratives talk about the survivors in the long term. We do not know what happens to their health, or, where applicable, what happens to their ability to access visas that allow them to settle in the countries to which they were trafficked. We do not know what happens after they are repatriated (if they are deported to their countries of origin). We do not know whether and how they struggle to build secure lives, that is, as we discuss in chapter 1, lives that are generally free of threats to survival and wellbeing. While we use the term "survivor" to describe people who were able to escape trafficking, we mostly do not know enough about the material conditions for their long-term survival. In other words, we might have to expand our understanding of victims and survivors temporally: we need to think about a long path of victimhood, and a longer path, with many potential impediments, to long-term survival. The key question we should ask is what happens *long-term* before, during, and after their victimhood.

Relatedly, we also need to reconsider whether the current emphasis on discrete forms of trafficking actually reflects the realities in which victims are positioned. We recognize that treating each form of trafficking separately has arisen from the lineage of trafficking as an international crime. The laws of criminal justice seek to prosecute individuals and gangs who traffic in human beings for different purposes. Some of the literature has begun to indicate that the actors in the trafficking chain are diverse; criminal networks operate trafficking rings, but a host of small actors, sometimes alone and sometimes in concert with others, act as cogs in the trafficking process.

Our reliance on discrete forms of trafficking minimizes and/or erases the continuities between different forms of trafficking and the broader context of victimization. It is important to keep in mind, as we have argued, that human beings who are trafficked *for one purpose can be trafficked for other purposes* within their lifetimes. Women who are trafficked for sexual exploitation can be "rescued," but, in the absence of viable options to rebuild their lives, they might be exploited later as domestic labor, or be recruited again for sexual exploitation as they search for economic security (Mahdavi 2013). We also know that trafficked victims, because they have few options to control their lives, can be exploited for different purposes *at the same time.* Women who migrate seeking jobs as domestic laborers, or are trafficked for domestic labor, are vulnerable to sexual exploitation as well. In addition, women who travel as temporary labor in the entertainment industry may find themselves caught in situations of sexual exploitation (Choo 2016). Sometimes, one person is trafficked for one type of exploitation, but the arena of exploitation expands and can draw other people in the victims' networks into the terrain of trafficking. The poor men who sell their kidneys in order to meet their family-provider obligations are often then unable to work as they did before their kidneys were harvested. If they are still in debt, other family members are asked to work to pay off their debt, opening up new channels for labor and sexual exploitation (Yousaf and Purkayastha 2015b).

Understanding trafficking in these linked ways opens up the field of inquiry beyond the emphasis on the prosecution of criminal gangs and individuals, and on counting trafficking cases on the basis of prosecutions. Most dominant actors currently describe the types of trafficking in ways that indicate the agendas of governments are different from the agendas of the law-breakers, such as smugglers and traffickers. The dominant anti-trafficking efforts are not indicting *governments and law-breakers* for creating the coalescing means, actions, and conditions of exploitation that are characteristic of trafficking for sex, labor, or organs. Yet unless we continue to ask "Who profits?" "Who benefits?" "Who and/or what obstructs victims' attempts to strive for human security in their lives?" from the perspective of a trafficking continuum, we will not be able to link trafficking to the series of transnational-national-local processes that shape the trafficking terrain.

Using a trafficking continuum approach also encourages us to critically examine the data and reports that, sometimes, obscure whether people are being re-counted because of the ways in which prosecution numbers contribute to discrete categories of trafficking. Such critical inquiry is important if we want to assess which types of policy and intervention, by governments and NGOs, are more successful in addressing whether victims are able to survive and build lives of dignity *over the long term.*

These changes – thinking of trafficking in terms of a continuum, and thinking of disjunctured and coalescing legal and illegal actions and processes that create trafficking terrains – are unlikely to happen quickly. But we have a growing body of academic research to support advocacy to reshape the discourse and efforts on trafficking. As an analogy, we can look at the trajectory of activism to combat violence against women. Through the last four decades of the twentieth century, feminist scholars pointed out that in order to understand domestic violence, we needed to move away from the overwhelming focus on deviant men and begin to examine how states facilitate violence by ignoring what happens within the private spheres of homes (see e.g. Katzenstein 1989). In every country, where anti-domestic-violence laws were passed, activists and scholars made these larger structures visible (see Ertürk and Purkayastha 2012 for an overview of these efforts). In some ways, the current focus on trafficking is similar to the early days of domestic violence scholarship and activism. The current policies and efforts are mostly directed toward criminal gangs and individual perpetrators, without an equal focus on the multiple, and sometimes contradictory, roles that states play in preventing *and* facilitating trafficking. We need to expand our focus.

Toward a trafficking-free world: a look at the resources for victims

The global awareness of trafficking, and the sheer numbers of countries that have signed up to the trafficking protocols, constitute a significant step in addressing trafficking globally. Yet it is important to ask: do we have enough political will and money to address the conditions that facilitate trafficking?

Laws and policies

While NGOs play important roles in creating awareness about trafficking, few have, as far as we are aware, systematically targeted their activism toward countries' migration laws. Yet, as we highlight throughout this book, and especially in chapter 3 on labor trafficking, the laws and policies that govern migration and the rights migrants are able to access prior to, during, and after migration are critical for victims' and survivors' long-term human security. Trafficking is forced migration, and these migrant-victims' statuses determine the type of rights they will be able to access substantively. These statuses stratify who can, without fear, access law enforcement agencies to report trafficking, and who are likely to be caught and punished by crimmigration systems as undocumented migrants. Even though the human rights protocols are meant to apply to everyone irrespective of their political status, the reality is that countries often ignore these expectations. Under the best circumstances, countries provide visas for trafficking victims. The reality is that the total number of such visas is typically limited.[3]

The gaps between migrants' human rights and the vision driving the protection of trafficking victims have been evident at the international level from the time when the UN and US anti-trafficking policies and protocols were being written. Mary Robinson, the UNHCR, issued an "informal note" pointing out that the trafficking persons protocols ought to pay particular attention to the existing conventions on the human rights of migrants (see DeStefano 2008 for a description of this conflict). More recently, in 2010, the heads of UN agencies jointly promulgated a statement on migration and human rights to remind countries that signed the declaration of human rights of their obligation on migrants' human rights. A key emphasis in the 2010 and subsequent statements are the duties of states toward migrants under the International Covenant on Economic, Social and Cultural Rights (OHCHR n.d., UNHCR 2016). Yet, like many other scholars, we have found that countries and large NGOs might talk about prevention (of trafficking) and protection (of victims), but in reality the solutions offered rarely address the long-term human security issues of different types of trafficking victims. Instead, the involvement of smugglers and traffickers in the process of migration has often been described by countries as a national (state) security crisis, and used as political rhetoric to create even more stringent controls on migration. Mindful of powerful countries' declarations that international human rights conventions are contingent upon their ability to ensure national security, even the UN statements are careful to note that countries have a sovereign right to decide who can enter and/or stay in their country, before reminding countries about their obligations to fulfil their human rights responsibilities. These claims of protecting national security are not always in alignment with the human security needs of migrants *who were not explicitly allowed into the country for permanent residence* at the beginning of their migration. As the discussion on labor trafficking has shown, the sovereign rights of countries to determine terms of entry and stay are often *the* source of the exploitative structures that negatively affect trafficked persons. Yet, in this power struggle over which actors determine migrants' human rights, the UN is very much at a disadvantage, since the countries, and not the UN, have the actual power to provide or withhold resources and substantive access to rights for migrants.

Money

The purpose of these human rights is to ensure people are able to access resources for survival and long-term needs of wellbeing. By signing up to the UN anti-trafficking protocols, countries commit, or are expected to commit, resources to combat trafficking. In the previous chapters we have not discussed the resources used in anti-trafficking efforts, but the resources offer another perspective on the ways in which these efforts are carried out. When we examine the reports on money and anti-trafficking efforts, what the total sums of money are and for what purposes these are spent are not always clear. Private foundations are involved, along with governments, in funding anti-trafficking efforts. A whole range of INGOs are also playing increasingly prominent roles, along with governments, in managing the money at different points of the anti-trafficking efforts. As we describe during our discussion of shelters in chapter 5, sometimes these INGOs are able to overshadow the local efforts.

According to Mike Dottridge, in 2011 the EU contributed USD15 million and the US contributed USD51 million to anti-trafficking efforts. In September 2013, three private foundations, including the Walk Free Foundation, announced the establishment of the Freedom Fund, "allocating USD30 million to the fund themselves and suggesting the fund should attract...and spend USD100 million by 2020" (Dottridge 2014, p. 5), to combat modern-day slavery. Pointing out that relatively little is known about the effectiveness of much anti-trafficking programming, the GAATW took on the responsibility of producing a fact sheet on funding – listing both the contributions and the spending by countries and corporations – to assess the effectiveness of the efforts. In the introduction to a special issue on money in anti-trafficking efforts, Dottridge (2014) reported that it is not always possible to trace the trajectory of the money spent on anti-trafficking efforts because of the varying terms and definitions used by different actors. For instance, Martina Ucnikova of the Walk Free Foundation reported on international spending *to combat modern slavery* (2014). In contrast, many country reports use the terms *anti-trafficking efforts*. These terms, as we have discussed earlier, are not synonymous. Sometimes, aid flows to countries and anti-trafficking money are conflated with anti-trafficking contributions. Since the identification of trafficking victims, specifically, might be the key to receiving some help and support from other governments or NGOs, the distinctions between terms such as "aid" and "anti-trafficking contributions" is important if we are to understand where the money flows. Thus, some of the ambiguities we discuss in earlier chapters about data on trafficking are also apparent in the reports on spending to combat "modern slavery" and/or "trafficking."

When specific accounts are available, the picture reflects many of the contradictions we have discussed in this book. In some cases, NGOs were funded to establish long-term support for victims; nonetheless, the money may not reach the victims. Surtees and de Kerchove (2014) noted that despite billions of dollars in EU funding on anti-trafficking measures, "only limited funds were available to support trafficked persons while they rebuilt their lives" (p. 9). Summarizing Hoff's article (2014), Dottridge pointed out that "a large proportion of donors' resources are channeled via international organizations (where a portion is consumed by administrative costs) and that not enough reaches trafficked persons or local communities" (Dottridge 2014, p. 9). Suzanne Hoff (2014) also described the complicated terrain of trafficking, where sometimes local NGOs are denied access to foreign funding because state governments are wary of the motivation behind foreign money. At other times, INGOs compete with local NGOs to provide the same services in order to meet the needs of their funding cycles, and during the period of competition, some local NGOs simply end their operations, thus curtailing the options for trafficking victims.

Is a trafficking-free world possible?

We have to hope so, and we build this hope on an awareness of the histories of human rights struggles. Despite the focus on the legal edifices of human rights, we know, from various accounts, that rights are substantively realized through struggles, and the terrain of struggle includes significant setbacks and conflict (e.g. Andersen 2003, Armaline et al. 2015, D'Angelo 2001). An important arena for the struggle to address trafficking has to focus on improving labor conditions, especially addressing the contemporary tendency of countries to delink the labor contribution of migrants from their access to rights and resources. Another, overlapping arena of struggle has to focus on interrupting the rapidly shrinking role of governments to provide social rights and benefits during the current phase of neoliberal globalization. For instance, a struggle to demand widespread provision of health care and increase the accessibility of health care for all those who live within the boundaries of a country would benefit trafficking victims. If the intention of trafficking protocols is to protect victims, then they have to be able to access political, civil, economic, social, and cultural rights to build secure lives so that they survive or are not trafficked repeatedly. But, as this book has shown, these objectives are often unreachable.

At present many international efforts, however well-intentioned, fail to address trafficking in ways that are cognizant of local conditions. For instance, as we discuss in chapter 7, afterword 1, establishing indicators for "modern-day slavery" in countries that have no histories (or language) of slavery equivalent to the language and histories in countries that have benefited from slavery means that these anti-slavery frames may not work effectively to address trafficking. Or sometimes, countries may have different sets of legal tools to prosecute people who smuggle human beings and people who severely exploit human beings. These might be the most effective tools locally and might address trafficking, without using the international trafficking language. It is not clear whether adoption – often translation – of the new language is more effective in achieving the desired result of prevention, prosecution, and protection. To what extent should anti-trafficking efforts be guided by international directives, and to what extent should awareness-building be achieved through international efforts while local laws and policies are strengthened through efforts from the ground up? The solutions advocated by the US or some INGOs may be less effective because they are based on conceptualizations and practices that work in countries with specific organizations of legal terrains, or specific sets of socially relevant solutions, and do not always work locally.

One utopian view that we would offer is to adopt a "curb-trafficking-by-steps" approach where numerous existing local efforts are supported and complemented by tweaks and extensions, in order to better assess what can be achieved locally. At the same time, anti-trafficking efforts cannot be treated as distinct ways to address discrete problems. We advocate working in multiple directions, and paying critical attention to the ways in which these advocacy efforts might impede the activism for social justice and human security of a wider swath of marginalized people, including internal and international migrants.

On a macro level, this curb-by-steps approach would require working for more peaceful worlds, or at least supporting or not impeding the efforts to lessen the wars, conflicts, environmental degradation, and state-sponsored routine violence that lead to displacement and insecure conditions of life. It would require addressing trafficking through better labor and immigration laws and policies. There is an urgent need to address the causes of vulnerability, which includes more resources to address poverty and other intersecting structures of inequality. This approach would require different types of coalition building as well as principled leadership locally and nationally.

Some of the anti-trafficking laws need to be localized. Laws akin to those developed to curb the "rent-a-womb" phenomenon in India might work to deter trafficking in organs. Making it illegal to go to another country for transplants (if your own country will not allow it or you have a long wait locally), at par with the severe punishment for those who buy organs or perform transplants for transnational organ transfers, would deter some of this practice. A lot of funding and efforts to set up registries of donors around the world might arrest some of the most flagrant human rights violations of this form of trafficking. (Although, as we point out in chapter 7, afterword 4, we have to resolve the question of who can access these registries.)

Making it easier, and cheaper, to complain about trafficking might improve the access of victims to channels of redress. Even in countries like the US, which has national hotlines for victims, it is not clear how exactly victims would be able to learn about the hotlines, or even use them. Some localities have done better in publicizing anti-trafficking efforts; for instance, the airports have many anti-trafficking prevention messages and hotlines on their billboards. Perhaps providing these numbers to everyone who enters a country, and promoting public service announcements across the country, in multiple languages, could help. Using some tactics that have been useful for partner violence, establishing training – or trained cells in law enforcement agencies – for people specifically to deal with trafficking for sexual, labor, or organ exploitation would help.

(However, this training would be effective only if the laws and policies were designed to address human rights violations.)

Insisting on more public reporting on the patterns of spending by governments and NGOs would act as an ongoing check on the spending for anti-trafficking efforts. Much like government budgets, transparent reporting and accounting of the proportion of money that goes to administrative costs vs. directly to victims could redirect some of the money into the hands of those who need it most.

Finally, using a tried and tested technique that is already in use at the UN might offer another way to find out more about trafficking locally. Creating a mechanism for issues "shadow reports" – parallel reports by the civil society – not simply on government efforts but on the efforts of some of the prominent NGOs, would also create the political pressures to directly help the victims, regularize how they are identified, and chart the actual paths for them to follow to access their human rights and security.

We know the answer to the question why, despite the legislation and money for combatting trafficking, trafficking continues to flourish in our times. The solution, however, is far more complex than the path we are now on, that is, vigorous efforts to prosecute individuals and gangs, and limited initiatives to protect some victims or minimize the conditions as part of the effort to prevent trafficking. With the long-term human security of trafficking victims as key to anti-trafficking efforts, our prevention and protection aspects of trafficking have to be significantly improved through political, economic, and social channels.

7
Afterwords: Ongoing Debates and Unresolved Questions

There are several ongoing debates in the field of scholars and practitioners who are interested and involved in mitigating trafficking. Here we present five sets of additional debates and additional information to illustrate the depth and directions of some of these unresolved questions.

Afterword 1: Modern-day slavery

In order to draw attention to exploitative conditions, many NGOs, policy makers, and media outlets have begun to use the phrase "modern-day slavery" to describe exploitation through forced labor and trafficking (see, for instance, *The Guardian*'s website on modern-day slavery, or Walk Free Foundation's (2014) definition in the Global Slavery Index or the ILO et al.'s (2017) discussion of modern-day slavery).

Are the material conditions and moral considerations of trafficked human beings the same as, or sufficiently similar to, slavery to warrant the descriptor "modern-day slavery"?

Exactly what was meant by slavery historically?

In 1927, the Slavery Convention emphasized two aspects of slavery in order to outlaw this practice:

(1) Slavery is the status or condition of a person over whom any or all of the powers attaching to the right of ownership are exercised.

(2) The slave trade includes all acts involved in the capture, acquisition or disposal of a person with intent to reduce him to slavery; all acts involved in the acquisition of a slave with a view to selling or exchanging him; all acts of disposal by sale or exchange of a slave acquired with a view to being sold or exchanged, and, in general, every act of trade or transport in slaves. (OHCHR n.d.)

The history of slavery shows a change from the time when people were captured during wars and subsequently enslaved, to the organization of slavery as a commercial enterprise in selling and profiting from the sale and ownership of human beings, from the Middle Ages (Palmiotto 2015). Obokata (2006) further emphasizes that the drawing of race boundaries defined who could be considered a slave. To foster this slavery, societies institutionalized the rights of buyers to become the legal owners of slaves and their descendants. Slaves were often geographically co-located with their owners, though under starkly unequal living circumstances, so they could provide labor for the owner's enterprise. Since owners controlled the slaves' destinies, they could be sold or sent elsewhere, for any purpose. The case of a pioneering physician and researcher, J. Marion Sims, stands testimony to the widespread belief slaves were not wholly human; Sims conducted medical experiments on slave women's bodies, without anesthesia (Holland 2017; also see Schiebinger 2017). Thus three sets of structures and processes structured slavery: racist ideologies about people who were considered less than wholly human; formal political and economic structures which upheld slavery because the dominant groups benefited from it; along with the actions of owners and people in their strata of society toward slaves.

"Slavery" today

Some NGOs and actors argue that the conditions of trafficked persons today are similar to the older forms of slavery. Walk Free Foundation (and the lead author of its Global Slavery Index Kevin Bales) popularized this descriptor; it is now being used by many governments and NGOs. Descriptors such as "modern-day slavery" act as frames for mobilizing a response from large swaths of societies. Social scientists consider frames to be sets of descriptors that enable people to link their own understanding and experiences with what is being claimed by social movements or NGOs. If there is frame alignment, people are more likely to act to support the agenda of the movement or organization. Thus evoking the symbolism of slavery has gotten many actors to think about trafficking as (unacceptable as) slavery.

Fiona David of Walk Free Foundation has argued that even though there are distinctions between political and legal definitions of human trafficking, forced labor, and slavery, for the victims of inhumane conditions, such "finer distinctions" have limited relevance. David (2015) cites the example of men who were discovered by the Indonesian government on an island where they had been kept in cages and regularly beaten. (The government acted quickly in favor of these men.) David says:

> Consider the value of the investigative journalism that shone a light on this situation and ultimately led to these men being rescued. Does it matter to the average reader whether these men were slaves, in forced labour or trafficked? I expect not. What matters is that the general public understands that situations of this nature still occur even today and that they have the capacity to influence these situations through their consumer choices and pressure on governments who continue to be complicit through inaction or willful blindness. (2015, pp. 150–1)

David's views are reflected in a large body of work created by Walk Free Foundation in their successful attempt to get NGOs and governments to recognize the social ill through the use of the language – "framing"– of modern-day slavery.

Not exactly slavery

Arguing from a different perspective, Janie Chuang (2015) points out that each of the terms "slavery," "trafficking," and "forced labor" is defined precisely within legal frameworks. In Chuang's opinion, using the descriptor "modern-day slavery" and citing extreme examples of labor and sexual exploitation hinder the process through which these types of exploitation can be addressed. Chuang argues that conflating all three forms raises the bar in terms of addressing forced labor and trafficking. If all forms of trafficking had to meet the legal criteria for slavery, it would make a victim's quest for justice even more difficult. The legal path to punishing slavery, in the areas where slavery exists, should be used to the fullest extent. Where the conditions do not meet the standard of slavery, evoking that symbolism does not help to resolve the situation of other types of victims who are exploited severely. Paavilainen (2015) uses a different argument. According to her, countries use different sets of laws, sometimes against forced labor, sometimes against labor trafficking, to address the forms of exploitation experienced by trafficked persons. She emphasizes that multiple routes are acceptable because the focus ought to be on *eradicating* the *causes* that lead to unacceptable levels of labor exploitation.

O'Connell Davidson (2017) raises other points. She points out that the use of this language co-opts the visual and textual history of transatlantic slavery for the purpose of fostering NGO and bystander activism.

> The large-scale, profitable, and legally sanctioned business of shipping human beings from Africa into chattel slavery in the New World that flourished between the fifteenth and nineteenth centuries relied on overwhelming physical force at every stage – from the moment of kidnap, through the journey to the West African coast, detention in the dungeons of fortresses and castles prior to shipment, during the Middle Passage itself, and on arrival. (p. 2)

The structures of trafficking (or forced labor) today do not resemble *these* structures of violence that were at the heart of slavery. O'Connell Davidson and her colleagues are also critical of the fact that the proponents of the idea of modern-day slavery rarely acknowledge that racism and capitalist exploitation existed alongside liberalism during slavery in countries such as the US. Selectively using the term "slavery," and relying on extreme cases to justify it, rarely shows a commitment to dismantling the *structures of racism* that led to slavery, and continue to harshly diminish the lives of racial minorities today.

In addition, we add the point about language and social realities. For countries that have histories of slavery, including struggles to abolish slavery, frames such as "modern-day slavery" make a moral claim to not participate in contemporary enslavement of human beings. For the countries in which slavery was not practiced historically, often, similar words do not exist for *this practice*. No country is free of histories of marginalization and inhumane treatment of their minorities, and the terms are likely to reflect those social realities. By evoking slavery symbolically, we can never be sure how it translates locally. We used Google Translate to translate "slavery" into Hindi and Bangla; the translation yielded the terms *ghulaami* and *dashattva*. Both terms suggest that the employer is in control, but the Hindi *ghulaami* means being under the control of another – even in ordinary low-level jobs – without an association with the extremely harsh, exploitative conditions of slavery. The Bangla term comes closer but it does not evoke a history similar, for example, to the US history of slavery.[1] So the symbolism evoked here also expresses a particular hierarchy of evoking histories of the Global North and uncritically applying it to all of the Global South.

The key issue that arises from these reflections is whether or not these frames translate locally, and, whether, in the absence of easy translations, these terms can be used to initiate effective local action against trafficking.

Resources

Chuang, Janie. 2015. "The Challenges and Perils of Reframing Trafficking as 'Modern-Day Slavery'." *Anti-Trafficking Review* 5:146–9.

David, Fiona. 2015. "When it Comes to Modern Slavery, Do Definitions Matter?" *Anti-Trafficking Review* 5:150–2.

O'Connell Davidson, Julia. 2017. "The Presence of the Past: Lessons of History for Anti-Trafficking Work." *Anti-Trafficking Review* 9: 1–13.

Paavilainen, Marja. 2015. "Towards a Cohesive and Contextualised Response: When Is It Necessary to Distinguish between Forced Labour, Trafficking in Persons and Slavery?" *Anti-Trafficking Review* 5: 158–61.

Plant, David. 2015. "When it Comes to Modern Slavery, Do Definitions Matter?" *Anti-Trafficking Review* 5: 150–2.

Notes on contemporary definitions

UNODC (2016) defines trafficking – as we present repeatedly in this book. But the report also states:

> Forms of exploitation specified in the definition of trafficking in persons include, sexual exploitation, slavery and forced labour, among others. Slavery and forced labour are also addressed in distinct international treaties.
>
> A victim of **forced labour** is any person in any form of work or service which is exacted from him/her under the menace of any penalty and for which the said person has not offered himself voluntarily.
>
> A victim of **slavery** is a person over whom any or all of the powers attached to the right of ownership are exercised...
>
> **Differences between victims of trafficking in persons and populations affected by forced labour and/or slavery**: trafficking victims may be exploited for other purposes than forced labour or slavery, enumerated in article 3(a) of the UN Trafficking in Persons Protocol. In addition, while forced labour requires coercion or threat of punishment, in the context of trafficking in persons, victims can be trafficked by other means, including abuse of power or a position of vulnerability. For minors, the consent is always irrelevant in the determination of a trafficking case. (pp. 14–16)

UNODC (2016) points out that in reality there is some overlap between these three forms of exploitation (but these are not synonymous terms).

The 2017 *Global Estimates of Modern Slavery* (ILO et al. 2017) defines slavery in this way:

> modern slavery covers a set of specific legal concepts including forced labour, debt bondage, forced marriage, other slavery and slavery like practices, and human trafficking. Although modern slavery is not defined in law, it is used as an umbrella term that focuses attention on commonalities across these legal concepts. Essentially, it refers to situations of exploitation that a person cannot refuse or leave because of threats, violence, coercion, deception, and/or abuse of power. The *Global Estimates of Modern Slavery* focus on two main issues: forced labour and forced marriage. The estimate of forced labour comprises forced labour in the private economy (forms of forced labour imposed by private individuals, groups, or companies in all sectors except the commercial sex industry), forced sexual exploitation of adults and commercial sexual exploitation of children, and state-imposed forced labor. (ILO et al. 2017)

Afterword 2: Feminist dissensions on how we should address trafficking for sexual exploitation

The issue of how to address trafficking – through identification and prosecution of perpetrators through criminal justice systems, or by focusing on some other direction – has been the grounds for significant debates among anti-trafficking actors. Here we focus on the debates among feminist scholars and activists who have been most involved in anti-trafficking efforts to address sexual exploitation. At one level, feminist scholars and activists have been at the forefront of identifying violence against women, including sexual violence, as an important subject that ought to be addressed systematically across the globe (see Ertürk and Purkayastha 2012). At another level, there are disagreements about the means of addressing trafficking for sexual exploitation. These debates are broader than the emphasis on trafficking for sexual exploitation, but the contours are interesting and important for thinking through anti-trafficking efforts.

As we noted in chapter 1, the religious right within the US was successful in bringing their anti-prostitution agenda to the heart of US anti-trafficking laws. This emphasis on abolishing prostitution meshed with the stream of feminism that identified all commercial sexual activity as violence by men against women. As Bernstein (2010) has noted, for many feminists, the issue was simple: who would be *for* sex trafficking?

While no feminist group is "for" sex trafficking, these groups differ significantly in how they envision the agency of women who are part of the industry that sells sex. One group sees women as victims and envisions all commercial sexual activity as violence against women. This group typically advocates the prosecution of traffickers as well as consumers or those who buy sex as a primary way to address prostitution.

Bernstein (2010, 2012) has argued that until the 1990s the sex workers' movement in the US was attempting to decriminalize sex work and demand rights for sex workers within a labor frame much like the demands of Darbar in Kolkata, India, that we have presented in chapter 2. Advocacy groups in the US, such as the Bay Area Sex Worker Advocacy Network, have pointed out that without strong labor and immigration protections, trafficking victims are vulnerable to deportation (Chang 2013). But as the national, local, and international reach of US laws and policies began to equate sex (human) trafficking with all forms of prostitution, the ground shifted to prosecution of traffickers and the clients of prostitution. With the rapid expansion of carceral systems during the 1980s and 1990s, these two streams of agendas – the neoliberal state's governance based on prosecution and punishment, and the dominant liberal feminist agenda to control all violence against women – came together, in the US and in other countries, to emphasize anti-trafficking efforts based on prosecution and punishment.

The debates about women's agency and violence against women lead to these questions:

- Should addressing trafficking be wholly or primarily based on punishment and prosecution?
- Should it be based on supporting human rights of victims along with punishing perpetrators?

These distinctions are important because the power of the liberal feminist (and state) agendas drives what happens within the US and globally. This power has led to the rising tide of prosecutions, which are an important tool in the anti-trafficking efforts. There is very little political effort, currently, to systematically establish human rights within countries so that victims can access these rights. Yet without access to rights, without finding ways to build human security, the needs of victims of trafficking are not addressed systematically.

Resources

Bernstein, Elizabeth. 2010. "Militarized Humanitarianism Meets Carceral Feminism: The Politics of Sex, Rights, and Freedom in Contemporary Antitrafficking Campaigns." *Signs: Journal of Women in Culture and Society* 36:45–71.

Chang, Grace. 2013. "This Is What Trafficking Looks Like." Pp. 56–78 in *Immigrant Women Workers in the Neoliberal Age*, edited by N. Flores-González, A. R. Guevarra, M. Toro-Morn, and G. Chang. Chicago, IL: University of Illinois Press.

Eyewitness News. n.d. *What Happened to the Girl Next Door.* (Documentary) https://www.youtube.com/watch?v=ljrselo4s1U

NETNebraska. n.d. *Sold for Sex: Trafficking in Nebraska.* (Documentary) https://www.youtube.com/watch?v=etao-pHnjUs

Afterword 3: Geopolitics, security, and trafficking for labor

While we have discussed forced labor and labor trafficking in chapter 3, we have indicated that the distinctions states make between trafficking and smuggling are very important for how migrants are likely to be treated if they escape exploitative situations. Here, we highlight how *geopolitical interests intersect with state interests* to sway the directions of state intervention on labor trafficking.

Many states across the world are engaged in tightening border controls, building crimmigration systems to manage "illegal migration," and creating or firming up temporary worker visa categories. Some of the examples in chapter 3 are of workers who were given temporary worker visas which led to their "near-slavery" experience. The exploitation of workers, including trafficking for labor, is often related to the nexus of migration policies and labor laws within countries.

What part do geopolitics play?

Lenore Lyons and Michele Ford's (2014) work on Malaysia offers a glimpse into the role of geopolitics in a less powerful nation. According to Lyons and Ford, Malaysia passed its Anti-Trafficking in Persons (ATIP) Act in 2007, and subsequently expanded this protocol to include migrant smuggling (in 2010). The ATIP Act was initially similar to the UN Protocol (OHCHR 2000). It included provisions for protection (of victims) and prosecution of perpetrators.

In 2009, Malaysia was placed in tier 3 by the TIP report for failure to address conditions of forced labor. As a result, Malaysia focused on border control, and on reducing the number of foreign workers who were more likely to be in forced labor situations. At the same time, Malaysia was under pressure from Australia to control the flow of asylum seekers – from conflict-torn countries such as Myanmar, Iraq, or Afghanistan – to Malaysia. Many asylum seekers were transiting through Malaysia to get to Australia, which was a signatory to the Refugee Convention, and, therefore, considered to be a place to seek asylum. But Australia had, based on a drift toward more conservative politics, been very aggressive in rebuffing asylum seekers before they reached the country (for a later report, see Innis 2015). Pressuring Malaysia to control its borders fit this agenda. While the Malaysian government recognized the interlinks between trafficking and smuggling in persons, the focus of its 2010 ATIP amendment redefined the idea of the illegal migrant to include many potential asylum seekers who were assumed to be self-financing their illegal entry into Malaysia. As a result, those who reached the country from conflict zones or other countries were given very little protection or access to rights. Both groups become "vulnerable to exploitation and trafficking" (Lyons and Ford 2014, p. 40).

Initially, many local NGOs, including those working to eliminate violence against women, for migrants' rights, or for labor rights, looked to ATIP as a path to address labor exploitation and violation of trafficked persons' human rights. However, the government did not want to pursue many labor rights cases under ATIP after 2009, since it would have worked against its border enforcement strategy. At the same time the government was interested in increasing the numbers of prosecutions of trafficking for sexual exploitation to improve its standing on the TIP report. Thus the direction of attention changed from addressing labor exploitation to border control, including smuggling.

Two related questions remain critically important:

- Are border controls and anti-trafficking measures antithetical? Miller and Baumeister (2013) ask this question.
- Is it possible to reconcile the rapid spread of security blocks (to control crimes and terrorism) while identifying and protecting victims of trafficking for labor? (Many scholars have been writing about this issue; a few appear in the following Resources list.)

Resources

FitzGerald, Sharron A. 2015. "Vulnerable Geographies: Human Trafficking, Immigration and Border Control in the UK and Beyond." *Gender, Place & Culture* 23(2):181–97. doi: 10.1080/0966369X.2015.1013441.

Hadjimatheou, Katerina, and Jennifer K. Lynch. 2017. "'Once They Pass You, They May Be Gone Forever': Humanitarian Duties and Professional Tensions in Safeguarding and Anti-Trafficking at the Border." *The British Journal of Criminology* 57(4):945–63. Document2 doi: 10.1093/bjc/azw027.

Innis, Michelle. 2015. "Australian Leader is Pressed on Whether Migrant Smugglers Were Paid to Turn Back." *New York Times*, June 13.

Miller, Rebecca, and Sebastian Baumeister. 2013. "Managing Migration: Is Border Control Fundamental to Anti-Trafficking and Anti-Smuggling Interventions?" *Anti-Trafficking Review* 2:15–32.

Moreno-Lax, Violeta. 2018. "The EU Humanitarian Border and the Securitization of Human Rights: The 'Rescue-Through-Interdiction/Rescue-Without-Protection' Paradigm." *JCMS: Journal of Common Market Studies* 56: 119–40. doi: 10.1111/jcms.12651.

Sandor, Adam. 2016. "Border Security and Drug Trafficking in Senegal: AIRCOP and Global Security Assemblages." *Journal of Intervention and Statebuilding* 10(4):490–512. doi: 10.1080/17502977.2016.1240425.

Afterword 4: If transplant registries exist in countries, should foreigners be able to receive transplants?

As many scholars have noted, there are multiple debates on buying and selling organs. As we discuss in chapter 4, a key issue is the extent to which the organ "sellers" provided their organs freely. Earlier we presented disagreements among scholars about the structures underlying choices. We argued, in tune with Kamala Kempadoo and others, that persons who are situated within severe structural constraints may make choices, but the contexts of their choices are qualitatively different from those of the person who makes choices from a position of privilege. The point was that the existing policies often use "choice" to separate those who participated voluntarily and those who were, in fact, coerced into trafficking worlds. The term "seller" implies choice without looking into the issues of structural location. We avoided this discussion by using the term "provider."

There are several debates about markets for organs and, if regulated markets existed, whether these would address some of the exploitative conditions under which organ sellers' decisions are made. Many authors focus on the issues of exploitation, harm, and the need to protect vulnerable individuals (e.g. Alpinar-Sencan, Baumann, and Biller-Adorno 2017, Cohen 1999, Scheper-Hughes 2003a, Yousaf and Purkayastha 2015b). Others argue that as long as the markets operate fairly, sellers receive a benefit that they would not have otherwise (e.g. Gregory 2011).

Here we would like to highlight a different aspect of the debate: an issue raised by Cohen (2014). *Should foreigners be able to receive organ transplants?* In an article where he distinguishes among many types of foreigners, Cohen concludes that foreigners should be included in the waiting lists for organ transplantation. Cohen's question is not explicitly tied to the issue of organ trafficking, nor is it tied to kidney transplants only. Nonetheless we think the article raises many questions about trafficking matters as well.

Many countries, like the US, or regions, like the EU, have national registries of donors and people waiting to receive organs. Many of the organs are obtained from the deceased based on their prior wish to donate organs. We know that some registries, e.g. Eurotransplant and Scandiatransplant, have reciprocity rules for sharing across registries. We also know about transplant tourism, where people travel to other countries to procure organs from live donors and receive transplants.

Who should be able to access the organs available via the registries? Cohen asks: should it only be citizens? Should non-citizen, legal residents be able to access organs?

As a corollary to this, we raise several related questions for reflection and debate.

- Since trafficking always includes the objective of exploitation, and the use of force or fraud or deception, do registries solve the problems of exploitation and fraud?
- Should migrants on temporary work permits be able to donate organs to these registries? This raises the complicated matter of the timing and residence of people who sign up to donate organs. If they happen to be residents of a country at a particular point in time, should they be allowed to donate to that country's registry or should the registry be contingent upon proof of citizenship?
- Further, should the registries be tied to the geographic boundaries of the state? Or can states create registry blocs, much like countries that cooperate and act collectively as global security blocs?
- Should states be allowed to expand the zones from which they can accept organ donations if the relations between the countries are not politically equal? Should the places

that are tied via colonial relationships with a country be part of the geography of these registries? Should American Samoa, Guam, or Puerto Rico (where people do not have full voting powers) be part of the US registry's geographical zone for the purposes of donation procurement?

- Should a powerful country be able to expand the geographic reach of its registry by working out multilateral agreements with countries to which it contributes significant amounts of foreign aid?[2] Would the citizens of these countries be assured of equal access to the registries of the powerful country?
- Should transplant tourism be allowed?

Resources

Cohen, Glenn. 2014. "Organs Without Borders? Allocating Transplant Organs, Foreigners, and the Importance of the Nation-State (?)." *Law and Contemporary Problems* 77:175–216.

Petrini, C. 2016. *Organ Allocation Policies 10 years after UNESCO's Universal Declaration of Bioethics and Human Rights.* Rome: Bioethics Unit, Office of the President, National Institute of Health.

WHO (World Health Organization). 2010. "WHO Guiding Principles on Human Cell, Tissue and Organ Transplantation." *Transplantation* 90(3):229–33.

Afterword 5: Two UN reports on human rights and human trafficking

We present here the main principles outlined in two UN reports on human rights and human trafficking. Readers who are interested should consult the full texts of the *Recommended Principles and Guidelines on Human Rights and Human Trafficking* (OHCHR 2002) and the more recent UN report on *Human Rights and Trafficking* (OHCHR 2014). However, the important point we wish to emphasize for further consideration, through public scrutiny, debate, and advocacy, is the extent to which trafficking efforts are meeting human rights standards. Since the initiatives, including the creation of the US TIP reports and the subsequent country reports, are intended to address trafficking, the principles of human rights in these reports continue to emphasize the need to center the needs of victims to create anti-trafficking initiatives.

Equally important, following our emphasis on access to rights substantively, these principles are not the responsibility of governments alone. Additional questions, especially based on the material we have presented in chapters 2, 3, and 4, are the following:

- Are we, i.e. humanitarian action groups and individual citizens, complicit in human rights violations, through the choices we make about the best efforts to address trafficking for sex, labor, and organs?
- Do we need to examine our cultural choices and worldviews about our entitlements and actions?
- Do we need to rethink our stance on immigration, to find out many more details about the migrant rights of trafficked persons, as we support or engage in anti-trafficking efforts?

From *Recommended Principles and Guidelines on Human Rights and Human Trafficking:*[3]

The primacy of human rights
1. The human rights of trafficked persons shall be at the centre of all efforts to prevent and combat trafficking and to protect, assist and provide redress to victims.
2. States have a responsibility under international law to act with due diligence to prevent trafficking, to investigate and prosecute traffickers and to assist and protect trafficked persons.
3. Anti-trafficking measures shall not adversely affect the human rights and dignity of persons, in particular the rights of those who have been trafficked, and of migrants, internally displaced persons, refugees and asylum-seekers.

Preventing trafficking
4. Strategies aimed at preventing trafficking shall address demand as a root cause of trafficking.
5. States and intergovernmental organizations shall ensure that their interventions address the factors that increase

vulnerability to trafficking, including inequality, poverty and all forms of discrimination.

6. States shall exercise due diligence in identifying and eradicating public sector involvement or complicity in trafficking. All public officials suspected of being implicated in trafficking shall be investigated, tried and, if convicted, appropriately punished.

Protection and assistance

7. Trafficked persons shall not be detained, charged or prosecuted for the illegality of their entry into or residence in countries of transit and destination, or for their involvement in unlawful activities to the extent that such involvement is a direct consequence of their situation as trafficked persons.

8. States shall ensure that trafficked persons are protected from further exploitation and harm and have access to adequate physical and psychological care. Such protection and care shall not be made conditional upon the capacity or willingness of the trafficked person to cooperate in legal proceedings.

9. Legal and other assistance shall be provided to trafficked persons for the duration of any criminal, civil or other actions against suspected traffickers. States shall provide protection and temporary residence permits to victims and witnesses during legal proceedings.

10. Children who are victims of trafficking shall be identified as such. Their best interests shall be considered paramount at all times. Child victims of trafficking shall be provided with appropriate assistance and protection. Full account shall be taken of their special vulnerabilities, rights and needs.

11. Safe (and, to the extent possible, voluntary) return shall be guaranteed to trafficked persons by both the receiving State and the State of origin. Trafficked persons shall be offered legal alternatives to repatriation in cases where it is reasonable to conclude that such repatriation would pose a serious risk to their safety and/or to the safety of their families.

Criminalization, punishment and redress

12. States shall adopt appropriate legislative and other measures necessary to establish, as criminal offences, trafficking, its component acts and related conduct.

13. States shall effectively investigate, prosecute and adjudicate trafficking, including its component acts and related

conduct, whether committed by governmental or by non-State actors.

14. States shall ensure that trafficking, its component acts and related offences constitute extraditable offences under national law and extradition treaties. States shall cooperate to ensure that the appropriate extradition procedures are followed in accordance with international law.
15. Effective and proportionate sanctions shall be applied to individuals and legal persons found guilty of trafficking or of its component or related offences.
16. States shall, in appropriate cases, freeze and confiscate the assets of individuals and legal persons involved in trafficking. To the extent possible, confiscated assets shall be used to support and compensate victims of trafficking.
17. States shall ensure that trafficked persons are given access to effective and appropriate legal remedies. (OHCHR 2002, pp. 1–2)

From *Human Rights and Human Trafficking*:

B. The human rights of trafficked persons

Both the Charter of the United Nations and the Universal Declaration of Human Rights confirm that rights are universal: they apply to everyone, irrespective of their race, sex, ethnic origin or other distinction. Trafficked persons are entitled to the full range of human rights. Even if they are outside their country of residence, international law is clear that trafficked persons cannot be discriminated against simply because they are non-nationals. In other words, with only some narrow exceptions that must be reasonably justifiable, international human rights law applies to everyone within a State's territory or jurisdiction, regardless of nationality or citizenship and of how they came to be within the territory.

International human rights law recognizes that **certain groups** require additional or special protection. This may be because of past discrimination or because their members share particular vulnerabilities. In the context of trafficking, relevant groups include women, children, migrants and migrant workers, refugees and asylum seekers, internally displaced persons, and persons with disabilities. Sometimes, members of a group will be specifically targeted for trafficking. **Children,** for example, may be trafficked for purposes related to their age such as sexual exploitation, various forms of forced labour and begging. **Persons with disabilities** can also be targeted for certain forms of exploitative labour and begging. **Women and girls** are trafficked into gender-specific situations of exploitation such as exploitative prostitution and sex tourism, and forced labour in domestic and service industries. They also suffer gender-specific forms of harm and consequences of being trafficked (for example, rape, forced marriage, unwanted or forced pregnancy, forced termination of pregnancy, and sexually transmitted diseases, including HIV/AIDS).

Individuals belonging to specific groups who are subject to trafficking may be in a position to claim different or additional rights. For example, international human rights law imposes important and additional responsibilities on States when it comes to identifying **child victims of trafficking** as well as to ensuring their immediate and longer-term safety and well-being. The core rule is derived from the obligations contained in the Convention on the Rights of the Child: the best interests of the child are to be at all times paramount. In other words, States cannot prioritize other considerations, such as those related to immigration control or public order, over the best interests of the child victim of trafficking. In addition, because of the applicability of the Convention to all children under the jurisdiction or control of a State, non-citizen child victims of trafficking are entitled to the same protection as nationals in all matters, including those related to the protection of their privacy and physical and moral integrity. Other treaties may further specify these rights. For example, the Trafficking Protocol requires certain special measures with regard to child victims, as does the Convention on Action against Trafficking in Human Beings (OHCHR 2014, pp. 6–7).

Notes

Chapter 1 Introduction

1 http://www.un.org/en/events/humantrafficking/index.shtml
2 In this first chapter we introduce important terms in **bold**.
3 While we discuss the policy-based definition of trafficking and its distinction from smuggling later in this chapter, the transportation of human beings for profit characterizes both operations. It is also important to mention that scholars disagree about the extent to which we should think of trafficking only in terms of the work of criminal networks (see e.g. David 2015 for a critique).
4 Recently, some focus on the victims/survivors' quality of life is being included in some international reports. Nonetheless, the main focus remains on prosecution.
5 While we provide a very basic outline of this process, we strongly recommend readers refer to DeStefano's (2008) excellent book on this subject.
6 The US policy on trafficking was developed earlier (in October 2000) than the UN protocol (which was passed in December 2000). But, we especially picked the US policy because the TVPA is globally influential in scope. The annual *Trafficking in Persons* (TIP) reports that the US Department of State issues rank countries on records of trafficking, and tie foreign aid to the standing of countries in these reports.
7 The core elements are quoted from http://www.unodc.org/unodc/en/human-trafficking/faqs.html#What_is_human_trafficking

8 For instance, according to the US Citizenship and Immigration services, among the 1,062 trafficking victims who applied for visas in 2015, only 632 were approved (US Citizenship and Immigration Statistics 2016).

Chapter 2 Trafficking for Sexual Exploitation

1 See for instance Nicolas Kristof's documentary *A Path Appears* (Kristof and WuDunn. 2015), or an ABC News report, *Hidden America: A Chilling New Look at Sex Trafficking in the US* (ABC News 2013).
2 We use this phrase, instead of the widely used term "sex trafficking," because "trafficking for sexual exploitation" emphasizes the *purpose* of trafficking. Critical scholars are using this phrase more often to open up discussions on the social structures that create and sustain the contexts in which trafficking occurs.
3 These narratives represent illustrative cases of trafficked persons. We are aware that the data on trafficked persons are often controversial (see e.g. Kempadoo et al. 2012, Yea 2015a), including iconic stories that are trafficking myths (Frederick 2012). These three narratives are intended to illustrate some key points we discuss, often critically, in this chapter. Here we picked examples from our own research, narratives from known groups or researchers, and cases that reflect the *conditions* reported by multiple sources.
4 Boys and men are also trafficked for sexual exploitation (see e.g. Maternick and Ditmore 2015), though our discussion here focuses on the trafficking of women and girls for sexual exploitation.
5 Uncikova (2014) states that between 2003 and 2012, the US, Norway, and Japan provided USD (US dollars) 91.7 million out of a total USD124 million annually to combat trafficking in general.
6 ILO (2012) contradicts this, pointing out that more people are trafficked into labor servitude including domestic labor and sweatshops. UNODC (2016) also reports that compared to trafficking for sexual exploitation, trafficking for labor is increasing relative to the data in 2007 (p. 28).
7 Henceforth, "gendered" refers to the intersecting structures of race/class/gender/age and other social hierarchies that create differing forms of marginalization or privilege for different groups of women and men.

8 See the literature on comfort women (e.g. Okamoto 2013).

9 We do not mean to fetishize the positive impact of known networks. After all, as the introductory vignettes showed, abuse within homes often occurs within these known networks. Here we mean networks to which people *may be* able to turn for help. When none exist, vulnerability to trafficking increases.

10 UNHCR (2016, p. 8): "Globally at the end of 2015, about half of refugees were children, requiring focused efforts to address their needs and minimize the impact of forced displacement upon them. The total number of unaccompanied or separated children who applied for asylum worldwide increased almost threefold to 98,400 during 2015, compared to 34,300 in 2014. This was the first time that UNHCR recorded such a large number of these claims within a single year since the agency started systematically collecting this information in 2006."

11 According to many reports, Norway has one of the best records for addressing trafficking. Consequently, it is interesting to examine Norway's case to understand some dimensions of trafficking.

12 See http://www.unrefugees.org/what-is-a-refugee for the definition of a refugee vs. an internally dispersed person. Getting the status of a refugee means the UNHCR has to recognize the migrant as a refugee. For more see http://www.unhcr.org/en-us/refugee-status-determination.html

13 For details see http://www.un.org/en/universal-declaration-human-rights and the associated charters and conventions.

14 These include groups that attempt to raise consciousness about human trafficking,

15 We are deliberately withholding the names of the countries because in most cases we found many staff members at the shelters try to work within impossible situations to provide a modicum of dignity to the trafficked women. But their efforts do not change the system in which they work.

16 According to the mandate of shelter homes in Pakistan, any woman who is in distress or a victim of violence may approach the homes. The majority of women who do so are referred to these shelters by courts while their cases are under trial. Other women are either referred by NGOs or come on their own. Residents of shelter homes are categorized with reference to types of violence, including: domestic violence, stove burning, attempted murder, rape, *vanni* or *swara* (marrying women to a hostile family as compensation for a relative's crime), gang rape, *karo-kari* (honor killing), abduction or kidnap, sexual harassment, forced marriage, psychological torture, and physical violence. Recently, trafficking has been added to the list, but individuals are rarely categorized as victims of trafficking.

17 We were told about this mechanism though we were not able to verify it independently. However, the process is frightening because shelters, like camps, can become new catchment areas for traffickers.

18 Sharon Zukin (1990) had pointed out almost thirty years earlier how products were increasingly sold because of the cultural tag attached to them. Thus, "made by former trafficking victims" transforms a less expensive product to a product worth more as people assume the money goes toward the rehabilitation of these women. While we did not discuss the case of boys who are trafficked, the emphasis on feminized work in the rehabilitation efforts also raises questions about the adequacy of their rehabilitation.

19 The complexities of these rescue-and-rehabilitate operations is not a simple story of the West vs. the rest. An early documentary, *The Selling of Innocents*, showed some of the rescued women working as domestic labor in the houses in which they had been placed after their rescue from brothels. Apne Aap: Women Worldwide, which has successfully rehabilitated some trafficking victims, has also been severely criticized by some students at Harvard who launched their rehabilitation project in India.

20 Darbar in Kolkata has been especially recognized for its HIV/STD prevention efforts.

21 See Dickenson (2006), Huda (2006), Samarasinghe (2008), and http://www.ungift.org/knowledgehub/en/about/human-trafficking-and-hiv-aids.html

22 There is a different literature on the HIV programs targeted at prostitutes and the biopolitics surrounding those campaigns. For more, see e.g. Lakkimsetti (2014).

Chapter 3   Trafficking for Labor Exploitation

1 Without further details it is not clear whether she became an undocumented individual at the end of six years when she escaped. Typically, tourist visas to the US are given for a maximum of six months; had she officially enrolled in college, she would have been on a different type of visa which would have been contingent upon her enrollment in school. Even if we imagine this family sponsored her for a longer-term visa, her escape, which is very similar to the path domestically abused women take, suggests she was unlikely to have actual access to her papers.

2 As we discuss later, organizing by domestic workers has led some countries to recognize domestic work as labor that ought to be

brought under the purview of labor laws. However, these formal shifts are still rare. In other cases, sending countries try to broker better work conditions, though the record of actual implementation in the destination countries is mixed, at best.

3 The Ghanaian region has emerged as having the highest concentration of child trafficking. The selling or "handing over" of 8-year-old children is clearly identifiable as child trafficking. However, Neil Howard (2014b) has pointed out that the use of age 18 – normalized in the Global North as a cut-off for childhood – does not always fit the local cultural expectation that 16–17-year-old boys are expected to contribute economically to the household. The UNODC (2016) also points out that because sub-Saharan African countries had trafficking laws that only applied to children until recently, the data may reflect anti-trafficking efforts still focused on children.

4 In contrast to the scholarship on the sexual exploitation of trafficking victims, as far as we are aware there is no systematic, growing body of research on the health consequences for people who are in forced labor situations.

5 The report acknowledges that the data should be interpreted with caution because the data for the Arab states and the Americas are not fully available.

6 Kevin Bales, who has been long associated with the development of this work on modern-day slavery, earlier argued that the "root causes of trafficking in persons include the greed of criminals, economic pressures, political instability and transition, and social and cultural factors" (2007, p. 269). The 2016 iteration of the Walk Free Foundation's GSI index, with which he is the lead researcher, expands the causes of labor exploitation, without focusing on the transnational factors (see the debate between Martinez 2009 and Bales and Soodalter 2009).

7 In many countries, structural adjustments have led governments to retreat from earlier social benefit provisions. Education and health care are being rapidly privatized so that, in these spheres too, at least two broad tiers have emerged, with good quality privatized education and health care for those who can pay, and inadequately government supported education and health provision for others.

8 These jobs were always performed by women or racialized low-status men. In the contemporary world, people are recruited in larger numbers *from other countries*.

9 Kubal (2014) describes similar forces in Europe and the experiences of Eastern Europeans who consider themselves to be not wholly legal or illegal. Kubal also cautions that some scholars, such as Aliverti (2012), have begun to argue that the coming

together of criminal justice and immigration systems is primarily symbolic in Europe, intended to warn migrants. Kubal's research refutes this position.

10 See for instance accounts of the organizing in the US (Toro-Morn 2013) or Singapore (Haider 2006).

11 The kind of arguments used prior to Brexit in the UK or the rise of the Trump presidency in the US.

12 http://www.un.org/en/universal-declaration-human-rights

13 http://www.ohchr.org/en/professionalinterest/pages/ccpr.aspx

14 http://www.ohchr.org/EN/ProfessionalInterest/Pages/CESCR.aspx

15 The case of refugees we discussed in chapter 1 reminds us about the overlap between legalities of migration and the illegalities associated with migrants' actual movement from and to camps.

16 Howard is very critical about labeling this form of work as trafficking. We discuss this issue further in chapter 5.

17 Immigrant advocates have pointed out that many detained persons are encouraged to plead guilty to "lesser charges" to escape a long period in prison. In this case others have also pointed out that the inadequate provision of translators – those who could presumably understand and adequately convey the intent of the charges – led to further violations of the rights of these workers.

18 These raids occur within a larger economic shift in the middle of the US. We had earlier documented the movement of Mexican workers to these meatpacking plants (Torres Stone and Purkayastha 2005). Labor recruiters within the country promised the seasonal workers – who are legally working at one type of job – that owners would provide the right papers for them to work long-term in these new destinations.

19 And the presence of temporary migrants undermines their labor security.

Chapter 4 Organ Trafficking

1 We have published on different aspects of organ trafficking earlier. Some of our arguments in this chapter were published in Yousaf and Purkayastha (2015a, 2015b).

2 The UNODC (2015) reports that in the 1980s there were stories of patients going from the Middle East to India to buy and get kidney transplants; Nancy Scheper-Hughes (2000) had also reported on body-snatching rumors in Brazil.

3 As we discuss later, organ trafficking is often associated with indentured labor. Men are more likely to be indentured laborers.

It is also possible fewer women are detected as victims of organ trafficking because of the ways in which this industry is organized.

4 The assumption in those discussions is that both the "donor" and the recipient get some benefits: one gets money, the other an organ.

5 While we did not find narratives of women to feature here, Budiani-Saberi and colleagues (2014) report that the Indian women they interviewed were selling kidneys for cash because of poverty. Lawrence Cohen (2003) also presents data on women selling their kidneys.

6 Gunnarson and Lundin suggest the following scholars as proponents of markets for organs: Friedlaender (2002), Matas (2004), Savulescu (2003), and Slabbert (2008).

7 These government drives often pay men and women money for undergoing sterilization or tubal ligation (Berry and Dugger 2016).

8 The term "transplant tourism" is used by some scholars to describe these short-term moves that are similar to the ways in which tourists travel to consume the resources of another place (and its people).

9 Here we use our preferred terms "buyer" and "provider" instead of "donor" and "recipient."

Chapter 5   The Other Side of Trafficking: A Look at the Data and Policies on Trafficking

1 For details, see http://www.undp.org/content/undp/en/home/sustainable-development-goals.html

2 We highlight some problematic issues by making the text **bold**. We have also removed the report's footnote numbers from the quoted text. Interested readers are very strongly encouraged to read the entire report and the methodological appendices.

3 Trafficking became an issue within a larger political concern about organized crime. Indeed most policy makers, scholars, and advocates think of trafficking as part of organized crime (see, for instance, Whitman and Gray 2015), yet others have begun to question this understanding, based on examining the data on prosecutions. Fiona David (2012) reported on diversity among traffickers: some are solo or small-scale operators, while at the other end of the spectrum are organized crime groups. Examining the data on Australia, she has argued that the evidence to date does not support the idea that trafficking is mostly operated

through organized criminal networks. Reviewing the ambiguities of the data, Weitzer (2011) has called for evidence-based legislation.

4 We pick Pakistan for pragmatic reasons. It is one of the top countries marked on the TIP reports, it houses one of the largest concentrations of refugees in the world, and it has seen a great deal of political and economic instability. Also, Yousaf has conducted extensive research in the country, including gathering data from trafficked persons, a variety of social justice persons, and stakeholders, and has extensive data on the country's policies and their operation in practice.

5 The UN Convention against Transnational Organized Crime is supplemented by three Protocols, which target specific areas and manifestations of organized crime: the *Protocol to Prevent, Suppress and Punish Trafficking in Persons, Especially Women and Children* (OHCHR 2000); the *Protocol against the Smuggling of Migrants by Land, Sea and Air*; and the *Protocol against the Illicit Manufacturing of and Trafficking in Firearms, their Parts and Components and Ammunition*.

6 Even a casual comparison of the TIP report (US Department of State 2016) on the USA and Norway, both Tier 1 countries, shows the persistent difference in how compliance with the TVPA's expectations are *interpreted*. In many places the US report appears more similar to Pakistan's report than to Norway's.

7 In the previous chapters we have used several examples from the US. Following the passage of the TVPA and the money allotted to addressing trafficking, there are a range of local laws and policies that cover aspects of trafficking too (see, for instance, Shih's 2016 description of California). Yet these policies and efforts, including those of missionaries, have not addressed trafficking, especially trafficking for labor.

8 According to section 3 of PACHTO:

> (i) Whoever knowingly plans or executes any such plan for human trafficking into or out of Pakistan for the purpose of attaining any benefit, or for the purpose of exploitative entertainment, slavery or forced labour or adoption in or out of Pakistan shall be punishable with imprisonment which may extend to seven years and shall also be liable to fine:
> Provided that in case of an accused who, in addition to committing an offence as aforesaid has also been guilty of kidnapping or abducting or any attempt thereto in connection with such offence, the imprisonment may extend to ten years with fine:
> Provided further that whoever plans to commit an offence under this clause but has not as yet executed the same shall be

punishable with a term of imprisonment, which may extend to five years and shall also be liable to fine.

(ii) Whoever knowingly provides, obtains or employs the labour or services of a person by coercion, scheme, plan or method intended to make such person believe that in the event of non-performance of such labour or service, he or any other person may suffer from serious harm or physical restraint or legal proceedings, shall be punishable with imprisonment which may extend to seven years and shall also be liable to fine:

Provided that if the commission of the offences under this clause involves kidnapping or abduction or any attempt thereto, the term of imprisonment may extend to ten years with fine:

Provided further that payment of any remuneration in lieu of services or labour of the victim shall not be treated as mitigating circumstance while awarding the punishment.

(iii) Whoever knowingly purchases, sells, harbours, transports, provides, detains or obtains a child or a woman through coercion, kidnapping or abduction, or by giving or receiving any benefit for trafficking him or her into or out of Pakistan or with intention thereof, for the purpose of exploitative entertainment by any person and has received or expects to receive some benefit in lieu thereof shall be punishable with imprisonment which may extend to ten years and shall also be liable to fine:

Provided that if the commission of the offences under this clause involves kidnapping or abduction or any attempt thereto of the victim, the term of imprisonment may extend to fourteen years with fine:

Provided further that plea, if any, taken by the biological parents of the child shall not prejudice the commission of offence under this clause.

(iv) Whoever knowingly takes, confiscates, possesses, conceals, removes or destroys any document related to human trafficking in furtherance of any offence committed under this Ordinance or to prevent or restrict or attempt to prevent or restrict, without lawful authority, a person's liberty to move or travel shall be punishable with imprisonment which may extend to seven years and shall also be liable to fine. (Federal Investigation Agency n.d.)

9 It is interesting to compare the reports on Pakistan over the years. The 2017 TIP report (US Department of State 2017) is an improvement because it notes the forms of trafficking – related to forced labor – that local stakeholders identified as bigger issues in Pakistan. Yet these examples of internal trafficking are presented alongside the international migration of Pakistanis to the Middle

East that sometimes leads to their exploitation for labor and sex (as Pakistan should be liable for the exploitation in the Middle East). Based on our research we agree that Pakistan needs significantly more sustained efforts, but the disorganized series of assertions in this report raises questions, as in the GSI, about the ways in which the data were collected.

10 Different agencies within the UN have developed plans for how to address the needs of victims. For instance, the OHCHR has drafted outlines of the basic principles for effective remedies for trafficked persons (OHCHR 2014, pp. 31-2), but countries have to live up to these obligations. Currently, very few countries do that.

Chapter 6　Envisioning a Trafficking-Free World

1 While we have not marked the effect of age explicitly in the preceding chapters, it is important to point out that older women and men are rarely trafficked for sexual exploitation, labor, or organ harvesting.

2 In the US, an iconic moment of the struggle for racial justice through the Civil Rights movement is the action of Mrs. Rosa Parks, who refused to give up her seat on a segregated bus. Mrs. Parks was a long-time activist and is correctly honored for her act. However, earlier, other people had fought back against bus segregation, including an unmarried pregnant teenager, Claudette Clovin (see D'Angelo 2001). Many of the prominent activists realized that Clovin's case would not attract as much support from people or persuade them to support the movement. They would point to Clovin's "social transgressions" rather than applaud her courage. So Clovin's stand against segregation never made history. The trafficking survivor stories are similar in that they often depict victims who had very few choices. Consequently, these simplified stories are able to garner much more sympathy from the larger public, and become a standard against which victimhood is understood. Yet unlike the situation of the anti-racist activists, who were being actively opposed during the Civil Rights struggle and had to choose stories that would not be discredited by powerful actors, the iconic stories of trafficking are being presented by the strongest actors – states, INGOs – long after trafficking has been recognized as a global problem, to further their agendas of focusing on some forms of

trafficking, some perpetrators, and some forms of redress and not others.

3 Within the US, of the 1,062 applications made by victims of trafficking, 610 T visas were approved in 2015 (US Citizenship and Immigration Services 2016).

Chapter 7   Afterwords: Ongoing Debates and Unresolved Questions

1 Another way to explain the linguistic conventions is to look at similarly unacceptable historical practices that were extant in Europe or the Americas. We searched for "genocide"; in Bangla it translates to *gana-hattwa* or "mass killing," which could easily result from riots or conflicts. The argument is not that extremely harsh and exploitative conditions are not known in the Global South. Instead, the argument is that the frames need to have local resonance.

2 The premise of this question is based on a very a different issue. We use the US as an example because the country has worked to bypass the jurisdiction of the International Criminal Court on the possibility of war crime charges against its soldiers and politicians. It has worked out bilateral agreements with countries that received US foreign aid to ensure the immunity of US soldiers who are charged with war crime violations under the jurisdiction of the International Criminal Court (see Global Policy Forum 2005).

3 "Trafficking" in the *Principles and Guidelines* follows the definition in the UN Trafficking Protocol (OHCHR 2000, article 3 (a)), quoted earlier.

References

ABC News. 2013. *Hidden America: A Chilling New Look at Sex Trafficking in the US*. http://abcnews.go.com/Nightline/video/hidden-america-chilling-sex-trafficking-us-28446981

Abraham, Yvonne, and Brian R. Ballou. 2007. "350 are Held in Immigration Raid: New Bedford Factory Employed Illegal, Says US." *The Boston Globe*, March 7.

Adepoju, Aderanti. 2005. *Migration in West Africa*. Global Commission on International Migration. https://www.iom.int/jahia/webdav/site/myjahiasite/shared/shared/mainsite/policy_and_research/gcim/rs/RS8.pdf

Adur, Shweta Majumdar. 2011. "Do Human Rights Endure Across Nation-State Boundaries? Analyzing the Experiences of Guest Workers." Pp. 162–72 in *Human Rights in Our Own Backyard: Injustice and Resistance in the United States*, edited by W. T. Armaline, D. S. Glasberg, and B. Purkayastha. Philadelphia, PA: University of Pennsylvania Press.

Agustin, L. M. 2007. *Sex at the Margins: Migration, Labor and the Rescue Industry*. London: Zed Books.

Ahmed, Aziza. 2011. "Feminism, Power, and Sex Work in the Context of HIV/AIDS: Consequences for Women's Health." *Harvard Journal of Law and Gender* 34(1):225–58.

Ahmed, Aziza. 2015. "Trafficked? AIDS, Criminal Law and the Politics of Measurement." *University of Miami Law Review* 70(1):96–251.

Ahmed, Aziza, and Meena Seshu. 2015. "'We Have the Right Not to Be Rescued': When Anti-Trafficking Programs Undermine the

Health and Well-Being of Sex Workers." Pp. 169–80 in *Global Human Trafficking: Critical Issues and Contexts*, edited by M. Dragiewicz. New York, NY: Routledge.

Ali, Masud A. K. M. 2005. "Treading along a Treacherous Trail: Research on Trafficking in Persons in South Asia." *International Migration* 43(1/2):141–64.

Aliverti, A. 2012. "Making People Criminal: The Role of the Criminal Law in Immigration Enforcement." *Theoretical Criminology* 16:417–34.

Allain, Jean. 2014. "No Effective Trafficking Definition Exists: Domestic Implementation of the Palermo Protocol." *Albany Government Law Review* 14. http://papers.ssrn.com/sol3/papers.cfm?abstract_id=2510719

Allais, Carol. 2013. "The Profile Less Considered: The Trafficking of Men in South Africa." *South African Review of Sociology* 44(1):40–54.

Alpinar-Sencan, Zumrut, Holger Baumann, and Nikola Biller-Andorno. 2017. "Does Organ Selling Violate Human Dignity?" *Monash Bioethics Review* 34(3):189–205.

Altink, Sietske. 1995. *Stolen Lives: Trading Women into Sex and Slavery*. London: Scarlet Press.

Alvarez, Priscilla. 2016. "When Sex Trafficking Goes Unnoticed in America." *The Atlantic*, February 23.

Ambagtsheer, Frederike, Damián Zaitch, and Willem Weimar. 2013. "The Battle for Human Organs: Organ Trafficking and Transplant Tourism in a Global Context." *Global Crime* 14(1):1–26.

Amirthalingam, Kopalapillai, Danesh Jayatilaka, Rajith W. D. Lakshman, and Nishadi Liyanage. n.d. *Victims of Human Trafficking in Sri Lanka: Narratives of Women, Children and Youth*. https://editorialexpress.com/cgi-bin/conference/download.cgi?db_name=IAFFE2011&paper_id=75

Andersen, Carol. 2003. *Eyes Off the Prize: The United Nations and the African American Struggle for Human Rights, 1944–1955*. Cambridge: Cambridge University Press.

Anitha, S., Anupama Roy, and Harshita Yalamarty. 2016. *Disposable Women: Abuse, Violence and Abandonment in Transnational Marriages: Issues for Policy and Practice in the UK and India*. Lincoln: University of Lincoln Press.

Argueta, Luis, and Vivian Rivas. 2010. *AbUSed: The Postville Raid*. (Trailer) Maya Media. http://www.abusedthepostvilleraid.com

Armaline, William T., Davita Silfen Glasberg, and Bandana Purkayastha. 2015. *The Human Rights Enterprise: Political Sociology, State Power, and Social Movements*. Malden, MA: Polity.

Bales, Kevin. 1999. *Disposable People: New Slavery in the Global Economy*. Oakland, CA: University of California Press.

Bales, Kevin. 2007. "What Predicts Human Trafficking." *International Journal of Comparative and Applied Criminal Justice* 31(2): 269–79.

Bales, Kevin. 2013. *The Methodology behind the Global Slavery Index.* https://www.theguardian.com/global-development-professionals-network/2013/oct/17/global-slavery-index-methodology

Bales, Kevin, and Ron Soodalter. 2009. *The Slave Next Door: Human Trafficking and Slavery in America Today.* Berkeley, CA: University of California Press.

Bangura, Zainab. 2013. *Sexual Violence in Conflict.* https://dfid.blog.gov.uk/2013/11/12/sexual-violence-in-conflict

Banovic, Bozidar, and Zeljko Bjelajac. 2012. "Traumatic Experiences, Psychophysical Consequences and Needs of Human Trafficking Victims." *Vojnosanitetski Pregled* 69:94–7.

Barnett II, William, and Michael Saliba. 2004. "A Free Market for Kidneys: Options, Futures, Forward, and Spot." *Managerial Finance* 30(2):38–56.

Barry, Kathleen. 1995. *Prostitution of Sexuality: The Global Exploitation of Women.* New York, NY: New York University Press.

Batstone, David. 2007. *Not for $ale: The Return of the Global Trade – and How We Can Fight It.* New York, NY: HarperCollins.

Bengali, Shashank, and M. N. Parth. 2016. "Duped into Selling His Kidney, This 23-Year-Old Exposed an Illegal Organ Racket in India." *Los Angeles Times*, September 15.

Bernat, Frances P., and Tatyana Zhilina. 2010. "Human Trafficking: The Local Becomes Global." *Women and Criminal Justice* 20(1–2):2–9.

Bernstein, Elizabeth. 2007. *Temporarily Yours: Intimacy, Authenticity, and the Commerce of Sex.* Chicago, IL: University of Chicago Press.

Bernstein, Elizabeth. 2010. "Militarized Humanitarianism Meets Carceral Feminism: The Politics of Sex, Rights, and Freedom in Contemporary Antitrafficking Campaigns." *Signs: Journal of Women in Culture and Society* 36:45–71.

Bernstein, Elizabeth. 2012. "Carceral Politics as Gender Justice? The 'Traffic in Women' and Neoliberal Circuits of Crime, Sex, and Rights." *Theory and Society* 41:233–59.

Berry, Ellen, and Celia Dugger. 2016. "India to Change Its Decades-Old Reliance on Female Sterilization." *New York Times*, February 20. https://www.nytimes.com/2016/02/21/world/asia/india-to-change-its-decades-old-reliance-on-female-sterilization.html

Bertone, Andrea Marie. 2000. "Sexual Trafficking in Women: International Political Economy and the Politics of Sex." *Gender Issues* 18(1):4–22.

Bindel, Julie. 2013. "Organ Trafficking: A Deadly Trade." *The Telegraph*, July 1.

Birkenthal, Sara. 2011. "Human Trafficking: A Human Rights Abuse with Global Dimensions." *Interdisciplinary Journal of Human Rights Law* 6(1):27–40.

Bodeau, Gary. 2013. *Haiti Questions the Findings of Walk Free Foundation's Report on Child Labor and Human Trafficking Conditions and Highlights Government Initiatives to Address the Issue.* https://www.prnewswire.com/news-releases/haiti-questions-the-findings-of-walk-free-foundations-report-on-child-labor-and-human-trafficking-conditions-and-highlights-government-initiatives-to-address-the-issue-228597941.html

Boris, Eileen, and Heather Berg. 2014. "Protecting Virtue, Erasing Labor: Historical Responses to Trafficking." Pp. 19–29 in *Human Trafficking Reconsidered: Rethinking the Problem, Envisioning New Solutions*, edited by K. K. Hoang and R. S. Parrenas. New York, NY: International Debate Education Association.

Bosworth, Mary, and Emma Kaufman. 2011. "Foreigners in a Carceral Age: Immigration and Imprisonment in the United States." *Stanford Law and Policy Review* 22(2):429–54.

Brace, Laura, and Julia O'Connell Davidson. 2000. "Minding the Gap: General and Substantive Theorizing on Power and Exploitation." *Signs* 25(4):1045–50.

Brennan, Denise. 2014. "Trafficking Scandal, and Abuse of Migrant Workers in Argentina and the United States." *The Annals of the American Academy of Political and Social Science* 653(1):107–23.

Broome, Andre, and Joel Quirk. 2015. "The Politics of Numbers: The Normative Agendas of Global Benchmarking." *Review of International Studies* 41(5):813–19.

Brownmiller, Susan. 1975. *Against Our Will: Men, Women and Rape.* New York, NY: Ballantine Books.

Bruggeman, W. 2002. *Illegal Immigration and Trafficking in Human Beings Seen as a Security Problem for Europe.* Paper presented at the European Conference on Preventing and Combating Trafficking in Human Beings, Brussels, September 19.

Brunwasser, Matthew. 2015. "A 21st-Century Migrant's Essentials: Food, Shelter, Smartphone." *New York Times*, August 25.

Budiani-Saberi, D. A., and F. L. Delmonico. 2008. "Organ Trafficking and Transplant Tourism: A Commentary on the Global Realities." *American Journal of Transplantation* 8:925–9.

Budiani-Saberi, Debra A., Kallakurichi Rajendiran Raja, Katie C. Findley, Ponsian Kerketta, and Vijay Anand. 2014. "Human Trafficking for Organ Removal in India: A Victim-Centered, Evidence-Based Report." *Transplantation* 97:380–4.

Burke, Mary C. 2013. "Introduction to Human Trafficking: Definitions and Prevalence." Pp. 3–23 in *Human Trafficking: Interdisciplinary Perspectives*, edited by M. C. Burke. New York, NY: Routledge.

Cagatay, Nilufer, and Sule Ozler. 1995. "Feminization of the Labor Force: The Effects of Long Term Development and Structural Adjustment." *World Development* 23(11):1883–94.

Campbell, Denis, and Nicola Davison. 2012. "Illegal Kidney Trade Booms as New Organ is 'Sold Every Hour'." *The Guardian*, May 27.

Carling, Jorgen. 2005. *Trafficking in Women from Nigeria to Europe.* Migration Policy Institute. https://www.migrationpolicy.org/article/trafficking-women-nigeria-europe

Carvajal, Doreen. 1996. "For Immigrant Maids, Not a Job but Servitude." *New York Times*, February 25.

Chang, Grace. 2000. *Disposable Domestics: Immigrant Women in the Global Economy.* Boston, MA: South End Press.

Chang, Grace. 2013. "This Is What Trafficking Looks Like." Pp. 56–78 in *Immigrant Women Workers in the Neoliberal Age*, edited by N. Flores-González, A. R. Guevarra, M. Toro-Morn, and G. Chang. Chicago, IL: University of Illinois Press.

Chapkis, Wendy. 2003. "Trafficking, Migration, and the Law: Protecting Innocents, Punishing Immigrants." *Gender and Society* 17(6):923–37.

Choo, Hae Yeon. 2016. *Decentering Citizenship: Gender, Labor, and Migrant Rights in South Korea.* Stanford, CA: Stanford University Press.

Chozick, Amy. 2017. "Raids of Illegal Immigrants Bring Harsh Memories, and Strong Fears." *New York Times*, January 2.

Chuang, Janie. 2015. "The Challenges and Perils of Reframing Trafficking as 'Modern-Day Slavery'." *Anti-Trafficking Review* 5:146–9.

Chun, Jennifer, George Lipsitz, and Young Shin. 2013. "Immigrant Women Workers at the Center of Social Change: Asian Immigrant Women's Advocates." Pp. 207–31 in *Immigrant Women Workers in the Neoliberal Age*, edited by N. Flores-González, A. R. Guevarra, M. Toro-Morn, and G. Chang. Chicago, IL: University of Illinois Press.

Clay, Megan, and Walter Block. 2002. "A Free Market for Human Organs." *The Journal of Social, Political and Economic Studies* 27(2):227–36.

Cohen, Cynthia B. 1999. "Selling Bits and Pieces of Humans to Make Babies: The Gift of the Magi Revisited." *Journal of Medicine and Philosophy* 24(3):288–306.

Cohen, Glenn. 2014. "Organs Without Borders? Allocating Transplant Organs, Foreigners, and the Importance of the Nation-State (?)." *Law and Contemporary Problems* 77:175–216.

Cohen, Lawrence. 2003. "Where it Hurts: Indian Material for an Ethics of Organ Transplantation." *Zygon* 38(3):669–88.

Cohen, Lawrence. 2011. "Migrant Supplementarity: Remaking Biological Relatedness in Chinese Military and Indian Five-Star Hospitals." *Body and Society* 17(2–3):31–54.

Collins, Patricia Hill. 1990. *Black Feminist Thought: Knowledge, Consciousness, and the Politics of Empowerment*. Boston, MA: Unwin Hyman.

Collins, Patricia Hill, and Sirma Bilge. 2016. *Intersectionality*. Malden, MA: Polity.

Columb, Sean. 2017. "Excavating the Organ Trade: An Empirical Study of Organ Trading Networks in Cairo, Egypt." *British Journal of Criminology* 57:1301–21.

Connell, R. W. 1985. "Theorizing Gender." *Sociology* 19(2):260–72.

Costa, Daniel. 2017. *Modern-Day Braceros: The United States has 450,000 Guestworkers in Low-Wage Jobs and Doesn't Need More*. Working Economics Blogs. Economic Policy Institute. http://www.epi.org/blog/modern-day-braceros-the-united-states-has-450000-guestworkers-in-low-wage-jobs

Cousins, Sophie. 2016. "Nepal: Organ Trafficking After the Earthquake." *The Lancet* 387:833.

Craig, Gary. 2010. "Flexibility, Xenophobia and Exploitation: Modern Slavery in the UK." Pp. 173–98 in *Social Policy Review 22: Analysis and Debate in Social Policy, 2010*, edited by I. Greener, C. Holden, and M. Kilkey. Bristol: Policy Press.

Crowley-Matoka, Megan, and Margaret Lock. 2006. "Organ Transplantation in a Globalised World." *Mortality: Promoting the Interdisciplinary Study of Death and Dying* 11(2):166–81.

Cullen, Miriam, and Bernadette McSherry. 2009. "Without Sex: Slavery, Trafficking in Persons and the Exploitation of Labour in Australia." *Alternative Law Journal* 34(1):4–10.

Cullen-DuPont, Kathryn. 2009. *Global Issues: Human Trafficking*. New York, NY: Infobase.

Cwikel, Julie, and Elizabeth Hoban. 2005. "Contentious Issues in Research on Trafficked Women Working in the Sex Industry: Study, Design, Ethics, and Methodology." *The Journal of Sex Research* 42(4):306–16.

D'Angelo, Raymond. 2001. "Brown and Beyond: Rising Expectations, 1953–1959." Pp. 222–78 in *The American Civil Rights Movement: Readings and Interpretations*, edited by R. D'Angelo. London: McGraw-Hill.

Datta, Ankur. 2016. "Rethinking Spaces of Exception: Notes from a Forced Migrant Camp in Jammu and Kashmir." *International Journal of Migration and Border Studies* 2(2):162–75.

David, Fiona. 2012. "Organised Crime and Trafficking in Persons." *Trends and Issues in Crime and Criminal Justice* 436. https://aic.gov.au/publications/tandi/tandi436

David, Fiona. 2015. "When it Comes to Modern Slavery, Do Definitions Matter?" *Anti-Trafficking Review* 5:150–2.

Davidson, Julia O'Connell, and Bridget Anderson. 2006. "The Trouble with 'Trafficking'." Pp. 11–26 in *Trafficking and Women's Rights*, edited by C. L. van den Anker and J. Doomernik. New York, NY: Palgrave Macmillan.

DeStefano, Anthony. 2008. *The War on Human Trafficking: US Policy Assessed*. Piscataway, NY: Rutgers University Press.

Dewey, Susan. 2008. *Hollow Bodies: Institutional Responses to Sex Trafficking in Armenia, Bosnia and India*. Sterling, VA: Kumarian Press.

Dickenson, Donna. 2006. "Philosophical Assumptions and Presumptions about Trafficking for Prostitution." Pp. 43–53 in *Trafficking and Women's Rights*, edited by C. L. van den Anker and J. Doomernik. New York, NY: Palgrave Macmillan.

Diner, Hasia. 1983. *Erin's Daughters in America*. Baltimore, MD: Johns Hopkins University Press.

Di Tommaso, Maria L., Isilda Shima, Steinar Strom, and Francesca Bettio. 2009. "As Bad as it Gets: Well-Being Deprivation of Sexually Exploited Trafficked Women." *European Journal of Political Economy* 25:143–62.

Doezema, Jo. 2001. "Ouch! Western Feminists' 'Wounded Attachment' to the 'Third World Prostitute'." *Feminist Review* 67(1):16–38.

Doezema, Jo. 2002. "Who Gets to Choose? Coercion, Consent, and the UN Trafficking Protocol." *Gender and Development* 10(1):20–7.

Doezema, Jo. 2010. *Sex Slave and Discourse Matters: The Construction of Trafficking*. London: Zed Books.

Dottridge, Mike. 2014. "Editorial: How Is the Money to Combat Trafficking Spent?" *Anti-Trafficking Review* 3:3–14.

Downe, Pamela J. 2007. "Strategic Stories and Reflexive Interruptions: Narratives of 'Safe Home' Amidst Cross-Border Sex Work." *Qualitative Inquiry* 13(4):554–72.

Dragiewicz, Molly, ed. 2015. *Global Human Trafficking: Critical Issues and Contexts*. New York, NY: Routledge.

Drew, Karen. 2017. *2 Children Saved, 22 People Arrested for Human Trafficking During Detroit Auto Show*. https://www.clickondetroit.com/news/defenders/2-children-saved-22-people-arrested-for-human-trafficking-during-detroit-auto-show

Dworkin, Gerald. 1994. "Markets and Morals: The Case for Organ Sale." Pp. 155–61 in *Morality, Harm and the Law*, edited by G. Dworkin. Boulder, CO: Westview Press.

Dworkin, Ronald. 1981. "Is there a Right to Pornography?" *Oxford Journal of Legal Studies* 1(2):177–212.

Ebbe, Obi N. I. 2008. "Introduction: An Overview of Trafficking in Women and Children." Pp. 3–16 in *Global Trafficking in Women and Children*, edited by O. N. I. Ebbe and D. K. Das. Boca Raton, FL: CRC Press.

Elkins, Julie, and Shareen Hertel. 2011. "Sweatshirts and Sweatshops: Labor Rights, Student Activism, and the Challenges of Collegiate Apparel Manufacturing." Pp. 9–21 in *Human Rights in Our Own Backyard: Injustice and Resistance in the United States*, edited by W. T. Armaline, D. S. Glasberg, and B. Purkayastha. Philadelphia, PA: University of Pennsylvania Press.

Elliott, Jessica. 2015. *The Role of Consent in Human Trafficking*. London: Routledge.

Equality Now. 2017. "Grace." Pp. 28–30 in Equality Now: Survivor Stories. https://www.equalitynow.org/campaigns/trafficking-survivor-stories/grace

Ertürk, Yakin, and Bandana Purkayastha. 2012. "Linking Research Policy and Action: A Look at the Work of the Special Rapporteur on Violence against Women." *Current Sociology* 60(2):142–60.

Espiritu, Yen Le. 2007. *Asian American Women and Men: Love, Labor, Laws*, 2nd edn. Lanham, MD: Rowman and Littlefield.

European Commission. n.d. *Trafficking Explained*. http://ec.europa.eu/anti-trafficking/citizens-corner/trafficking-explained_en

European Commission. 2016. *Report from the Commission to the European Parliament and the Council: Report on the Progress Made in the Fight Against Trafficking in Human Beings*. https://ec.europa.eu/home-affairs/sites/homeaffairs/files/what-we-do/policies/organized-crime-and-human-trafficking/trafficking-in-human-beings/docs/commission_report_on_the_progress_made_in_the_fight_against_trafficking_in_human_beings_2016_en.pdf

Federal Investigation Agency. n.d. *Prevention and Control of Human Trafficking Ordinance, 2002*. http://www.fia.gov.pk/en/law/Offences/22.pdf

Ferree, Myra Marx. 1990. "Beyond Separate Spheres: Feminism and Family Research." *Journal of Marriage and the Family* 52(4):866–84.

FitzGerald, Sharron A. 2010. "Biopolitics and the Regulation of Vulnerability: The Case of the Female Trafficked Migrant." *International Journal of Law in Context* 6(3):277–94.

Flores-González, Nilda, Anna Romina Guevarra, Maura Toro-Morn, and Grace Chang, eds. 2013. *Immigrant Women Workers in the Neoliberal Age*. Chicago, IL: University of Illinois Press.

Folbre, Nancy. 2006. "Measuring Care: Gender, Empowerment, and the Care Economy." *Journal of Human Development* 7:183–99.

Forced Migration Review. 2013. "Detention, Alternatives to Detention, and Deportation." Special issue. *Forced Migration Review* 44.

Ford, Michele, Lenore Lyons, and Willem van Schendel, eds. 2012. *Human Trafficking in Southeast Asia: Critical Perspectives*. New York, NY: Routledge.

Fouladvand, Shahrzad. 2018. "Decentering the Prosecution-Oriented Approach: Tackling Both Supply and Demand in the Struggle against Human Trafficking." *International Journal of Law, Crime and Justice* 52:129–43.

Fowler, Jeanna, Nicollete Che, and Lindsay Fowler. 2010. "Innocence Lost: The Rights of Human Trafficking Victims." *Procedia Social and Behavioral Sciences* 2:1345–9.

Frederick, John. 2012. "The Myth of Nepal-to-India Sex Trafficking: Its Creation, Its Maintenance, and Its Influence on Anti-Trafficking Interventions." Pp. 127–48 in *Trafficking and Prostitution Reconsidered: New Perspectives on Migration, Sex Work, and Human Rights*, edited by K. Kempadoo, J. Sanghera, and B. Pattanaik, 2nd edn. Boulder, CO: Paradigm.

Friedlaender, Michael M. 2002. "The Right to Sell or Buy a Kidney: Are We Failing Our Patients?" *Lancet* 359(9310):971–3.

Fullerton, Andrew, and Dwanna Robertson. 2011. "Labor Rights After the Flexible Turn: The Rise of Contingent Employment and the Conditions for Workers Rights in the United States." Pp. 22–33 in *Human Rights in Our Own Backyard: Injustice and Resistance in the United States*, edited by W. Armaline, D. Glasberg, and B. Purkayastha. Philadelphia, PA: University of Pennsylvania Press.

GAATW (Global Alliance Against Traffic in Women). 2007. *Collateral Damage: The Impact of Anti-Trafficking Measures on Human Rights Around the World*. Bangkok: GAATW.

Gallagher, Anne T. 2010. *The International Law of Human Trafficking*. New York, NY: Cambridge University Press.

Ganguly-Scrase, Ruchira. 2003. "Paradoxes of Globalization, Liberalization, and Gender Equality: The Worldviews of the Lower Middle Class in West Bengal, India." *Gender and Society* 17(4):544–66.

Gekht, Anna. 2008. "Shared but Differentiated Responsibility: Integration of International Obligations in Fight against Trafficking in Human Beings." *Denver Journal of International Law and Policy* 37:29–62.

Gibson, Owen. 2016. "Migrant Workers Suffer Appalling Treatment in Qatar World Cup Stadiums, says Amnesty." *The Guardian*, March 30. https://www.theguardian.com/global-development/2016/mar/31/migrant-workers-suffer-appalling-treatment-in-qatar-world-cup-stadiums-says-amnesty

Glenn, E. 2002. *Unequal Freedom: How Race and Gender Shape American Citizenship*. Cambridge, MA: Harvard University Press.

Global Policy Forum. 2005. *US Opposition to International Criminal Court*. https://www.globalpolicy.org/international-justice/the-international-criminal-court/us-opposition-to-the-icc.html

Golash Boza, Tanya. 2015. *Deported: Immigrant Policing, Disposable Labor and Global Capitalism.* New York, NY: New York University Press.

Goldberg, Michelle. 2014. "Should Buying Sex Be Illegal?" *The Nation*, July 30. http://www.thenation.com/article/should-buying-sex-be-illegal

Goldman, Emma. 1910. *The White Slave Traffic.* New York, NY: Mother Earth. http://theanarchistlibrary.org/library/Emma_Goldman_The_White_Slave_Traffic.html

Gowans, Allison. 2017. "Iowa's Hometown to the World: Postville Immigration Raid Leaves Lingering Fears, New Hopes." *The Gazette*, March 26. http://www.thegazette.com/subject/news/iowas-hometown-to-the-world-20170326

Gozdziak, Elzbieta. 2015. "Data Matters: Issues and Challenges for Research on Trafficking." Pp. 23–38 in *Global Human Trafficking: Critical Issues and Contexts,* edited by M. Dragiewicz. New York, NY: Routledge.

Gozdziak, Elzbieta. 2016. *Trafficked Children and Adolescents in the United States.* New Brunswick, NJ: Rutgers University Press.

Gregory, Anthony. 2011. "Why Legalizing Organ Sales Would Help to Save Lives, End Violence." *The Atlantic*, November 9.

Guevarra, Anna. 2010. *Marketing Dreams, Manufacturing Heroes: The Transnational Labor Brokering of Filipino Workers.* New Brunswick, NJ: Rutgers University Press.

Guinn, David E. 2008. "Defining the Problem of Trafficking: The Interplay of US Law, Donor, and NGO Engagement and the Local Context in Latin America." *Human Rights Quarterly* 30(1):119–45.

Gunnarson, Martin, and Susanne Lundin. 2015. "The Complexities of Victimhood: Insights from the Organ Trade." *Somatechnics* 5(1):32–51.

Gurung, Shobha Hamal. 2015. *Nepali Migrant Women: Resistance and Survival in America.* Syracuse, NY: Syracuse University Press.

Gurung, Shobha Hamal, and Bandana Purkayastha. 2013. "Gendered Labor: Experiences of Nepali Women within Pan-Ethnic Informal Labor Markets in Boston and New York." Pp. 81–95 in *Immigrant Women Workers in the Neoliberal Age*, edited by N. Flores-González, A. R. Guevarra, M. Toro-Morn, and G. Chang. Chicago, IL: University of Illinois Press.

Guth, Andrew, Robyn Anderson, Kasey Kinnard, and Hang Tran. 2014. "Proper Methodology and Methods of Collecting and Analyzing Slavery Data: An Examination of the Global Slavery Index." *Social Inclusion* 2(4):14–22.

Haag, Matthew. 2017. "Driver in Deadly Human Smuggling Case Pleads Guilty in San Antonio." *New York Times*, October 16. https://www.nytimes.com/2017/10/16/us/truck-driver-guilty-trafficking.html

Hadjimatheou, Katerina, and Jennifer K. Lynch. 2017. "'Once They Pass You, They May Be Gone Forever': Humanitarian Duties and Professional Tensions in Safeguarding and Anti-Trafficking at the Border." *The British Journal of Criminology* 57(4):945–63. doi: 10.1093/bjc/azw027.

Haider, Romana. 2006. "Economic Rights of Migrant Domestic Workers in Singapore and the United States." Honors thesis, University of Connecticut.

Haken, Jeremy. 2011. *Transnational Crime in the Developing World.* Washington, DC: Global Financial Integrity.

Harris, Catherine E., and Stephen P. Alcorn. 2001. "To Solve a Deadly Shortage: Economic Incentives for Human Organ Donation." *Issues in Law & Medicine* 16(3):213–33.

Haynes, Dina Francesca. 2014. "The Celebritization of Human Trafficking." *The Annals of the American Academy of Political and Social Science* 653(1):25–45.

Hepburn, Stephanie, and Rita J. Simon. 2013. *Human Trafficking Around the World: Hidden in Plain Sight.* New York, NY: Columbia University Press.

Hicks, George. 1995. *The Comfort Women: Japan's Brutal Regime of Enforced Prostitution in the Second World War.* New York: W. W. Norton.

Hoff, Suzanne. 2014. "Where Is the Funding for Anti-Trafficking Work? A Look at Donor Funds, Policies and Practices in Europe." *Anti-Trafficking Review* 3:109–32.

Holland, Brynn. 2017. *The "Father of Modern Gynecology" Performed Shocking Experiments on Slaves.* https://www.history.com/news/the-father-of-modern-gynecology-performed-shocking-experiments-on-slaves

Holmes, Ryan Connelly, and Dan Sagalyn. 2017. "One Doctor's War against Global Organ Trafficking." *PBSO News Hour.* https://www.pbs.org/newshour/world/one-doctors-war-global-organ-trafficking

Howard, Neil. 2014a. "Keeping Count: The Trouble with the Global Slavery Index." *The Guardian*, January 13.

Howard, Neil. 2014b. "Teenage Labor Migration and Antitrafficking Policy in West Africa." *The Annals of the American Academy of Political and Social Science* 653(1):124–40.

HRW (Human Rights Watch). 2002. "U.S. State Department Trafficking Report Missing Key Data, Credits Uneven Efforts." https://www.hrw.org/news/2002/06/06/us-state-department-trafficking-report-missing-key-data-credits-uneven-efforts

HRW (Human Rights Watch). 2018. *Hidden Chains: Rights Abuses and Forced Labor in Thailand's Fishing Industry*. https://www.hrw.org/report/2018/01/23/hidden-chains/rights-abuses-and-forced-labor-thailands-fishing-industry

Hua, Julietta, and Holly Nigorizawa. 2010. "US Sex Trafficking, Women's Human Rights and the Politics of Representation." *International Feminist Journal of Politics* 12(3–4):401–23.

Huda, S. 2006. "Sex Trafficking in South Asia." *International Journal of Gynecology & Obstetrics* 94:374–81.

Hughes, Donna M. 2014. "Trafficking in Human Beings in the European Union: Gender, Sexual Exploitation, and Digital Communication Technologies." *Sage Open* October–December: 1–8.

Hussein, Maliha, and Shazreh Hussain. 2012. *Internal Trafficking of Women and Girls in Pakistan: A Research Study*. Islamabad: Aurat Foundation.

Hyland, Kelly E. 2001. "The Impact of the Protocol to Prevent, Suppress and Punish Trafficking in Persons, Especially Women and Children." *Human Rights Brief* 8(2):30–1, 38.

Ikels, Charlotte. 2013. "The Anthropology of Organ Transplantation." *Annual Review of Anthropology* 42:89–102.

ILO (International Labour Organization). 2012. *ILO Global Estimate of Forced Labour: Results and Methodology*. Geneva: International Labour Organization.

ILO (International Labour Organization). 2014. *Profits and Poverty: The Economics of Forced Labour*. Geneva: International Labour Organization.

ILO (International Labour Organization), Walk Free Foundation, and IOM (International Organization for Migration). 2017. *Global Estimates of Modern Slavery: Forced Labour and Forced Marriage*. Geneva: International Labour Organization.

Innis, Michelle. 2015. "Australian Leader is Pressed on Whether Migrant Smugglers Were Paid to Turn Back." *New York Times*, June 13.

Jeffreys, Sheila. 1997. *The Idea of Prostitution*. North Melbourne: Spinifex Press.

Jeffreys, Sheila. 2009. *The Industrial Vagina: The Political Economy of the Global Sex Trade*. New York, NY: Routledge.

Jones, Tonisha R. 2010. "The Empirical Assessment of Human Trafficking in Washington State: Challenges, Roadblocks, and Barriers." PhD dissertation, Program in Criminal Justice, Washington State University.

Joralemon, Donald, and Phil Cox. 2003. "Body Values: The Case against Compensating for Transplant Organs." *Hastings Center Report* 33(1):27–33.

Joralemon, Donald, and Kim Mika Fujinaga. 1997. "Studying the Quality of Life after Organ Transplantation: Research Problems and Solutions." *Social Science and Medicine* 44(9):1259–69.

Jordan, Mary. 1995. "In Okinawa's Whisper Alley, GIs Find Prostitutes are Cheap and Plentiful." *The Washington Post*, November 23.

Jureidini, Ray. 2010. "Trafficking and Contract Migrant Workers in the Middle East." *International Migration* 48(4):142–63.

Kara, Siddharth. 2011. "Supply and Demand: Human Trafficking in the Global Economy." *Harvard International Review* 33(2):66–77.

Katzenstein, Mary Fainsod. 1989. "Organizing Against Violence: Strategies of the Indian Women's Movement." *Pacific Affairs* 62(1):53–71.

Kelly, Annie. 2015. "US Human Trafficking Report Under Fire as Cuba and Malaysia Are Upgraded."*The Guardian*, July 27. https://www.theguardian.com/global-development/2015/jul/27/us-human-trafficking-in-persons-report-under-fire-cuba-malaysia-upgraded

Kelly, Emily. 2013. "International Organ Trafficking Crisis: Solutions Addressing the Heart of the Matter." *Boston College Law Review* 36(2):1317–49.

Kempadoo, Kamala, ed. 1999. *Sun, Sex and Gold: Tourism and Sex Work in the Caribbean*. Lanham, MD: Rowman and Littlefield.

Kempadoo, Kamala. 2001. "Women of Color and the Global Sex Trade: Transnational Feminist Perspectives." *Meridians* 1(2):28–51.

Kempadoo, Kamala. 2012. "Abolitionism, Criminal Justice, and Transnational Feminism: Twenty-First-Century Perspectives on Human Trafficking." Pp. vii–xlii in *Trafficking and Prostitution Reconsidered: New Perspectives on Migration, Sex Work, and Human Rights*, edited by K. Kempadoo, J. Sanghera, and B. Pattanaik, 2nd edn. Boulder, CO: Paradigm.

Kempadoo, Kamala. 2016. "'Bound Coolies' and Other Indentured Workers in the Caribbean: Implications for Debates about Human Trafficking and Modern Slavery." *Anti-Trafficking Review* 9:48–63.

Kempadoo, Kamala, Jyoti Sanghera, and Bandana Pattanaik, eds. 2005. *Trafficking and Prostitution Reconsidered: New Perspectives on Migration, Sex Work, and Human Rights*. Boulder, CO: Paradigm.

Kempadoo, Kamala, Jyoti Sanghera, and Bandana Pattanaik, eds. 2012. *Trafficking and Prostitution Reconsidered: New Perspectives on Migration, Sex Work, and Human Rights,* 2nd edn. Boulder, CO: Paradigm.

Kibria, Nazli. 2000. "Ethnic Options, Ethnic Binds: Identity Negotiations of Second Generation Chinese and Korean Americans." *Sociological Perspectives* 43:77–95.

Knepper, Paul. 2013. "History Matters: Canada's Contribution to the First Worldwide Study of Human Trafficking." *Canadian Journal of Criminology and Criminal Justice* 55(1):33–54.

Kotiswaran, Prabhan. 2014. "Beyond Sexual Humanitarianism: A Postcolonial Approach to Anti-Trafficking Law." *UC Irvine Law Review* 4(1):353–406.

Kreidenweis, Alex, and Natalie F. Hudson. 2015. "More Than a Crime: Human Trafficking as Human (In)security." *International Studies Perspectives* 16:67–85.

Kristof, Nicholas D. 2004. "Going Home, With Hope." *New York Times*, January 24.

Kristof, Nicholas D., and Sheryl WuDunn. 2015. *A Path Appears.* (PBS series) http://apathappears.org/film

Kubal, Agnieszka. 2014. "Struggles Against Subjection: Implications of Criminalization of Migration for Migrants' Everyday Lives in Europe." *Crime, Law and Social Change* 62:91–111.

Laczko, Frank. 2005. "Introduction: Data and Research on Human Trafficking: A Global Survey." *International Migration* 43(1/2):5–16.

Laczko, Frank, and Elzbieta Gozdziak, eds. 2005. "Introduction: Data and Research on Human Trafficking: A Global Survey." *International Migration* 43(1/2).

Lakkimsetti, Chaitanya. 2014. "'HIV Is Our Friend': Prostitution, Biopower, and the State in Postcolonial India." *Signs: Journal of Women in Culture and Society* 40(1):201–26.

Landesman, Peter. 2004. "The Girls Next Door." *New York Times Magazine*, January 25.

Lange, Andrea. 2011. "Research Note: Challenges of Identifying Female Human Trafficking Victims Using a National 1-800 Call Center." *Trends in Organized Crime* 14(1):47–55.

Lee, Maggy. 2007. "Introduction: Understanding Human Trafficking." Pp. 1–25 in *Human Trafficking*, edited by M. Lee. Cullompton, UK: Willan.

Leenders, Reinoud. 2009. "Refugee Warriors or War Refugees? Iraqi Refugees' Predicament in Syria, Jordan and Lebanon." *Mediterranean Politics* 14(3):343–63.

Liempt, Ilse van. 2006. "Trafficking in Human Beings: Conceptual Dilemmas." Pp. 27–42 in *Trafficking and Women's Rights*, edited by C. L. van den Anker and J. Doomernik. New York, NY: Palgrave Macmillan.

Lima de Perez, Julie. 2015. "Examining Trafficking Statistics Regarding Brazilian Victims in Spain and Portugal." *Crime, Law and Social Change* 63(3–4):159–90.

Limoncelli, Stephanie A. 2010. *The Politics of Trafficking: The First International Movement to Combat the Sexual Exploitation of Women.* Stanford, CA: Stanford University Press.

Lisborg, Anders. 2014. "The Good, the Bad and the Ugly: In the Name of Victim Protection." Pp. 19–34 in *Human Trafficking in Asia: Forcing Issues*, edited by S. Yea. Abingdon: Routledge.

Lock, Margaret. 2001. "The Alienation of Human Tissue and Biopolitics of Immortalized Cell Lines." *Body & Society* 7(2–3):63–91.

Loff, Bebe, and Jyoti Sanghera. 2004. "Distortions and Difficulties in Data for Trafficking." *The Lancet* 363:566.

Longman, Jere. 2017. "Report Finds 17 Deaths and Labor Abuses at Russia's World Cup Stadiums." *New York Times*, June 14.

Lovell, Vicky, Heidi Hartmann, and Misha Werschkul. 2007. "More than Raising the Floor: The Persistence of Gender Inequalities in the Low-Wage Labor Market." Pp. 35–58 in *The Sex of Class: Women Transforming American Labor*, edited by D. Cobble. Ithaca, NY: Cornell University Press.

Lydersen, Kari. 2008. "Former CEO of Iowa Kosher Meatpacking Plant is Arrested." *The Washington Post*, October 31.

Lyman, Rick, and Alison Smale. 2015. "Migrant Smuggling in Europe Is Now Worth 'Billion'." *New York Times*, September 3.

Lyons, Lenore, and Michele Ford. 2014. "Trafficking versus Smuggling: Malaysia's Anti-Trafficking in Persons Act." Pp. 35–47 in *Human Trafficking in Asia: Forcing Issues*, edited by S. Yea. Abingdon: Routledge.

MacKinnon, Catharine A. 1987. *Feminism Unmodified: Discourses on Life and Law*. Cambridge, MA: Harvard University Press.

Mahdavi, Pardis. 2013. "Gender, Labour and the Law: The Nexus of Domestic Work, Human Trafficking and the Informal Economy in the United Arab Emirates." *Global Networks* 3(4):425–40.

Majic, Samantha. 2014. "'Beyond Victim-Criminals': Sex Workers, Nonprofit Organizations, and Gender Ideologies." *Gender and Society* 28(3):463–85.

Mandic, Danilo. 2017. "Trafficking and Syrian Refugee Smuggling: Evidence from the Balkan Route." *Social Inclusion* 5(2):28–38.

Manzano, Ana, Mark Monaghan, Barbara Potrata, and Michelle Clayton. 2014. "The Invisible Issue of Organ Laundering." *Transplantation* 98(6):600–3.

Martin, Dominique. 2012. *Action to Stop Thriving Global Organ Trade Must Start at Home*. The Conversation. https://theconversation.com/action-to-stop-thriving-global-organ-trade-must-start-at-home-7333

Martinez, Samuel. 2009. "Book Review: The Slave Next Door." *Connecticut Journal of International Law* 25:119–23.

Matas, Arthur J. 2004. "The Case for Living Kidney Sales: Rationale, Objections and Concerns." *American Journal of Transplantation* 4(12):2007–17.

Maternick, Anna, and Melissa Hope Ditmore. 2015. "Sex, Violence, and the Border: Trafficking for Sex Work from Mexico to the

U.S." Pp. 43–56 in *Global Human Trafficking: Critical Issues and Contexts,* edited by M. Dragiewicz. New York, NY: Routledge.

McGrath, Siobhan. 2012. "Many Chains to Break: The Multi-Dimensional Concept of Slave Labour in Brazil." *Antipode* 45(4):1005–28.

McGrath, Siobhan, and Fabiola Mieres. 2014. *Mapping the Politics of National Rankings in the Movement Against "Modern Slavery."* https://www.opendemocracy.net/beyondslavery/siobh%C3%A1n-mcgrath-fabiola-mieres/mapping-politics-of-national-rankings-in-movement-again

Merry, Sally Engle. 2011. "Sex Trafficking and Global Governance in the Context of Pacific Mobility." *Law Text Culture* 15:187–208.

Meyer, Silke. 2006. "Trafficking in Human Organs in Europe: A Myth or an Actual Threat?" *European Journal of Crime* 14(2):208–29.

Miller, Rebecca, and Sebastian Baumeister. 2013. "Managing Migration: Is Border Control Fundamental to Anti-Trafficking and Anti-Smuggling Interventions?" *Anti-Trafficking Review* 2:15–32.

Ministry of Interior, Government of Pakistan. 2005. *Pakistan Action Plan for Combating Human Trafficking.* Islamabad: Ministry of Interior, Government of Pakistan.

Missbach, Antje, and Frieda Sinanu. 2014. "People Smuggling in Indonesia: Dependency, Exploitation and Other Vulnerabilities." Pp. 165–82 in *Human Trafficking in Asia: Forcing Issues,* edited by S. Yea. Abingdon: Routledge.

Moazam, Farhat, Riffat Moazam Zaman, and Aamir M. Jafarey. 2009. "Conversations with Kidney Vendors in Pakistan: An Ethnographic Study." *Hastings Center Report* 39(3):29–44.

Moghadam, Valentine. 2015. "Gender and Globalization: Female Labor and Women's Mobilization." *Journal of World System Research* 5:366–89.

Moniruzzaman, Monir. 2010. "'Living Cadavers' in Bangladesh: Ethics of the Human Organ Bazaar." PhD thesis, University of Toronto.

Moniruzzaman, Monir. 2012. "'Living Cadavers' in Bangladesh: Bioviolence in the Human Organ Bazaar." *Medical Anthropology Quarterly* 26(1):69–91.

Montgomery, David, Manny Fernandez, and Yonette Joseph. 2017. "Journey Fatal for 9 Migrants Found in Truck in San Antonio Parking Lot." *New York Times,* July 23. https://www.nytimes.com/2017/07/23/us/san-antonio-truck-walmart-trafficking.html

Moreno-Lax, Violeta. 2018. "The EU Humanitarian Border and the Securitization of Human Rights: The 'Rescue-Through-Interdiction/Rescue-Without-Protection' Paradigm." *JCMS: Journal of Common Market Studies* 56: 119–40. doi: 10.1111/jcms.12651.

Mugge, Daniel. 2017. *40.3 Million Slaves? Four Reasons to Question the New Global Estimates of Modern Slavery.* https://www.opendemocracy.net/beyondslavery/daniel-m-gge/403-million-slaves-four-reasons-to-question-new-global-estimates-of-moder

Mullins, E. 2007. "Pakistan Fights Organ Trading." *Irish Medical Times* 41(6):8.

Musalo, Karen, and Eunice Lee. 2017. "Seeking a Rational Approach to a Regional Refugee Crisis: Lessons from the Summer 2014 'Surge' of Central American Women and Children at the US–Mexico Border." *Journal on Migration and Human Security* 5(1):137–79.

Musto, Jennifer Lynne. 2010. "The NGO-ification of the Anti-Trafficking Movement in the United States: A Case Study of the Coalition to Abolish Slavery and Trafficking." Pp. 23–36 in *Sex Trafficking, Human Rights and Social Justice*, edited by T. Zheng. New York, NY: Routledge.

Naqvi, Syed Ali Anwar, Bux Ali, Farida Mazhar, Mirza Naqi Zafar, and Syed Adibul Hasan. 2007. "A Socioeconomic Survey of Kidney Vendors in Pakistan." *Transplant International* 20(11):934–39.

National Assembly of Pakistan. 2012. *The Constitution of the Islamic Republic of Pakistan.* http://www.na.gov.pk/uploads/documents/1333523681_951.pdf

National Institute of Justice. 2014. *Expert Working Group on Trafficking in Persons Research Meeting.* https://www.ncjrs.gov/pdffiles1/nij/249914.pdf

New York Times. 2010. "Editorial." *New York Times*, June 28.

Njiru, Roseanne. 2018. "Outsiders in Their Own Nation: Electoral Violence and Politics of Internal Displacement in Kenya." *Current Sociology* 66(2):226–40.

Njiru, Roseanne, and Bandana Purkayastha. 2015. *Voices of Internally Displaced Persons in Kenya.* London: Frontpage.

Nonnenmacher, Sophie. 2014. "Trafficking at Sea: The Situation of Enslaved Fishermen in Southeast Asia." Pp. 141–64 in *Human Trafficking in Asia: Forcing Issues*, edited by S. Yea. Abingdon: Routledge.

Oblinger, D. G. 2015. "Sex Trafficking in Sexually Oriented Businesses." Pp. 129–48 in *Combating Human Trafficking: A Multidisciplinary Approach,* edited by M. J. Palmiotto. Boca Raton, FL: CRC Press.

Obokata, Tom. 2006. *Trafficking of Human Beings from a Human Rights Perspective: Towards a Holistic Approach.* Leiden: Koninklijke Brill.

O'Connell Davidson, Julia. 2015. "On Broken Chains and Missing Links: Tackling the 'Demand Side of Trafficking.'" Pp. 153–66 in *Global Human Trafficking: Critical Issues and Contexts*, edited by M. Dragiewicz. New York, NY: Routledge.

O'Connell Davidson, Julia. 2017. "The Presence of the Past: Lessons of History for Anti-Trafficking Work." *Anti-Trafficking Review* 9:1–13.

OHCHR (Office of the United Nations High Commissioner for Human Rights). 2000. *Protocol to Prevent, Suppress and Punish Trafficking in Persons, Especially Women and Children.* http://www.ohchr.org/EN/ProfessionalInterest/Pages/ProtocolTraffickingInPersons.aspx

OHCHR (Office of the United Nations High Commissioner for Human Rights). 2002. *Recommended Principles and Guidelines on Human Rights and Human Trafficking.* http://www.ohchr.org/Documents/Publications/Traffickingen.pdf

OHCHR (Office of the United Nations High Commissioner for Human Rights). 2014. *Human Rights and Human Trafficking.* http://www.ohchr.org/Documents/Publications/FS36_en.pdf

OHCHR (Office of the United Nations High Commissioner for Human Rights). n.d. *Slavery Convention 1927.* http://www.ohchr.org/EN/ProfessionalInterest/Pages/SlaveryConvention.aspx

Okamoto, Julia. 2013. "The 'Comfort Women' of the Pacific War." *Journal of Scientific Initiation on International Relations* 1:91–108.

O'Neill Richard, Amy. 2000. *International Trafficking in Women to the United States: A Contemporary Manifestation of Slavery and Organized Crime.* Washington, DC: Center for the Study of Intelligence.

Ong, Aihwa. 1987. *Spirits of Resistance and Capitalist Discipline: Factory Women in Malaysia.* Albany, NY: State University of New York Press.

Outshoorn, Joyce. 2005. "The Political Debates on Prostitution and Trafficking of Women." *Social Politics* 12(1):141–55.

Outshoorn, Joyce. 2015. "The Trafficking Policy Debates." Pp. 7–22 in *Global Human Trafficking: Critical Issues and Contexts,* edited by M. Dragiewicz. New York, NY: Routledge.

Paavilainen, Marja. 2015. "Towards a Cohesive and Contextualised Response: When Is It Necessary to Distinguish between Forced Labour, Trafficking in Persons and Slavery?" *Anti-Trafficking Review* 5:158–61.

Palmiotto, Michael J. 2015. "Introduction: Human Trafficking – Modern Slavery." Pp. xvii–xxv in *Combating Human Trafficking: A Multidisciplinary Approach,* edited by M. J. Palmiotto. Boca Raton, FL: CRC Press.

Panjabi, Ranee Khooshie Lal. 2010. "The Sum of a Human's Parts: Global Organ Trafficking in the Twenty-First Century." *Pace Environmental Law Review* 28(1):1–44.

Parreñas, Rachel. 2001. *Servants of Globalization: Women, Migration and Domestic Work.* Stanford, CA: Stanford University Press.

Patil, Vrushali, and Bandana Purkayastha. 2017. "The Transnational Assemblage of Indian Rape Culture." *Ethnic and Racial Studies.* doi: 10.1080/01419870.2017.1322707.

Pattanaik, Bandana. 2002. "Where Do We Go from Here?" Pp. 217–30 in *Transnational Prostitution: Changing Patterns in a Global Context,* edited by S. Thorbek and B. Pattanaik. London: Zed Books.

Pearson, Elaine. 2004. *Coercion in the Kidney Trade? A Background Study on Trafficking in Human Organs Worldwide.* Eschborn: GTZ.

Pentinnen, Elina. 2008. *Globalization, Prostitution and Sex Trafficking: Corporeal Politics.* New York, NY: Routledge.

Permoser, Julia Mourao. 2017. "Redefining Membership: Restrictive Rights and Categorisation in European Union Migration Policy." *Journal of Ethnic and Migration Studies* 43(15):2536–55.

Peters, Alicia W. 2013. "'Things that involve Sex are Just Different': US Anti-Trafficking Law and Policy on the Books, in Their Minds, and in Action." *Anthropological Quarterly* 86(1):221–55.

Peters, Alicia. 2014. "Challenging the Sex/Labor Trafficking Dichotomy with Victim Experiences." Pp. 30–40 in *Human Trafficking Reconsidered: Rethinking the Problem, Envisioning New Solutions,* edited by K. K. Hoang and R. S. Parrenas. New York, NY: International Debate Education Association.

Petrini, C. 2016. *Organ Allocation Policies 10 years after UNESCO's Universal Declaration of Bioethics and Human Rights.* Rome: Bioethics Unit, Office of the President, National Institute of Health.

Plant, David. 2015. "When it Comes to Modern Slavery, Do Definitions Matter?" *Anti-Trafficking Review* 5:150–2.

Polaris Project. 2015. *Survivor Story.* https://polarisproject. org/blog/2015/06/17/survivor-story-promised-education-forced-work-instead

Preston, Julia. 2008. "Workers on Hunger Strike Say They Were Misled on Visas." *New York Times,* June 7.

Purkayastha, Bandana. 2005. *Negotiating Ethnicity: South Asian Americans Traverse a Transnational World.* New Brunswick, NJ: Rutgers University Press.

Purkayastha, Bandana. 2012. "Intersectionality in a Transnational World." *Gender and Society* 26(1):55–66.

Purkayastha, Bandana. 2018. "Migration, Migrants, and Human Security." *Current Sociology.* doi: 10.1177/0011392117736302.

Purkayastha, Bandana, and Shweta Majumdar. 2009. "Sex Trafficking in South Asia." Pp. 185–202 in *Globalization and Third World Women: Exploitation, Coping and Resistance,* edited by L. Lindio-McGovern and I. Wallimann. Farnham: Ashgate.

Quirk, Joel. 2007. "Trafficked into Slavery." *Journal of Human Rights* 6:181–207.

Rajan, S. Irudaya, V. Varghese, and M. Jayakumar. 2011. *Dreaming Mobility and Buying Vulnerability: Overseas Recruitment Practices in India*. New Delhi: Routledge.

Ray, M. 2017. "Crossing Borders: Family Migration Strategies and Routes from Burma to the US." *Journal of Ethnic and Migration Studies*. Epub ahead of print. doi: 10.1080/1369183X.2017.1314815.

Raymond, Janice G. 2002. "The New UN Trafficking Protocol." *Women's Studies International Forum* 25(5):491–502.

Reitano, Tuesday. 2017. "Does 'Human Trafficking' Need a New Definition?" *ISS Today*, July 31. https://issafrica.org/iss-today/does-human-trafficking-need-a-new-definition?utm_source=BenchmarkEmail&utm_campaign=ISS+Today&utm_medium=email

Renzetti, Claire M. 2015. "Service Providers and Their Perceptions of the Service Needs of Sex Trafficking Victims in the United States." Pp. 138–52 in *Global Human Trafficking: Critical Issues and Contexts*, edited by M. Dragiewicz. New York, NY: Routledge.

Richards, Kelly, and Samantha Lyneham. 2015. "Bride Traffic: Trafficking for Marriage to Australia." Pp. 105–20 in *Global Human Trafficking: Critical Issues and Contexts*, edited by M. Dragiewicz. New York, NY: Routledge.

Richardson, Ruth. 2006. "Human Dissection and Organ Donation: A Historical and Social Background." *Mortality* 11(2):151–65.

Richmond Justice Initiative. 2016. *Barbara Amaya's Story*. Survival Stories. http://richmondjusticeinitiative.com/human-trafficking/survival-stories

Robinson, Mary. 2005. "Connecting Human Rights, Human Development and Human Security." Pp. 308–16 in *Human Rights in the War on Terror*, edited by R. Wilson. Cambridge: Cambridge University Press.

Romero, Mary. 1992. *Maids in the USA*. New York, NY: Routledge.

Roth, Silke. 2015. *The Paradoxes of Aid Work*. London: Routledge.

Saadatmand, Yassaman, Michael Toma, and Shyam Menon. 2007. "Female Labor Participation in India and Structural Adjustment." *Journal of Global Business Issues* 1(2):65–73.

SAARC (South Asian Association for Regional Cooperation). 2002. *SAARC Convention on Preventing and Combating Trafficking in Women and Children for Prostitution*. http://saarc-sec.org/digital_library/detail_menu/saarc-convention-on-preventing-and-combating-trafficking-in-women-and-children-for-prostitution

Samaddar, Ranabir. 2015. "Returning to the Histories of the Late 19th and Early 20th Century Immigration." *Economic and Political Weekly*, January 10.

Samarasinghe, Vidyamali. 2008. *Female Sex Trafficking in Asia: The Resilience of Patriarchy in a Changing World*. New York, NY: Routledge.

Sandor, Adam. 2016. "Border Security and Drug Trafficking in Senegal: AIRCOP and Global Security Assemblages." *Journal of Intervention and Statebuilding* 10(4):490–512. doi: 10.1080/17502977.2016.1240425.

Sanghera, Jyoti. 2016. "Unpacking the Trafficking Discourse." Pp. 3–24 in *Trafficking and Prostitution Reconsidered: New Perspectives on Migration, Sex Work, and Human Rights*, edited by K. Kempadoo, J. Sanghera, and B. Pattanaik, 2nd edn. New York, NY: Routledge.

Sassen, Saskia. 2013. *The Global City: New York, London, Tokyo*. Princeton, NJ: Princeton University Press.

Savulescu, J. 2003. "Is the Sale of Body Parts Wrong?" *Journal of Medical Ethics* 29(3):137–8.

Schauer, Edward J., and Elizabeth M. Wheaton. 2006. "Sex Trafficking into the United States: A Literature Review." *Criminal Justice Review* 32(2):146–69.

Scheper-Hughes, Nancy. 2000. "The Global Traffic in Human Organs." *Current Anthropology* 41(2):191–224.

Scheper-Hughes, Nancy. 2001. "Commodity Fetishism in Organs Trafficking." *Body & Society* 7(2):31–62.

Scheper-Hughes, Nancy. 2002. "The Ends of the Body: Commodity Fetishism and the Global Traffic in Organs." *SAIS Review* 22(1):61–80.

Scheper-Hughes, Nancy. 2003a. "Keeping an Eye on the Global Traffic in Human Organs." *The Lancet* 3617:1645–8.

Scheper-Hughes, Nancy. 2003b. "Rotten Trade: Millennial Capitalism, Human Values and Global Justice in Organ Trafficking." *Journal of Human Rights* 2(2):197–226.

Scheper-Hughes, Nancy. 2004. "Parts Unknown: Undercover Ethnography of the Organs-Trafficking Underworld." *Ethnography* 5(1): 29–73.

Scheper-Hughes, Nancy. 2006. "Organs Trafficking: The Real, the Unreal and the Uncanny." *Annals of Transplantation* 11(3):16–30.

Scheper-Hughes, Nancy. 2008. "llegal Organ Trade: Global Justice and Traffic in Human Organs." Pp. 106–21 in *Living Donor Organ Transplantation*, edited by R. W. G. Gruessner and E. Bendini. New York, NY: McGraw-Hill.

Scheper-Hughes, Nancy. 2013. "Organs Trafficking: A Protected Crime." *Al Jazeera*, November 5.

Schiebinger, Londa. 2017. *Secret Cures of Slaves: People, Plants, and Medicine in the Eighteenth-Century Atlantic World*. Stanford: Stanford University Press.

Seedat-Khan, Miriam. 2012. "Tracing the Journey of South African Indian Women from 1860." Pp. 35–47 in *Contemporary India and South Africa: Legacies, Identities, Dilemmas,* edited by S. Patel and T. Uys. New Delhi: Routledge.

Segrave, Marie, Sanja Milivojevic, and Sharon Pickering. 2009. *Sex Trafficking: International Context and Response.* Portland, OR: Willan.

Shahrokhi, Sholeh. 2010. "Beyond 'Tragedy': A Cultural Critique of Sex Trafficking of Young Iranian Women." Pp. 37–46 in *Sex Trafficking, Human Rights and Social Justice,* edited by T. Zheng. New York, NY: Routledge.

Shamshad, Rizwana. 2017. "Bengaliness, Hindu Nationalism and Bangladeshi Migrants in West Bengal, India." *Asian Ethnicity* 18(4):433–51.

Shih, Elena. 2014. "Globalizing Rehabilitative Regimes: Framing the Moral Economy of Vocational Training in After-Trafficking Work." Pp. 64–78 in *Human Trafficking in Asia: Forcing Issues,* edited by S. Yea. Abingdon: Routledge.

Shih, Elena. 2016. "'Not in My 'Backyard Abolitionism': Vigilante Rescue against American Sex Trafficking." *Sociological Perspectives* 59(1):66–90.

Shimazono, Yosuke. 2007. "The State of the International Organ Trade: A Provisional Picture Based on Integration of Available Information." *Bulletin* 85(12):955–62.

Shrivastava, Aseem, and Ashis Kothari. 2012. *Churning of the Earth: The Making of Modern India.* New Delhi: Random House.

Silverman, Jay, Niranjan Saggurti, Debbie Cheng, Michele Decker, Sharon Coleman, Carly Bridden, Manoj Pardeshi, Anindita Dasgupta, Jeffry Samet, and Anita Raj. 2014. "Associations of Sex Trafficking History with Recent Sexual Risk among HIV-Infected FSWs in India." *AIDS and Behavior* 18:555–61.

SIPRI. 2013. *SIPRI Yearbook 2013: Armaments, Disarmament and International Security.* Oxford: Oxford University Press on behalf of Stockholm International Peace Research Institute.

Slabbert, Magda. 2008. "Combat Organ Trafficking: Reward the Donor or Regulate Sales." *Koers* 73(1):75–99.

Sleightholme, Carolyn, and Indrani Sinha. 1996. *Guilty without Trial: Women in the Sex Trade in Calcutta.* Calcutta: Stree.

Smale, Alison, and Melissa Eddy. 2015. "Grisly Discovery in Migrant Crisis Shocks Europe." *New York Times,* August 27.

SPLC (Southern Poverty Law Center). 2013. *Close to Slavery: Guest Work Programs in the United States.* Montgomery, AL: Southern Poverty Law Center.

Srikantiah, Jayashri. 2007. "Perfect Victims and Real Survivors: The Iconic Victim in Domestic Human Trafficking Law." *Boston University Law Review* 87:157–211.

Stats, Katrina. 2015. "Welcome to Australia? A Reappraisal of the Fraser Government's Approach to Refugees, 1975–83." *Australian Journal of International Affairs* 69(1):69–87.

Steen, Richard, Smarajit Jana, Sishena Reza-Paul, and Marlise Richter. 2015. "Trafficking, Sex-Work, and HIV: Efforts To Resolve Conflict." *The Lancet* 382(9963):94–6.

Surtees, Rebecca, and Fabrice de Kerchove. 2014. "Who Funds Re/integration? Ensuring Sustainable Services for Trafficking Victims." *Anti-Trafficking Review* 3:64–86.

Sutton, Barbara, Sandra Morgen, and Julie Novkov, eds. 2008. *Security Disarmed: Critical Perspectives on Gender, Race, and Militarization.* New Brunswick, NJ: Rutgers University Press.

Toro-Morn, Maura. 2013. "Elvira Arellano and the Struggles of Low-Wage Undocumented Latina Immigrant Women. Domestic Workers Organizing." Pp. 38–55 in *Immigrant Women Workers in the Neoliberal Age*, edited by N. Flores-GonzaiezGonzález, A. R. Guevarra, M. Toro-Morn, and G. Chang. Chicago, IL: University of Illinois Press.

Torres-Stone, Rosalie, and Bandana Purkayastha. 2005. "Predictors of Earnings for Mexican Americans in the Midwest." *Great Plains Research* 15:101–16.

Transplantation Society and International Society of Nephrology. 2008. *The Declaration of Istanbul on Organ Trafficking and Transplant Tourism.* https://ars-els-cdn-com.ezproxy.lib.uconn.edu/content/imag e/1-s2.0-S0140673608609678-mmc1.pdf

Tripp, Aili Mari, Myra Marx Ferree, and Christina Ewig, eds. 2013. *Gender, Violence, and Human Security: Critical Feminist Perspectives.* New York, NY: New York University Press.

Tseng, Hsun-Hui. 2014. "Victims of Human Trafficking or Perpetrators of Fraudulent Marriage? Foreign Spouses Engaging in the Sex Industry in Taiwan." Pp. 49–63 in *Human Trafficking in Asia: Forcing Issues*, edited by S. Yea. Abingdon: Routledge.

Tsutsumi, Atsuro, Takashi Izutsu, Amod K. Poudyal, Seika Kato, and Eiji Marui. 2008. "Mental Health of Female Survivors of Human Trafficking in Nepal." *Social Science and Medicine* 66:1841–7.

Tuan, Mia. 1998. *Forever Foreigners or Honorary Whites? The Asian Ethnic Experience Today.* New Brunswick, NJ: Rutgers University Press.

Turner, Simon. 2015. "What Is a Refugee Camp? Explorations of the Limits and Effects of the Camp." *Journal of Refugee Studies* 29(2):139–48.

Tyldum, Guri. 2013. "Dependence and Human Trafficking in the Context of Transnational Marriage." *International Migration* 51(4):103–15.

Tyldum, Guri, and Anette Brunovskis. 2005. "Describing the Unobserved: Methodological Challenges in Empirical Studies on Human Trafficking." *International Migration* 43(1–2):17–34.

Ucnikova, Martina. 2014. "OECD and Modern Slavery: How Much Aid Money Is Spent to Tackle the Issue?" *Anti-Trafficking Review* 3:133–51.

UN (United Nations) Department of Economic and Social Affairs. 2016. *International Migration Report 2015*. New York, NY: United Nations.

UN (United Nations) Development Programme. 2007. *Human Trafficking and HIV: Exploring Vulnerabilities and Responses in South Asia*. Colombo: UNDP Regional Centre.

UN (United Nations) Voluntary Trust Fund on Contemporary Forms of Slavery. 2014. *The Human Faces of Modern Slavery*. http://www.ohchr.org/Documents/Issues/Slavery/UNVTCFS/UNSlaveryFund.pdf

UNHCR (United Nations High Commissioner for Refugees). 2016. *Global Trends: Forced Displacement in 2015*. Geneva: United Nations High Commissioner for Refugees.

UNODC (United Nations Office on Drugs and Crime). 2009. *Global Report on Trafficking in Persons*. Vienna: United Nations Office on Drugs and Crime.

UNODC (United Nations Office on Drugs and Crime). 2012. *Guidance Note on "Abuse of a Position of Vulnerability" as a Means of Trafficking in Persons in Article 3 of the Protocol to Prevent, Suppress and Punish Trafficking in Persons, Especially Women and Children, Supplementing the United Nations Convention against Transnational Organized Crime*. www.unodc.org/documents/human-trafficking/2012/UNODC_2012_Guidance_Note_-_Abuse_of_a_Position_of_Vulnerability_E.pdf

UNODC (United Nations Office on Drugs and Crime). 2014. *Global Report on Trafficking in Persons*. Vienna: United Nations Office on Drugs and Crime.

UNODC (United Nations Office on Drugs and Crime). 2015. *Assessment Toolkit: Trafficking in Persons for the Purpose of Organ Removal*. Vienna: United Nations Office on Drugs and Crime. https://www.unodc.org/documents/human-trafficking/2015/UNODC_Assessment_Toolkit_TIP_for_the_Purpose_of_Organ_Removal.pdf

UNODC (United Nations Office on Drugs and Crime). 2016. *Global Report on Trafficking in Persons*. Vienna: United Nations Office on Drugs and Crime.

US (United States) Citizenship and Immigration Services. n.d. *Victims of Human Trafficking: T Nonimmigrant Status*. https://

www.uscis.gov/humanitarian/victims-human-trafficking-other-crimes/victims-human-trafficking-t-nonimmigrant-status

US (United States) Citizenship and Immigration Services. 2016. *Number of I-914 Applications for T Nonimmigrant Status (Victims of Severe Forms of Trafficking and Family Members) by Fiscal Year, Quarter, and Case Status 2008–2016.* https://www.uscis.gov/sites/default/files/USCIS/Resources/Reports%20and%20Studies/Immigration%20Forms%20Data/Victims/I914t_visastatistics_fy2016_qtr2.pdf

US (United States) Department of State. 2000. *Victims of Trafficking and Violence Protection Act of 2000.* https://www.state.gov/j/tip/laws/61124.htm

US (United States) Department of State. 2016. *Trafficking in Persons Report 2016.* http://www.state.gov/j/tip/rls/tiprpt/2016

US (United States) Department of State. 2017. *Trafficking in Persons Report 2017.* http://www.state.gov/j/tip/rls/tiprpt/2017

US (United States) Immigration and Customs Enforcement. 2013. *Human Trafficking and Smuggling.* https://www.ice.gov/factsheets/human-trafficking

Vakulavaranam, Vamsi, and Purendra Prasad. 2017. "Babu's Camelot: Amaravati and the Emerging Capitalist Dynamics in 'New' Andhra Pradesh." *Economic and Political Weekly*, January 14.

Varghese, Linta. 2006. "Constructing a Worker Identity: Class, Experience, and Organizing in Workers' Awaaz." *Cultural Dynamics* 18(2):189–211.

Vatican Radio. 2017. *Vatican Organ Trafficking Summit Issues Statement.* http://en.radiovaticana.va/news/2017/02/09/vatican_organ_trafficking_summit_issues_statement/1291387

Veen, Marjolein van der. 2001. "Rethinking Commodification and Prostitution: An Effort at Peacemaking in the Battles over Prostitution." *Rethinking Marxism* 13(2):30–51.

Vora, Kalindi. 2008. "Others' Organs: South Asian Domestic Labor and the Kidney Trade." *Postmodern Culture* 19(1). doi: 10.1353/pmc.0.0036.

Walk Free Foundation. 2013. *Global Slavery Index.* Nedlands: Walk Free Foundation.

Walk Free Foundation. 2014. *Global Slavery Index.* Nedlands: Walk Free Foundation.

Walk Free Foundation. 2016. *Global Slavery Index.* Nedlands: Walk Free Foundation.

Waring, Marilyn. 1988. *If Women Counted.* New York, NY: HarperCollins.

Weitzer, Ronald. 2011. "Sex Trafficking and the Sex Industry: The Need for Evidence-Based Theory and Legislation." *Journal of Criminal Law and Criminology* 101(4):1337–69.

Whitman, Amy, and David H. Gray. 2015. "Transnational Human Trafficking." *Global Security Studies* 6(3):11–18.

WHO (World Health Organization). 2010. "WHO Guiding Principles on Human Cell, Tissue and Organ Transplantation." *Transplantation* 90(3):229–33.

WHO (World Health Organization). 2017. *Women on the Move: Migration, Care Work and Health*. Geneva: World Health Organization.

Wooditch, Alese. 2011. "The Efficacy of the Trafficking in Persons Report: A Review of the Evidence." *Criminal Justice Policy Review* 22(4):471–93.

Wuebbels, Mark. n.d. *Demystifying Human Smuggling Operations Along the Arizona–Mexican Border*. http://traccc.gmu.edu/pdfs/publications/human_trafficking_publications/wuebbe01.pdf

Yea, Sallie. 2010. "Trafficking in Part(s): The Commercial Kidney Market in a Manila Slum, Philippines." *Global Social Policy* 10(3):358–76.

Yea, Sallie, ed. 2014. *Human Trafficking in Asia: Forcing Issues*. Abingdon: Routledge.

Yea, Sallie. 2015a. "Trafficked Enough? Missing Bodies, Migrant Labour Exploitation, and the Classification of Trafficking Victims in Singapore." *Antipode* 47(4):1080–1100.

Yea, Sallie. 2015b. "Masculinity Under the Knife: Filipino Men, Trafficking and the Black Organ Market in Manila, the Philippines." *Gender, Place, and Culture* 22(1):123–42.

Yousaf, Farhan Navid. 2016. "Fleeing Violence: Gender, Human Rights and Trafficking in Women in Pakistan." PhD dissertation, Department of Sociology, University of Connecticut.

Yousaf, Farhan Navid. 2018. "Forced Migration, Human Trafficking, and Human Security." *Current Sociology*. doi:10.1177/0011392117736309.

Yousaf, Farhan Navid, and Bandana Purkayastha. 2015a. *Human Trafficking Amidst Interlocking Systems of Exploitation: A Focus on Pakistan*. London: Frontpage.

Yousaf, Farhan Navid, and Bandana Purkayastha. 2015b. "'I Am Only Half Alive': Organ Trafficking in Pakistan Amid Interlocking Oppressions." *International Sociology* 30(6):637–53.

Yousaf, Farhan Navid, and Bandana Pukayastha. 2016. "Social World of Organ Transplantation, Trafficking, and Policies." *Journal of Public Health Policy* 37:190–9.

Yu, Szde. 2015. "Human Trafficking and the Internet." Pp. 61–74 in *Combating Human Trafficking: A Multidisciplinary Approach*, edited by M. J. Palmiotto. Boca Raton, FL: CRC Press.

Zhang, Sheldon X. 2007. *Smuggling and Trafficking in Human Beings: All Roads Lead to America*. Westport, CT: Praeger.

Zheng, Tiantian. 2010. "Introduction." Pp. 1–22 in *Sex Trafficking, Human Rights and Social Justice*, edited by T. Zheng. New York, NY: Routledge.

Zimmerman, Cathy, Mazeda Hossain, and Charlotte Watts. 2011. "Human Trafficking and Health: A Conceptual Model to Inform Policy, Intervention and Research." *Social Science and Medicine* 73(2):327–35.

Zukin, Sharon. 1990. *The Cultures of Cities*. New York, NY: Blackwell.

Zutlevics, T. L. 2001. "Markets and the Needy: Organ Sale or Aid?" *Journal of Applied Philosophy* 18(3):297–302.

Index